# Praise for *The Departe*

The Departed Among the Living is ............. ....g. to the as-
sumption that human consciousness is annihilated with the death of
the brain and body. Dr. Erlendur Haraldsson's meticulous, fascinating
research will validate those who already believe in life after death, and
should stimulate serious reflection in those who do not. This book will
almost certainly become a classic in the field of survival research.

—Larry Dossey, M.D.
Author of *Healing Words* and *Reinventing Medicine*

With nearly three quarters of Icelanders stating a belief in some form
of survival of bodily death, we might expect a substantial amount of
evidence to be reported. Thanks to Erlendur Haraldsson, one of the
outstanding field researchers of our time, much of this evidence is now
available to us, in one of the most important books of its kind since the
classic 1886 survey *Phantasms of the Living*.

—Guy Lyon Playfair,
Author of *The Flying Cow* and *Twin Telepathy*

"When you start thinking about the meaning of your life and the best
way to live, the question of whether it's all material, you die and everything is over, versus whether we continue on in some form as part of
a spiritual existence, becomes very important. Do I really care about
meaning and the consequences of my actions since it all ends suddenly and I'm gone, no regrets, no real satisfactions? It would mean a lot
to think you can plan for a long existence of spiritual evolution, but
is that all a myth as we think science says, an opiate for the masses to
keep them obedient while the smart exploit them? Genuine science
says investigate, not dogmatically affirm or deny survival, and while the
survival question is generally ignored by those supposedly practicing
science, a very few scientists, of whom Erlendur Haraldsson is a ster-
ling example, search out and analyze the relevant evidence suggesting
survival. You will, to put it mildly, be fascinated by what he presents in
this book - and perhaps the plan of your life will be changed.....

—Charles T. Tart, Ph.D.
Author of *The End of Materialism*

# The Departed Among the Living

## An Investigative Study of Afterlife Encounters

BY

# Erlendur Haraldsson, Ph. D.

# CONTENTS

1. Have You Ever Perceived the Presence of a Person Who Has Died?.... 1

2. Visual Experiences............................................................................ 5

3. Auditory Perceptions ...................................................................... 19

4. Someone Touched Me! ..................................................................... 27

5. That Smells Familiar ....................................................................... 31

6. Sensing an Invisible Presence......................................................... 37

7. Experiences at the Moment of Death.............................................. 41

8. How soon after Death were the Deceased Encountered?................. 53

9. Who were the Deceased Persons? ................................................... 59

10. Who or What is the Source of the Apparitional Experience?.......... 67

11. Accidents and Violent Deaths: Sailors and Death by Drowning ..... 71

12. Accidental Deaths on Land ............................................................. 83

13. Suicide ............................................................................................ 91

14. Murder or Manslaughter ................................................................ 97

15. Circumstances, State of Mind and Consequences ......................... 99

16. Widows and Widowers.................................................................... 105

17. How did the Phenomena Appear and Disappear and How
    Long Did it Last?........................................................................... 115

18. How Physically Real was the Experience?...................................... 121

19. Was the Whole Body Visible or only Part of It? ............................. 125

20. Unusual Behaviour of Animals....................................................... 127

21. Meaning and Messages................................................................... 131

22. Experiences from Childhood .......................................................... 137

23. Localized Apparitions .................................................................... 145

24. Person-Centered Apparitions ................................................. 153

25. Warnings and Rescue at Sea ................................................. 157

26. Guidance and Words of Warning ......................................... 161

27. Healers and Cures ................................................................. 165

28. Mediums and Psychics .......................................................... 173

29. Is Someone Watching Over Us? ........................................... 177

30. I've Got a Bad Feeling About This ....................................... 185

31. They Showed up For Their Funeral ..................................... 193

32. Obtaining Information Unknown Before the Encounter .............. 199

33. Multiple Witnesses ............................................................... 201

34. Indirect Verification ............................................................. 209

35. Representative Surveys on Approaches to the Afterlife ................. 219

36. Belief in Life After Death Among Participants ...................... 227

37. Crucial Features of After-Death Encounters ......................... 231

38. Arguments For and Against an Afterlife .............................. 235

39. Personal Experiences. ........................................................... 239


Appendix A: Comparison of the two surveys ........................... 243

References .................................................................................. 249

Acknowledgements ................................................................... 253

Appendix B: The Questionnaire .............................................. 255

# 1

# Have You Ever Perceived the Presence of a Person Who Has Died?

ROM earliest times, people have speculated about what happens when they and their loved ones die. Their views will have varied from certainty about life after death to utter disbelief. Today, many continue to believe in existence after physical death with some claiming actual experiences of the departed or contact with them of some kind.

As we have suggested, such experiences are nothing new. Historical and literary sources bear ample witness to this. We find such encounters in the Icelandic sagas, in the plays of Shakespeare and in the writings of Goethe (Puhle 2006). Yet we also find them in society today, which might surprise many. The present time is seen as the enlightened era of science, education and widespread secularism. But in a survey around 1980 that was conducted in most countries of Western Europe 25 percent, every fourth person, reported that they had been in contact with some one who had died (Haraldsson and Houtkooper 1991). In the United States the figure was 31 percent (Greeley 1975).

We sought an answer to this question even earlier in the modern and educated society of Iceland, one of the Scandinavian countries. In a survey conducted in 1974-1975, we asked: "Have you ever been aware of the presence of a deceased person?" 31 percent of a representative national sample of 902 persons from all over the country answered "yes". These participants all reported that they had had an experience of a deceased man or woman.

1

These results led to further questions about the nature and details of these experiences. What form did this "presence of a deceased person" take? Was it only a vague feeling? Did it mean that people had seen the dead, heard them or perceived them in some other way? Were some of the dead only encountered in a dream? Who were the dead? Did they belong to a particular group of people? Were they first and foremost friends and relatives? In what circumstances did such an experience occur - in a resting state or at work, in light or in darkness? And did those who had these experiences differ from other people?

During the following years, detailed personal interviews were conducted with over 450 people who responded with a 'yes' to questions about personal experiences of the deceased while in a waking state. These accounts form the basis for this book. Technical information about samples and procedure can be found in Appendix A.

Those who shared their experiences with us were first asked to describe their experience in their own words. If they had more than one encounter to report they were asked to describe only their most vivid or remarkable experience. After that, we went with them through a long list of questions. We asked in what manner our informant had experienced the deceased person, even if it was already clear in their description. Was the deceased person seen, heard, smelled, touched or encountered in another way? Was the deceased person perceived in more than one sensory way at the same time? For example, was the deceased both seen and heard? Several such possibilities were offered in the questionnaire.

Our interviews yielded a variety of experiences. It was most common to have perceived the deceased person with only one of the senses, with 48 percent experiencing them visually. However, when all the visual cases are added up, either as the only sensory perception or as one of them, it showed that a great majority – 67 percent - of reported encounters with the deceased involve visual experiences. It is much less common to have experiences of the deceased through only hearing, touch or smell; or to merely sense the presence of a deceased person. For details see table 1.

| Table 1. How the deceased were perceived. Sensory modalities of reported encounters. N = 449. | | | | |
|---|---|---|---|---|
| | No of cases: One modality | More than one modality | Total number Of cases | % |
| Visual | 218 | 85 | 303 | 67 |
| Auditory | 53 | 74 | 127 | 28 |
| Tactual | 18 | 42 | 60 | 13 |
| Olfactory | 18 | 3 | 21 | 5 |
| Only vivid sense of presence | 49 | | 49 | 11 |

In about a fifth of the accounts the perception involved more than one of the senses. Some for instance both saw and heard the deceased person (10 percent). Other combinations were sight, sound and touch (6 percent), sight and touch (3 percent) or sound and touch (2 percent). Other combinations were rare.

In the following chapters we will describe cases in which the deceased were perceived through each of the different senses and discuss the prominent characteristics of such incidents.

# 2

# VISUAL EXPERIENCES

THE most frequent experience of the deceased was visual. With 303 of our correspondents claiming visual sightings, these accounted for about 67 percent of the reported incidents. 218 of the apparitions were only perceived by sight but in 85 cases the deceased person was encountered with more than one of the senses. Let the examples speak for themselves.

**The parents**

My father died at the age of 67. He was rather short and thin, had a dark complexion but his hair had turned grey. He had a bad temper. I saw him after he died. The door connecting my room and my mother's bedroom was open. He came in, glanced at me and went into my mother's room. My mother died much later at the age of 81. She was short, stout, her hair had turned white, very good-tempered, light-hearted and content with little, made the best of things, was kind to everyone. The year after she died I was sitting late in the evening in my living-room and saw her coming. She walked around the living-room and then she disappeared in front of me - right before my very eyes. I was very pleased and grateful for having seen her. (756)

**The Police Officer**

My husband and I were sitting in the kitchen one morning having coffee when we saw a neighbour of ours come up the steps, right by the window as if he was going home. He was in uniform, had been on the police force but had died in an accident in his thirties. He lived on the floor above. We had been good neighbours for 4 or 5 years. He was about average height, handsome, light-hearted and very easy to get along with. We missed him very much. I sensed him often, but as time passed further from this accident, it dwindled and then stopped. This experience did not have much effect, but it was nice, it was lovely, to have seen him... (764).

### Man dressed in grey

I often heard footsteps and a few times I saw the same man, though I did not know him. This happened both here at home and in the hospital where I was being treated. One time, in the middle of the night, I went to the kitchen to heat up a snack, when I heard footsteps that sounded like someone was coming in and then a man dressed in grey appeared in the kitchen doorway. He was a very large man, with an ordinary grey hat, kind and it was like he wanted to let me know something. This made me feel rather uneasy. It did not feel pleasant and I was always a little frightened... (815)

### The birthday

This happened three years ago. I sat in a chair in my room and was reading. Then I looked up and saw my deceased grandmother standing in front of me, as fully was when she was alive. I told my mother about this the following day. She said, "That is nice. It was her birthday yesterday." I had not remembered it. (5018)

In the next example the perceiver also looks up from reading a book.

### Father and grandmother

I had the flu and lay in bed reading a book. I looked up from what I was reading and saw my deceased father's face. It looked real but it did not look like he was trying to tell me anything. Then I became aware of my father's deceased mother and I guess he was showing her to me. (293)

### The clock from Eyrarbakki

This happened shortly after my father died. I was in bed sleeping but woke up and felt there was something at my side. I saw my father there and looked at him, reached out and touched him. He was just as he had been, wearing a blue shirt over his underwear.... He got out of the bed and walked to the room he had lived in and which was across from mine. As he walked, he pointed to the wall without saying a word. On that wall there was a large clock that he had earlier asked me to deliver to his grandson in Reykjavík. (2010)

## Picture on the wall

It happened a few years ago, my sister had been dead for three years. She died at the age of sixty. One evening, when I had turned off the lights, a picture of my sister appeared on the wall at the foot of my bed, not as she was when she died but as she was at the age of seventeen. This was accompanied by a very pleasant feeling and a bright light that seemed to come from behind the picture and illuminate it. Then it disappeared just like when one turns off a camera or a projector. But the light seemed to be within me or somehow inside of me and it lasted for quite a while. (5033)

## A man from Nordfjord

I had just started work at sea here in Neskaupstad and did not know all the people working on the boat. We all slept in the forecastle. We were line-fishing south of the country and I was watching over a buoy. Then I saw a man come up from one of the cabins. I could see him very clearly, both his clothes and his physical appearance. It was quite light and he was standing in the light shining through the open cabin door. He stood there for a while before walking off across the deck. I thought it was somebody who had just started working on the boat and decided to go and speak to him but there was no one there. I did not really give it much thought at the time, just finished my shift. Then I asked the men about it and the man I thought I had seen. I described the man I had seen and the men from Nordfjord recognised the description. This person had died some years earlier and had worked on the boat until he died. I had not known anything about him before that... (7626)

The next story is unusual in that the participant sees the deceased person in the mirror.

## In the mirror

My brother drowned when he was 22 years old. I was 17 at the time and afterwards I started seeing him and other things. Two or three days after he drowned I was combing my hair in the hall and in the mirror I saw him - he was wet from the sea and very sad. I turned around and saw him disappear right there in the hall. He had planned to own his own boat and had finished a course in engineering. He was blond, rather tall and coarse, with a big temper but had learned to control it, had a strong sense of justice and was kind.... (708)

In the following two cases no person was seen but those who had the visual experience believed they knew what it was about. In the second case a strange movement is thought to be related to a woman who had passed away.

### Ball of fire

We had just moved to Hafnarfjord and a colleague of mine, who came from the same area where we were from, called me up and we planned for him to visit next Thursday. The night before, Wednesday, we were both asleep when I was suddenly awakened and all I could see was fire - or a ball of fire - because I did not see the source of the fire at the door. It seemed to be below the middle of the door and spread to the sides and filled the doorway up to the middle of the door.

I jumped up, waking my wife. I grabbed the bedcover because I was going to use it to shield myself from the fire but the fire suddenly disappeared. The next day I found out that this had happened about the same time that the man who was going to visit us on Thursday died. My explanation is that this was some sort of an energy transmission at the time of his death or shortly after. (7003)

### The spinning rock

I was sitting in the living room with two others and we were watching television. Then when a certain tune was heard on the TV a spinning rock, next to the TV set, started moving and we watched this happen. The tune was a special favorite of my mother who was dead when it happened. I associated the movement of the rock with my mother; she was telling us she was with us. The rock had belonged to my mother's mother. I think that my mother never owned it but without doubt had often seen it. (2)

Visual apparitions were usually perceived without any other sensory experience. However, it was quite common for sound to accompany them

(47 incidents). In several examples the vision was experienced along with touch (15 cases) or both touch and sound (20 cases). Only three incidents were reported in which the deceased person was both seen and smelled.

In the following two stories the encounters with the dead are experienced as if they are a normal experience. It is only after the deceased person has left that the perceiver realises that they are no longer living.

### The fourth man

I met four friends when I was taking a walk downtown and I spoke with them awhile. After our conversation my fiancé asked me what I had been looking at in the window of the shop. I had been looking at the fourth man in the group, but as she asked I suddenly remembered that he had died some time ago. (587)

### The Cousin

I was in the kitchen in the afternoon and had just finished breast-feeding my child. I felt weak and sat down. There was a knock on the door and in came my cousin with another man and said: "Hello cousin". I thought he was more nimble than usual, but he was always an amusing boy and very good-natured. He introduced his companion as our grandfather, who just smiled. My cousin said he was hurrying home and I wanted to go along with them, but he did not want me to. But I was in the hall anyway putting on my coat when the newcomers disappeared. At that moment my mother arrived and she did not see a thing. While I was talking with my cousin I had forgotten that he was dead. He had drowned a few months earlier when he was about twenty. He had planned to go to navigation college. I was very frightened to begin with, but later it did not have any effect on me, either good or bad. I did not look upon this as a haunting. (596)

The accounts above were transcribed from recorded interviews. Only a portion of the text has been displayed – the core of the incident. Repetitions and near meaningless words have been deleted but nothing else has been changed or removed. The next three accounts have been printed in full length, just as they were told, verbatim.

### Meeting on the stairs

It was about a week after my mother was buried. She died here in the house in the attic. She had a room there. I just met her on the stairs. She had just had a stroke – a brain hemorrhage – so she moved slowly and used to move to the side when she met someone on the stairs. In that incident she moved just as usual. It was so normal. Of course I knew immediately that I had made a perceptual mistake or something else. And I kept walking upstairs and it did not have an effect on me. That was all but it was not unclear or anything. I saw all of her and it had a good effect on me or something like that.

This happened in the year 1955. My wife was sewing. I went up the stairs and told my wife about it immediately. Afterwards I continued walking upstairs because I knew right away that this was in some way normal. She was dressed pretty much the same way as usual. The stairs are quite narrow and I saw that her skirt touched the upper step, and then I looked up and saw the whole picture. She was wearing normal clothes and looked just like she did before she died. That was it really - I just saw her. I looked up and just saw her, first the skirt and then I looked up and decided not to stop. I just kept going upstairs and did not look back because I was sure I would not see any more. It happened at the end of the day, as it was getting dark, but it was not that dark on the stairs. It was as if we had met on the stairs. I went past her. I think I looked back when I got to the top of the stair. I walked slowly up the steps – I did not stop. I seem to recall looking back down – but she would have been downstairs by then under normal circumstances. We met on the third or fourth step. (361)

## "Beggi dear"

I lost a young boy and have seen him at least twice around here – very clearly. I was so surprised myself that I said "Beggi dear" and walked towards him. I saw him through some bars between the lounge and the kitchen. I walked around from the kitchen, past a solid wall and into the lounge beside the kitchen. At the time I had forgotten that he had passed away. I know that his grandmother had seen him at my house. The boy was nine years old and had drowned two years earlier.

His grandmother was alone at my house, and when she saw him she simply told him: "I think you should use the time well and go and play in your room". And that was that.

When I saw him I was on my own at home – alone. I was washing the kitchen floor and suddenly I saw him through the bars in the lounge and I just felt him looking at me. I have seen him twice, always at the same place. I was washing the floor and I just looked up and it felt as if he was just standing there, looking at me. I especially remember the second time it happened. Then I said "Oh, Beggi dear" and ran into the lounge and then I just realised how far fetched it was, and thought to myself: "Oh well then, that's alright". He was wearing his normal clothes he had here. He suffered a violent death, drowned along with a girl. They went together the two of them. He was just as I remember him – he was not sad, but not laughing either – just sort of normal.

How long did I see him? No, it cannot have been long. When I looked up and saw him I took a long look and it took me a while to realise – but I walked over and then he was gone. But I remember I was so surprised that I stared for a while – did not say anything. It was just for a moment. I saw him close to me but through the bars. I was not thinking about him or anything – even had the radio on. It was in the middle of the afternoon. I seem to recall it having been a bright day. He disappeared as suddenly as I had noticed him.

It is really strange. The fact is that the girl who died with him had lost her mother half a year earlier. We lived in a different apartment buildings and the girl lived in the building across from us. When she had lost her mother she seemed to look to me for support and my boy and she became best friends. It was great fun to listen to them. They were always talking about God and God and God. The mother was supposed to be there and they talked about it a lot just before he died – only a few days before. He was a bit introverted. It was hard to get close to him as they say. Then one morning he said: "I dreamt about God last night". "Well, son" I answered, and thought it was quite funny, "What did he look like?". "That does not really matter", he replied and we never found out. But he had definitely had some sort of dream because he was very thoughtful and said: "I dreamt about God last night". He was quite introverted and not very social.

Some say that it is all finished when you die but I, on the other hand, have always taught my children that there is something on the other side. Yes, and my boy believed it – because her mother had died and then when they would also go there they would all meet up. Yes there is a life after this one.

I was not thinking of him especially when it happened – I have often thought of him more. He kept things secret and was not a very social type of person, and quite introverted for a child. To tell the

11

truth, he died a very unhappy child. There's no doubt about it. He was not learning to read properly so the principal suggested that I move him down a class at school, and that is what I did. He had only been there for a few days when it happened. And there was so much crying, endless crying taking him to class. And then I take him down there that last day – to school – and the boy cries and behaves badly and was quite stubborn. The principal comes along and says that such boys need to be taken care of and lifts him up rather harshly and says that children are not supposed to control their parents. No, I say, that's quite right. And there could be a reason for him being like that – his father drank a lot... and you know. So I said to the principal that I was against that sort of behaviour. Then he comes home that day and the following day he is supposed to go to school again. And then he says: "I am never going to school". And he ran down all the stairs and said: "I wish I was dead, I wish I was dead". And that evening he died. Those were his last words as he ran down the stairs. I had not felt sad when I saw him, because probably two or three years had passed since he died. (1066)

### Father in the chair

My father died a sudden death in the year 1969. Now he often sits in his chair at home. I don't think it is not just my imagination. At least, I walk past the chair and do not sit in it when he is there. This has happened quite often, especially soon after he died. He died very suddenly, just came back home, lay down on the sofa and died. So it happened very quickly. He died in their bedroom but I have never seen him there. After that I felt for a long time that I was trying to overcome it. But I felt that he was always trying to come towards us.

She, my mother, and both of them, lived not far away. When I was coming over and still to this day, I often felt that he opened the door and came to greet us. I think I can say for certain that I first saw him shortly after he passed away. It was around Christmas time. We came over on Christmas day for an evening meal. It was hard for me, I felt he had to sit in his chair and somehow I had not quite realised that he was gone. It is hard when people go so quickly. He was a healthy man, you really did not expect it, but death will not be mocked.

The first time I felt that he had approached me was just after he had died. My mother had heart problems and was ill shortly after his death. She came to our place and stayed at our house first after, but then she wanted to go back just before Christmas. She left the hospital just before Christmas – and really wanted us to come over for a Christmas meal. But I went over before she went back and cleaned the apartment and then he simply greeted me when I approached. And I was not scared of him. He was strong in this way. People probably differ in how they seek worldly contact after they die. I do not know. He was very religious.

I know a man in the next house. He claims that he has often seen my father there. I do not know, but perhaps the deceased differ in how strong they are in making themselves felt. Maybe it varies how much the deceased look back. I really believe there is life after this life. Other people have not seen him at the same time as I have seen him. I did not have that pleasure.

A friend came over and a couple was here and a few of us were sitting together. Then the friend comes into the kitchen – I was making us coffee – and says: "Did your father like music?" He said the father had been playing and was sitting here in the chair. I did not know what chair – this furniture is old stuff from them. It had always been with them and was passed on to me. I did not know if this was related to that. So I said to him: "Yes, he did enjoy music". "Yes, shows that he does", said our friend.

When I first saw him at the house I told my husband about it. He said something like: "Wow, it did not take long". Then I replied: "I am not surprised, for my dad was helping me". I think he took it more as a joke but I said: "I often feel he comes to greet me", and he said: "I have felt so too". He had been out on some errand.

But as I say, people are different personalities – but I have seen him, there is no question about it. I have also smelled him, a scent related to him, he took snuff. I have smelled tobacco. To tell the truth, I do not really think much about these matters but I have never in my life been scared of them. When I saw him he was exactly as when he was alive, just wearing his normal clothes. He was an extremely calm man. I just felt he was there and I saw him - met him in the hall that first time. I expect I did not see him for long. It is hard to put a time on such things. However, I felt he was around me the whole time. I felt it was very normal and quite alright. I told my mother about it; she just smiled and said: "Well, well".

When I saw him he was about one or two meters away from me. He just came towards me as soon as I opened the door to the hall.

That is, opened the front door to my mother's house and then he was right in front of me.

The light in the hall came from the bathroom where there was a window to the east and from a southern window facing the front door. The hall was quite bright – although this was in December. I guess it was around the middle of the month but it was still quite light. It was probably between three or four in the afternoon. When I opened the door I felt it was perfectly normal for him to be there. Then suddenly I realised: he was dead. Then I felt that he followed me around. We had been close, talked a lot – perhaps that is why we had a closer relationship than is typical of a father and daughter – I do not know.

My father was 76 when he died. He had been a skipper and ran a fishing company in Olafsfjord for many years. He was very religious – most definitely. He believed in the afterlife. I do not know if I was thinking of him especially before I met him in the hall that day. I was first and foremost trying to get what I had to get done as fast as possible. He was very knowledgeable about genealogy and I had been saying to him about two months before he died that now he should use the time and write down his genealogical table, as much as he could remember. And he had just started doing this when he died. It was a shame to lose that ocean of knowledge. He was an especially good-tempered man. (593)

At this point, many readers will wonder: Did people see what they perceived with their eyes open just like they perceive any other thing or person in sight? We asked about this specifically. The answer was 'yes'. People did not hesitate to state that this was indeed so. 272 informants, 90 percent of them, said they had seen the apparition with their eyes open. Only two had their experience with their eyes closed and 12 perceived the dead as if in their mind's eye. 16 people reported not being sure how the vision had appeared to them.

A man who is well known in Iceland describes his encounter with a friend who was one of the most famous poets of the past century:

### David

I was in hospital and it was either just before or just after I had my operation. I think it was before. It was in August and the weather was very good. I was looking out of the window at the clouds as they kept changing shape and I could see all sorts of strange figures in the clouds. That was pretty much all I had to keep me occupied, lying in bed, I had my own room. I do not know but I must have been influenced by something. I was very calm, looking at the clouds, thinking poetic thoughts which did not really surprise me. Then I sensed a strong force and I saw a grey-patterned jacket in the southeast corner of the room, no man but just the jacket and I smelled tobacco. I knew who it was, both sensed it and I knew the jacket as well as the smell. This man was David Stefansson. We were great friends and acquaintances. I could feel that strong force from the southeast corner which moved to the northwest across the bed and over me... (2210)

And now there follow several short accounts.

## On Gotta

I worked aboard a boat called Gotta. The first time I went to bed a man looked me in the eye. I guess he was about 27 or 28 years old. I saw him clearly. He had brown eyes and a pale complexion. He was calm and seemed to feel fine and he had on an English cap which leant to the right. I could only see him down to his chest. He just seemed to sit there in the bunk to the side... (7005)

## Christmas day

This was a few years ago, on Christmas day. The man I thought I had seen, or his outlines, had died the summer before. He was an old man related to my brother but my brother and his family were visiting that day. I was walking from lounge into the hall, and then I felt this man standing there. I knew him immediately. He was rather unusual in his appearance and very strongly built. I felt I saw the outlines of his body but then they disappeared. I was quite shocked and went into the kitchen to calm myself down. I saw the exact outlines in a room where my brother´s daughter was playing. She was very favoured by the old man who was almost a grandfather to her. But then it happened again in the evening, when I had quite stopped thinking about it. It happened in just the same way and in the exact same spot. I thought that was quite strange. (7574)

## The stepfather

I often perceive images of deceased people. Sometimes I wake up in the night and notice these things. One night I awoke and sat up in bed and saw my mother-in-law's stepfather standing at the bed at my wife's side. He had passed away many years ago. I had never met him alive. I only saw him that one time but I have often sensed his presence. (2136)

## Haraldur Níelsson

I have only once seen the vision of a dead man and it was in a place where I had never been to before. I have also felt a touch, a sort of feeling of heat, like a light or warmth on the side of my head or my cheek, and I saw something like a light shadow, which of course is a paradox but I saw this white or light "shadow". I have often sensed my grandfather, Haraldur Níelsson, sometimes many evenings in a row and sometimes for 5 to 10 minutes at a time. (5034)

## In his chair

My father always used to sit in a specific chair in the kitchen. Some time after his death when I came home and opened the kitchen door, I saw him sitting in his chair. I could not touch him, I only saw him. He did not say anything, he was simply there, sitting in his chair like he used to. (2017)

## A beautiful woman

I bent down to tie my shoe-laces. I was on my way out, when I felt someone standing beside me. I looked up and saw this woman very clearly, she was very beautiful and I felt as if I was standing there staring at her. I thought she was connected to me in some way but I did not recognize her. I also somehow knew that she had died a long time ago. I remember quite well how she wore her hair and the clothes she wore.... (2008)

## A little distracted

I was in a house the other day. I saw an old couple there, and it was later confirmed that they were the housewife's grandparents. I also heard them. I have often experienced this, seen, heard or sensed the presence of the deceased. One is always a little distracted when things like this happen. (2005)

## What a beautiful child

I have only had a psychic experience at one time. It was regarding a boy who died when he was four years old and happened about half a year after he died. My husband was his grandfather. I once lay awake in bed at home and was wide awake. Then suddenly I saw a child's face and thought to myself: "What a beautiful child". At the same time I felt myself thinking: "Oh, that's little Siggi" and at that he disappeared. (2024)

## My husband's friend

A few of the men in the village were going to a country dance and my husband was among them. I myself was in such a state that I could not go and that was fine. They were going to get there by truck and they were going to stand on the back of the truck. When the car got to our house and stopped there were about five or six men in the back. It was during the spring and the evening sun was shining. I stared at one of the men. The sun was shining on his hair. I could not believe my eyes. I also knew all the other men, they were friends of my husband and this man had also been my husband's friend but he had died during the autumn. He was standing there looking happy but suddenly disappeared when the truck started up. (307)

## An old friend

We were renovating an old house that we were living in. My husband had gone out and I was alone and lay down on a sofa. I was wondering what it would look like when it was finished. Then I heard a knock at the door and I opened it. Outside the door was an old man who used to live close to me when I was a child. While alive he used to come over to this house quite a lot, but now he was dead. I was not surprised to see him when I opened the door and he did not speak to me. He simply thought, you know, I understood and I did not speak to him with words but with thoughts. "What are you doing here?" "I've come to stay with you, Magga dear." I said "There's no space for you here now my friend, you can see what this place looks like." I felt he was a little angry with me: "I will have to come back later then", he said and went out and slammed the door. He was standing there just as if he was alive, in front of me, wearing nice dark clothes, a white shirt and tie, in his best suit, as they say. He was in good spirits and just as I remember him. He was happy when he saw me and called me "my dear Magga", as he used to do when I was a child and I used to spend time with him. I was surprised that he wanted to come... (7606)

## The welcome

This was after my mother died. I had a little child out east in Lit-li-Saurbær in Olfus, where she had lived. This was in the evening and it happened very suddenly. I was in my mother's bedroom. She appeared to me and I rushed out of bed and said:"Mummy!" I felt her come to me and hug me. I did not hear her, only felt I saw her. But this happened so quickly. I was a little frightened, although she seemed to be just as she used to be and she seemed to be welcoming me... (2054)

## The lighthouse

I remember a very clear incident. At that time I had a shop. I was at home drinking coffee when a tiny little boy comes over. I imagined he was about 10 years old. He stood there for a long time looking at me. I saw that this was a bit unusual and other than it should be. It was obviously a boy who had passed away and was not alive. Then he disappeared. I did not know why he had been there but I was a bit of a spiritualist back then, and actually I still am but not in the sense that I was at that time. We often spoke about such things in the shop back then and perhaps the shop was some sort of tiny lighthouse for those souls who were roaming about somewhere. (5029)

## Thorgerdur

An old woman died in my home village. I had known her well since I was a child. She died in a house in the middle of the village and there she was "kept" in a room in the house, as they used to do, as there was no morgue there at that time. I was walking down the road. It was bright and sunny and I was walking along the road. I cannot remember if it was the day after she died or one of the following days. Anyway I met the lady outside that house and walked a little towards her and I nodded my head towards her, just as you do when greeting. When I met her I was completely unaware of the fact that she had died. I had quite forgotten about it. It was just like normal. But as soon as she had passed by me I thought to myself: "How can that be? Thorgerdur is dead." That was her name. I looked right back but then I could not see her... I remember the incident so vividly. (5114)

# 3

## Auditory Perceptions

I N about a quarter of cases people heard sounds that they associated with a deceased person. In 53 of the 127 cases, only sounds were heard, but in 74 incidents the deceased person was also perceived by other senses. Auditory perceptions can be divided into two groups. In 58 percent of cases only a voice was heard and in 42 percent only some sound or noise was heard. These sounds had been typical of the deceased person, such as footsteps or were related to his or her former job and activities. Here are a few accounts:

### She will take care of it

My mother died 21 years ago when she was 64 years old. I have twice heard her very clearly. This has happened when I had been very worried and was very ill at ease, and both times just as I was falling asleep. My nickname was Dolla and I clearly heard her call to me: "Dolla dear". I knew the voice and she said my name so kindly. I felt just as if she were here and both times I lay calmly and thought: "She will take care of it." I felt as if she knew what I was thinking and had come to help me. (2034)

### "You have no business here"

I moved north to Akureyri at a time when there was great unemployment there and I had recently got engaged. Sometimes I got work at the harbour, mostly shovelling snow. Then a man came to see me, somebody I knew who ran a fishing company. He had a small boat called Hengill and was about to set of on a fishing trip to Siglufjord. He asked me if I would like to go on the trip as the **engineer** of the boat because the man who had been hired had fallen ill. 'Yes, yes", I said for I had nothing else to do, but first I wanted to see the boat. There was no problem with that, the boat was at the harbour and there was a lamppost right above the boat. It was a 10 tonn fishing boat and I really liked the look of it. It had a new layer of paint and it seemed it have been well looked after. I said to myself that I could work on the boat, I had nothing else to do anyway and I could go on a few trips. Then I went down to look at the engine. I had a habit of running my hand under the flywheel. I bent down and ran my hand under the wheel and felt that the space was about the width of a hand, space for the sea between the wheel and the belt and I say to myself: "I will have them make a tray under this when we get to Siglufjord." Then I hear somebody loudly and clearly say:"Palmar (my name), you have no business here." I was surprised to hear the voice. I looked up through the entrance but there was nobody there. I did not recognise the voice. When I got back up to the pier, both the ship owner and the skipper were waiting for me. I was quite flustered and said to myself: "I am not going on this boat." When we got back to town, the shipowner said to me: "Well, have you decided?" "Yes", I said, "I have decided not to go." They were very disappointed because they had decided to set off that same evening. But they managed to get another engineer and the boat sailed to Siglufjord. Four or five days later the boat was leased to fetch milk from Saudarkrok. They collected the milk but the boat was shipwrecked in the evening by Siglufjord with 8 men on board. (7634)

**A familiar voice**

I was in hospital when a woman very dear to me died. I had been with her in another hospital... She was about fifty when she died. I was awakened by her voice. I distinctly heard her voice and she said something about the bulbs we had given her... I do not remember if she had already been buried... (2042)

**Voices and archeological remains**

When I was a teenager I often heard strange noises and here is one example. I was raised up in the country. Below the field there was a small stream and I often sat by the stream fishing for trout. Up from the stream there is a small hill and I always felt as if I could hear people talking around there. One time I was sure I could hear people arguing and I thought I heard my name mentioned. I got scared and ran up onto the hill to check if I could see anyone but there was no one there. Later I found out that some archeological remains were discovered there, a grave or a shallow gravemound with several heathen and Christian artifacts. They were around a thousand years old. The area was known to be haunted. My father, for example, had heard similar things at the same hill, both male and female voices... (5047)

### The farewell

I was working with a girl with whom I was well acquainted. She lived on the next farm to mine. There had been an assembly in the Youth house on Sunday and refreshments were served. The next day we went together to clean up. Afterwards she came home with me and we had a cup of coffee in the kitchen. Then I went upstairs to the library. I was librarian and was putting away books while my friend was downstairs speaking with my mother. My mind was on the books, but all of a sudden I thought I heard a voice whispering to me, 'Why did not you say goodbye to Stina?" At first I ignored this but I thought there was something strange about it. Then I heard the voice again and it said firmly: "Why did not you say goodbye to Stina?" I was so startled that I threw away the book I was holding, rushed down the stairs and ran into my mother who was coming up. I asked her if Stina had left and she said she had. I went outside; the earth was covered with ice. I was very upset. She was already on her way and I watched her leave. I was upset the whole evening, I kept thinking about the voice but I did not tell anyone about it. That same night the girl became very ill. It was diphtheria and she passed away on Thursday. So I never got a chance to say goodbye to her. I have often imagined that it was my sister, who died when she was 19, who spoke to me. She had died a couple of years earlier. (5007)

In a few cases only breathing, singing or even whistling was heard. These sounds were recognised by the participant and gave them an idea of who was making the sound.

### In the mind

It used to happen more often that I became aware of my grandfather when I started playing. If it was not going so well, or if it was

taking me a long time to get something done and I was getting im-
patient, then I always felt that there was someone in the room with
me and I could hear him sighing or something like that. Therefore
I looked up. Then it was more like if I did see him but as if it were
in my mind... (5052)

### The stepfather

I went at least twice to a seance with Hafsteinn, the medium,
and was expecting my stepfather to come through. He had died one
or two years earlier in his seventies. At the seance all sorts of men
who had lived in the same area came through.... Then once when
my brother was staying with me we talked about how remarkable it
was that our father had not come through at the seance. One morning I woke up and heard him breathing. He had suffered from some
sort of shortness of breath when he lived and breathed in a special
way, and I clearly recognized it.... He let me know of his presence
in this way. (2046)

### A helpful man

I was in hospital, and one day I awoke from a nap and heard some
sort of strong, heavy and laboured breathing, I could both hear the
breathing and feel somebody's presence in a strong and definite way.
It felt as if the breathing person leant over me. I felt some sort of power as if I were being held but I could not feel any touch. After this my
illness got better in some ways and my swelling and other symptoms
improved. I told one of the sisters in the hosital about my experience.
She said the breathing belonged to an older man who used to occupy
my bed just before me. She said this man had always been wandering
about and had always wanted to help other people. (1053A)

### Fond of music

I lost my son four years ago. I have been aware of him here at
home. On one of these occasions his son was staying with me during the evening and we could hear somebody whistling in the kitch-
en. I knew just what it was; my son was always whistling. He was
so fond of music. Then the boy said to me: "Grandmother, who is
whistling?" I did not want to tell him what it was and said: "It must
be something outside." "No, no, somebody is whistling here and is
whistling a tune", he said. "Sure, it is somewhere", I just said. It was
very clear. I knew it well for I was aware of it so often. (5054)

Accounts of footsteps and sounds of movements are the most frequently reported sounds.

### I am coming

I often perceived my deceased husband. Sometimes when the kids were at school and came back late and I was getting worried he would come back just before them. I could hear the way he walked and I could hear him take off his coat. Then I knew they would be back soon. (2006)

### In Hvitarnes

I was on a trip with other people up in the highlands. We all slept in the loft at the small shelter at Hvitarnes. I heard someone trying to crawl up the ladder to the loft.... This was in the night and it was pitch-dark. When this being had crawled up half way up the ladder, it was like it did not have any more energy to go further. I never heard it descend, it was like its movements just slowly faded away and died down. Then it started again. It was like two or three attempts had been made to get up the ladder, but the being could not get any higher than to the middle. Downstairs I heard doors being slammed and benches were thrown around. Another man was awake and he also heard this. He is now deceased. This shelter has the reputation of being haunted. It is said to be haunted by the ghost of a woman who walks about in the hut. Some people have even seen her. (2072)

### An unusual walking style

I especially remember one incident. A man had been killed in an accident. I recall him being around forty years old. His mother lived in the same house as me. I heard his footsteps, he used to drag his feet a bit. I heard him walk up to the loft three times after he had had his fatal accident. The last time I went to check this for I did not like it. I was home alone and I could not see anything, I only heard him... (5002)

### In Trostansfjord

We were camping in Trostansfjord with some other people. I was awakened early in the night by a terrible noise. It sounded like a busload full of drunk people - laughing and crying - had arrived at the campsite. My husband was awake and he had also heard the same noise as I. He went outside but then everything went dead quiet and he did not see anything. I would not want to camp there again. (834A)

The author of this book has since been told that sometimes people in the neighbouring areas would in earlier times gather at this uninhabited fjord for dancing and amusement.

### A knock at the front door

I heard a knock at my front door and went to answer it but there was nobody there. A little later my young daughter, who had just started to talk, told me there was a man in the lounge. I guessed that it was my father who had passed away some years earlier. I have often heard knocks where I have been staying and this was especially common when I was a teenager. (5017)

### The neighbour

I was aware of some sort of footsteps. I recognised them as the footsteps of a woman who had died some days earlier. We were in the kitchen, me and my partner, and the window was open. We then heard the footsteps on the pavement outside and it sounded like somebody had used the door handle to open the door and close it again. I went to check but there was nobody there. We both believed it sounded like the way our neighbour used to walk. She used to drag her feet a little. Then, only about five or ten minutes later the woman's grandaughter came to fetch her little sister who bore the deceased woman's name... (7560)

### In Thorshofn

I was working as a manager in the cooperative shop in Thorshofn. I was in the office when I very distinctly heard somebody moving about, heard someone walking around in the shop. This was in the evening. I think it was during the weekend and I thought it must be one of the employees. I went into the shop and walked all around the shop but there was nobody there. The weather was dreadful and I did not expect anyone to come in. But suddenly a light was turned on. I called and looked but could not find anyone. I turned off the light and went back into the office section, where you enter the shop but there were no footprints in the snow outside the door. Next morning I asked the staff whether they had been in but they all said they had not. I heard similar sounds later under certain circumstances, when I was working alone in the evenings, for example. It sounded as if somebody was walking about and I know that others have had similar experiences and even seen something. In this building one of my prececessors had died suddenly in the office. That is how I explained the phenomena to myself. (7044)

### Mother's manner of walking

My mother lived in the same house as I did until she died. A few days after her death I started to hear her walk up the stairs in the apartment. The footsteps I heard sounded typical for her manner of walking. I have often heard this since and sometimes with my husband. He has also heard this even when I have not been near. (2004)

We contacted the husband and here is his version of this incident:

From the day my mother-in-law died and until today I have often heard sounds in my apartment where she lived for 40 years. I mostly hear noises coming from one of the staircases in the flat and it often sounds like somebody is walking up the steps. Sometimes I have heard these sounds with my wife, and after she told me of her experience I have associated the sounds with my mother-in-law.... (6020A)

Usually the deceased person was not only heard but also perceived by another of the senses. The most common of these combinations is both hearing and seeing the dead (47 cases). Less common is hearing, seeing and touching (20 cases) and in only seven cases is the deceased person both heard and touched. Finally, here are two examples of incidents where auditory and visual perceptions are experienced together:

### Sounds of someone moving about

I often hear someone walking about my apartment, everything creaks and cracking noises can be heard. My wife and I have often heard such noises, like someone is moving about. One evening I was at home alone watching television and I heard these sounds. I went into the hall to check it out and it was as if my father was in the hall. He appeared as a face, not as a body and he was higher up from the floor than people are. He was 56 years old when he died. (7588)

The last account is from a young couple who live in an area of Reykjavík called Breidholt.

### Footsteps

I woke up and had a vision. It was as if it was disintegrating into some sort of a fog. I only saw the face, although it was unclear because it looked like it was disappearing into smoke. We heard footsteps outside the bedroom door as if somebody was dragging their feet. (2130)

Her husband had this to say about the incident:

My wife and I lived in Breidholt and one evening it sounded like somebody was outside our bedroom door. We were just about to go to bed. It was as if somebody was walking about. I went to check but could not see anything. It was most definitely the sound of somebody walking about. My wife said she had seen something which gradually disappeared at the foot of our bed but I did not see it. Shortly after that we heard the noises. (2001)

# 4

## SOMEONE TOUCHED ME!

IN a total of 60 cases the encounters with the deceased involved touch. Tactile perceptions were usually experienced along with another type of sensory experience (42 incidents), whereas touch alone was experienced in no more than 18 cases. In most instances, the deceased person was both felt by means of touch as well as being seen and heard (20 accounts). Sometimes the dead were both seen and felt by touch (15 accounts); and in a few cases the deceased person was only felt and heard (7 accounts). The following few cases have been randomly chosen to represent tactile perceptions.

### Embrace and a dream

I had just woken up. A deceased woman, whom I knew very well, came to me and took me in her arms. This perception only lasted a few moments. When I was talking about this that same morning, my daughter said, "I also dreamt about her last night." (2013)

### A deceased female friend

I went to a séance with the medium Hafsteinn Bjornsson and my deceased friend spoke through the medium. My mother-in-law was with me. She is very interested in these sorts of things. Then there was that time when I came back from work, nobody was home and I lay down for a nap. Then this event came to my mind and I started wondering whether she would be able to make me aware of her.

And that is what she did just then. I could feel her touch as she put her hand on my shoulder. It was a very strange feeling. I could feel some sort of energy go through me and I was very scared... (2027)

## To comfort

My mother and my father-in-law died only a few months apart and I sensed one of them; I think it was my mother. I sat at a table and was working when I felt someone come up behind me, bend down and tightly grab my shoulder. At first I naturally thought it was someone in the household. I looked back but did not see anyone. Then I realized what it was. It was a cold and tight grip and it was not from anyone in the household. In a strange way I was astounded; I sort of jumped up when I realized what it was. I thought this would have intimidated the person who was trying to comfort me, someone who was trying to get close to me because I was probably a little depressed. I felt as if someone had come to comfort me. I never had an experience like this again. (2062)

## The mother-in-law

My mother-in-law died very suddenly. We received a telegraph message about her death. Of course, my wife was very sad that evening and so was I. My mother-in-law was from Germany. We were in bed and were trying to fall asleep but we were still thinking of her. We had our backs to each other and suddenly I felt a strong blow to my back. It really hurt so I turned around and asked: "What are you hitting me for?" She swore that she really was not in the sort of mood to start hitting me. It had been quite a blow between the shoulder blades. The morning after my wife told me that she had dreamt of her mother and that said she had seen her quite clearly in the dream. (5015)

## The rescue

I was on a sinking ship, the "Sula" from Akureyri, and we were off the coast of Gardskagi. The steer house was full of sea and I was there practically unconscious, probably hit by a floorboard. I knew everyone had gone up on the steer house-roof, through the window. I was the only one left. Then it was as if somebody grabbed my shoulder and suddenly before I knew it I was up on the roof... Later I was told by a medium, though not at a seance, that my grandfather said he often watched over me. And concerning this incident she said my grandfather said:"Yes, I pulled you out my boy." (7534)

28

### Grabbed around the waist

I was on a ship and was lying on my knees up in my bunk and was looking out the porthole, when I suddenly felt I was grabbed by the waist from behind. I immediately thought it was my husband and turned around, but I saw no one and no one could have left the cabin so quickly. I was talking about this and some members of the crew told me it was an Italian, who had died while building the ship and that he was now aboard. (454A)

### Dignity and peace

I was lying on the sofa and was resting when a being came to me. It seemed to walk slowly and calmly towards me. I did not see it but there was something beautiful about it, dignified and peaceful. Tears came to my eyes. Then I felt this being come closer to me and rest its arm on my shoulder. It then made the sign of the cross over my head. This made me very peaceful. One senses this somehow; it is very extraordinary... (2092)

### On the boat Ver

I was living in Siglufjord. I had just come off a boat that had been stranded and was 'between ships' as they say. Then a ship came in and they needed a deck officer. I was so pleased to get a job so soon. The ship was called Ver EA 401 and was from Hrisey. It used to be called Lif and was originally from Norway. In these boats the skipper, the cook, the deck officers and the engineers usually stayed in certain cabins and the bunks were assigned to the various members of the crew. When I came down the skipper was in the bunk that I thought should be mine. I did not make a big deal about it but took the next bunk which was not being used. This was a so-called upper bunk, which the skipper had been using before he moved. We either unloaded in Dalvik or Hrisey. I was the only non-local person on the boat and so when we had some time off after unloading all the men went home and I was on my own in the boat.

Sometimes I had been awakened suddenly from a deep sleep but never thought twice about it. Then there was one time when I was on my own there and I lay down for a nap. I woke up suddenly when somebody pulled forcefully at me and I was told to get up. I thought to myself that the lads must be back but then there was nobody there. I was really tired and fell fast asleep again and I really sleep deeply when I am tired. The next thing was that I am pulled out of the bunk and thrown to the floor. I did not seem to be welcome in this bunk... It was not a figment of my imagination and I packed up my things the morning after, left the boat and went home. A few years later I met a man on the boat Ellidi from Siglufjord who had been a deck officer on Ver. He was not one of the locals either, and for some reason he had also had to stay in that same bunk. He had exactly the same story to tell... (5108)

# 5

# THAT SMELLS FAMILIAR

PERCEPTIONS of the deceased involving smell or scent are not experienced often. Only 21 cases were reported. Many of these, however, are very interesting. In these incidents people perceived a smell which was in some way associated with a deceased person or representative of them in some way. The perception was thus experienced or interpreted as representing the presence of this person. In most of these cases only a smell was perceived but in three cases the deceased person was also seen.

### The herbalist

I was preparing herbal medicine for a man and was not thinking of anything else. All of a sudden I felt my deceased father standing next to me. I was going to turn to face him, but it did not work out, I just could not do that. His presence made me stop thinking about what I was doing, although it was not intentional. A certain man came quite vividly to my mind, whom I had not spoken to for six weeks and I said out loud to myself: "Why, he has not been here." At the same time it went through my mind, like the thought was being sent from the one standing next to me, that I should prepare a broth for this man whom I had not seen for a long time and whose present whereabouts I knew nothing about. Well, I stopped what I was doing and started on this. I did not sense the person who was next to me anymore. Two hours later there was a knock on my door. It was this man and he said: "I really must have one more of your bottles. When do you think you can have it ready?" I told him it just so happened that it had been pointed out to me that he would need this and that it was ready. And he got the bottle.... Yes, I often do feel the presence of my father. You could say I was in direct contact with him. There often was a strong odour of herbs from his fingers while he was involved in this. Sometimes, when I sense him sitting next to me, I smell this herb odour... I often sense the deceased as well as the living that are far away, see them and hear them and sense them in other ways... (2050)

## As if in the woods

My wife and I have had it for a habit to go to the cemetery once a week. And when these tree branches become available, we cover my mother-in-law's grave with them. She was from Latvia and came to Iceland as a refugee after the war. We have always done this. We saw in Eastern Germany how they cover their graves. Once, after having covered the grave only a few days earlier, we enter our car to find such a strong smell in the car, just as if we were in the middle of the woods. We both perceived this smell and we felt it was in some way related to the old lady. The car smelt all the way to our home. Then there was another time that we came back home and had just sat down when we both experienced this strong smell of soil, of de-caying soil. It was very distinct. We associated it with the old lady who had lived with us for 25 years. (5043)

## Bad smell

Most people with serious lung or digestion diseases have a bad odour, the smell of something rotting. My niece died young from lung cancer. One Sunday morning, sometime after she passed away, I smelled this stink very clearly in the kitchen where I was working. I looked around to see if something in the kitchen could cause this but found nothing. Not an hour had passed when her husband came to visit unexpectedly. I associated this smell with his visit for it was clearly her odour, exactly the smell she had after she became very ill.... I first thought of her when her husband arrived. (5058)

## The headmaster

I worked at this primary school for a long time, when this head-master was in charge. It was strange but he always smelt a certain way. Then he died. Once Hafsteinn the medium had a séance here and I went out of curiosity and sat on one of the benches. Suddenly I could smell strongly that smell I associated with the headmaster and I really could not understand what was going on. I looked around and saw his widow sitting there close by me. I felt it was a bit strange that just about this time this man was described by the medium, strange that it should happen just then. It was as if the smell followed me after he was a dead man and buried, always when I entered the headmaster's room there was that same smell, even though nobody else could smell it... (5072)

## Letting me know

My father died a few years ago and I have since been aware of several things that I associate with him. I went south so I could be present at his funeral and stayed in the apartment that had belonged to him. When I was about to fall asleep I perceived this really strong smell. I could not fall asleep because of it. His briefcase smelled of this certain smell - a smell of leather. But in that instant, the smell was so strong, so powerful that it kept me awake. I thought to myself that first thing in the morning I would air out the apartment but when I woke up the smell was gone. Then this smell appeared, for example, when I visited his sister, in a certain place where he used to sit when he was there. Then I smelled it when I was going through some of his papers. When I started checking out the briefcase I realised it was the same smell. I most definitely associate the smell with my father, who he was letting me know he was there. (5062)

## Snuff man

I was travelling alone in a car across the Hols mountains. I do not smoke or use tobacco and neither had been used in the car for a very long time. Suddenly I could smell this strong smell of snuff and it was so powerful that it really could not have been my mistaken perception. I cannot imagine that was the case. I thought of my father who died when I was a child and I never knew. I thought of him and I felt like I was not alone, it was a very strong feeling. My mother told me that he used a lot of snuff. You associate these things with what is closest to you. (7048)

## A peculiar smell

It was about a week after my father-in-law died here at home, that I went out to shop. When I came back I could smell such a strange odour all over the apartment. I recognised the smell immediately. He needed to take a lot of medicine and used to carry it in a box – and walked around with it – and took it at various times. And this smell was so strong when I walked in the door. And this I could smell for many days but nobody else could smell the odour. But one day a friend of mine comes over and says: "What a strange smell – it smells like medicine." So it was not just me – and she said: "It smells just like the medicine the old man used to use." It was very strong - every so often it would become really bad, but not always in the same place. He had lived with us for six years.

Is this the old man trying to tell me something? No, I am not sure about that. He probably worried about me. I could somehow feel that he was around me – was sure of it. My older daughter also noticed the smell and I was a bit surprised when she said: "It is just like the smell of grandfather". She only smelled it in the lounge – she is twelve. I was very surprised when other people could also smell it. But then it disappeared. I cannot quite remember when. It lasted for ten or twelve days but no more. By that time I had thrown away the medicine box and it was all gone.

Once I remember coming back home from the shop with my younger daughter. I had a fright when I opened the door. I cannot remember how long a time had passed then since his death. Whether it was half a month or three weeks – or a month – I cannot quite remember now, although I may have remembered when I answered the questionnaire you sent me. It arrived so soon afterwards. I was a bit restless. I went to look in all the rooms and so on – no one was there. Soon after I sensed the smell I always felt as if somebody was around. I sometimes felt I heard noises, such as doors being opened and closed and went to look. Nothing was there. I really did not let myself think about it too much because I was not exactly scared. When you are aware of something like this for the first time, you are more surprised – you do not know whether it is real or not. You are just so surprised. I wrote to his daughter, my sister-in-law, about all of it, because it had such an effect on me. I felt it was all extremely peculiar. (1065)

## Dead man's smell

A girl once stayed at my house for a while. When she was leaving my wife, my mother in law and I smelled this thing that smelled like a death odour. Shortly afterwards we heard that the girl's uncle had died at about the same time as we smelled this odour and I associated these two incidents....... (7518)

## Strong smell

About half a month after my father died, I could often sense this strong smell of him, especially if I was sitting where he used to sit. Other people could not smell it. (5032)

## The cumin coffee

I have often smelled peculiar odours that are very familiar. When I was a child my grandmother was alive but she is long dead by now. Her kitchen always smelled strange because she often made cumin coffee and the odour was very strong. Then it was on my girl's birthday last March..... The guests had gone and I was there with my mother. She was in the living room and I was alone in the kitchen. Then I smelled this odour, quite distinctly, but I could not associate it with anything in there. I called my mother and she came into the kitchen. I asked her if she smelled anything peculiar and, yes, she smelled something but she did not want to talk more about it. This odour was in there for some time but then it just vanished. (7516A)

And finally an incident where the deceased person was perceived both by smell and sight and the informant felt that the smell was just as important as the vision.

## Smoke in my face

Of course I have had all sorts of experiences through the years but I have only been aware of a deceased man this one time, perceived it so clearly... I was lying on a bench and this happened on a Sunday. Then I saw my deceased father who had died some months earlier. I could see his upper body, down to his chest. I could see him very vividly, just for a short while, but I could feel peace and satisfaction along with the vision. My father used to smoke the pipe quite a lot and this used to give off a very peculiar smell. Once I sensed this smell very clearly, just as if somebody had blown smoke in my face. It happened in his room, where he used to live... (2112)

# 6

# SENSING AN INVISIBLE PRESENCE

A ROUND one in nine of the incidents (49 accounts) consisted solely of subjective experiences without any actual sensory perception. This group was problematic for us to begin with as it fell outside the definition that had originally been formed for encounters with the deceased. However, it became clear quite early in the interviews that this sensing of an invisible presence can be a powerful and convincing experience for many people and thus plays an important role in alleged encounters of the deceased - or 'afterlife encounters' as it has become referred to in the USA (Archangel, 2005). Therefore we decided to include this group after some accounts had been removed that seemed particularly unclear.

## Perception

Shortly after the death of one of my female neighbours I sensed her presence every so often for a few months. She died in an accident forty years old. This was a keen awareness of her presence but there was no direct sensory perception of her. (209)

## The lady from Myrar

I have heard my name being called out loud when there was no one near. A few times I could smell a strange odour but more often I felt the presence of someone with me. It was that way with the woman from Myrar. I used to be a midwife there. When I sensed her I had the feeling that she had something to tell me but I did not know what it was. She was with me quite a lot. I did not know why. Then I learned of her death, and I still kept sensing her and it lasted for about two weeks.... (2039)

## Night guard in the house of parliament

I was working as a night guard in the house of the parliament. I had taken over from a friend of mine who had arranged for me to get the job. He had died of cerebral haemorrhage when he was 72 or 73 years old. He was a straightforward person, free-and-easy and cheerful. He died just one week before getting his pension. That week I felt his presence at various hours. The cleaning woman had also felt his presence. . (376)

## Teasing

I rented an apartment Reykjavík. I was frequently aware of the presence of a man and felt as if he was teasing me. Both the landlord and a medium told me that some time before me a man who had rented the flat had died in the living room, where I was most aware of him. I know that more people had been aware of his presence... (2030x)

## Out by the Westfjords

My grandmother died when she was 82 years old and I was 11 years old. Since then I have often felt that she has followed me. She has often shown me the way. Once I fell off a motorboat when we were out by the Westfjords. As soon as I fell in the water she came into my mind and said: "It is all right, it is all right." And that was the case for I managed to keep myself afloat and after a while the boat turned around and I was saved. (2126)

## At my father-in-law's

I was at my father-in-law's and was sitting beside him. We were talking about all sorts of things and he said something along the lines of: "There is a lot in this world that we cannot see." Then I felt as if a man was standing beside him and I said: "Yes, like that man who is standing beside you." I could feel it was a man wearing a hat and a grey jacket. I could not see him, I just felt him; it is hard to explain. I just knew exactly what the man looked like. I would not have thought much of it or remembered it, if my father-in-law had not died the following day. I have never managed to obtain information about who that man was. 7004)

## At home

This relates to an acquaintance of mine who died about eight years ago. I was never in any position to say goodbye to him which I felt I should have done. Then I was staying close to home in really good weather during the summer. It was a very beautiful place. It was sunny, still and peaceful. Then I felt he came to me like a storm through the calm weather. I could really feel him all around me... (7610)

## The grandfather

This relates to my grandfather. I lived in Reykjavik and he had a room in the basement for he wanted to be on his own and he died there. About nine years after the old man had died I started putting together some bookshelves downstairs in that room. When I was a small boy I had often visited him and he would let me hammer together some wood. I was making bookshelves which I was going to use upstairs. This was during the evening and it was quiet and still. Then I suddenly felt such a presence that I stopped and left. This was accompanied by some sort of fear, probably I was scared. I really felt he was there at my side. I often felt this after this first occasion but the fright disappeared. (2214)

## My grandmother's presence

I believe I was once aware of my grandmother's presence. I was outside enjoying nature and was engrossed in looking at some flowers and herbs. I just perceived her in some way. It was just some sort of presence. (2182)

## Dark and heavy

Once I went into the hall during the night and pretty much walked right through a deceased man, or it felt I did. I felt as if he came towards me not in an evil frame of mind but with a heavy presence, perhaps worried or whatever it was, as if he was having a hard time. And in order to face it I just kept going. I felt he stayed still and I walked through him. Then it was as if this being disintegrated or faded away. It became much darker around me when that happened, sort of dark and heavy. This was a very strong feeling and a strong perception first and foremost. It was dark and I could not see anything. (5049)

### Pleased with the work

I was building a house and my father-in-law was very helpful with advice. He used to be a mason and I was doing that work myself. He died while I was still building the house. Before he died he had told me to speak to him before I started tiling the bathroom and he would give me some advice. I tiled the bathroom and one day after I had finished, I was alone in the apartment. I could feel that he was there but I could not see him. He was standing in the doorway looking over the work and I felt as if he was pleased. I was extremely frightened but still, I could feel he was there... (5064)

Finally, here is an example where the informant is grateful to his grandfather for the success on the repairs of his boat.

### A condemned boat

I happened to be working on a boat as the chief engineer. Both engines had been declared unusable, and there seemed really to be no way we could finish the fishing-season. But things changed for the better. It was unbelievable how well things worked out. I clearly felt that it was not all my doing. There was someone with me. I was distinctly aware of it and I knew it was my grandfather who has been with me all my life. He died about the time when I was born. I do not want to describe his appearance here, but I had a very keen sense of him and it gave me such trust and strength to know that he was there and to feel his presence. (7528)

A few incidents were set aside which were not classified as experiences with the dead but may still be of interest. One person told of an experience with automatic writing. A carpenter had come across a shelf which had fallen from a wall along with all its fastenings, including the plastic rawlplugs in which the screws had been fastened. The girl who owned the shelf believed that this had happened because of an interruption from "the other side" and the carpenter agreed. These are examples of experiences which are often interpreted as stemming from the people 'on the other side' as some of our participants would have phrased it.

# 7

# EXPERIENCES AT THE
# MOMENT OF DEATH

IN many cases the deceased were perceived at the time they died. Every ninth encounter took place within 24 hours of the moment of death. It is very interesting to note that in 86 percent of these cases the informant had not known that the person had died when he or she had the experience. Let us first consider these cases.

**Encounters at the moment of death when the participant was unaware of illness or mortal danger**

### My name is Margret
My wife and I had living with us a little girl about two and a half years old whom we fostered. One night I woke up and felt as though a woman were standing beside the bed. She said to me, "My name is Margret." Then she vanished out the door. I looked at the clock and saw that it was exactly three thirty. The day after, or the same day, I learnt that the girl´s grandmother had died at that same moment from a heart attack at a town in another part of the country. Her name was Margret. I knew nothing about her health. I am not even sure if I knew her name. I had never seen her when she was living. (2180)

### You were lucky
I was a Member of the Parliament for 18 years and during that time I was in contact with many men who later became good

acquaintances of mine. One of them was Karl Kristjansson. We were friends and kept in touch on and off after we retired. One day in the winter I went out to the stable as I usually did after lunch. When I had been shovelling manure for a while, I suddenly felt that Karl Kristjansson standing in front of me in one of the stalls in the stable. He said something rather peculiar: "You were lucky, you did fine," and that was all because he then disappeared. That evening his death was announced on the radio. While pondering about the incident and trying to figure it out, I learnt that he had suffered a heart attack and been brought to the Reykjavik City Hospital where he died. I had been admitted to that hospital a year earlier after suffering a similar attack. I luckily recuperated and could go home, whereas he died. In that context I understood his words, "You were lucky, you did fine." (7030)

This participant told us that he had written down a description of what occurred just after he had his experience. This article was in the keeping of one of his sons and is printed here with his permission:

It was Tuesday, March 7th 1978 and the time was getting on for three o'clock and I had gone out to muck out the stables, here to the north of the farm. I had just begun to work on this when all at once my thoughts turned very strongly to Karl Kristjansson, a former member of Parliament, who was in parliament at the same time as me for many years. I had the feeling that Karl had come to me and I saw him in my mind, standing in front of me and saying "You were lucky, you did well." The tone of this speech was as if Karl was unhappy; that either he or someone else had not been so lucky.

What I saw and heard in my mind lasted no longer than the blink of an eye, but I found it quite an uncomfortable experience. However, I soon turned my thoughts to other things, although the occurrence did pop into my head once or twice during the day, as if I could not quite banish the memory altogether. I was, therefore, a bit upset, when, that same evening, I was sitting at the kitchen table eating my dinner and listening to the radio, when I heard the news of Karl Kristjansson's death. He had died at Borgarspítali that same day, and I must also admit to feeling rather strange on hearing this. I could not help but remember that the year before, I had lain in that same hospital, due to a coronary condition, but was lucky enough to make a full recovery. It occurred to me that perhaps Karl had got news of this while in hospital, and was thinking of me around the time he died. It could certainly be said of my stay there and the events leading up to it, that I had been lucky and had done well.

I wrote down the above account immediately that evening, just as it appears here. I also wish to make it clear that, as far as I can remember, Karl Kristjansson had not entered my mind for the past weeks or even months, even although he and I were friendly and I respected him greatly. Neither did I know anything about his illness or his spell in the hospital. Therefore, I cannot connect the incident in the stables with any pre-knowledge of this. (7030)

## The old man

I was really fond of an old man on the next farm but he was not related to me at all. What happened was that he came in and I could see his face and two knocks followed or something like that. Then he walked back out and closed the door behind him. It was a very strange incident which only lasted for a short time. The next day I found out that he had died at about the same time as I was aware of him. He was only letting me know, that is all... (2156)

## The call

I was working on the road construction up in the country. One night I woke up and felt that somebody was calling me, and I felt it was my mother. I went outside but could not see anyone. It was only three in the morning when I checked, so I went inside and went back to sleep. My mother was at Vifilsstadir hospital and as far as I knew she was about to return home. However, she had died about the same time that I heard someone call me. (2178)

## The nanny

It happened when I was a boy and lived in Bolungarvik. An old lady lived by the harbour and she used to look after me. Once I was ill and at home alone because my mother had gone shopping. By chance I walked to the door and opened it. Then I could see in front of me this old lady who looked after me. It did not last for long and we did not say a word but it felt as if she smiled to me. I went back into my room and a little later my mother came home. She told me that old Ingibjorg, my nanny, had died. It happened at about the same time that I saw her. (2176)

### At Hjorsey

When I was in my twenties I stayed at Hjorsey. One time in the middle of the night I woke up and saw an elderly man from the district, a farmer, standing on the middle of the floor. I watched him for quite a while. He did not move and then he disintegrated and disappeared as soon as I was about to speak to him. In the morning I told the household members of my experience and thought that this farmer was most likely dead now. In the evening we received a message by post informing us of the death of this farmer. About two months later I met this farmer's widow and she told me that she had dozed off after his death and dreamt her husband said to her: "I have already been to Hjorsey, but no one was aware of me there except Gisli (the informant)" (2011)

The man who gave us this account, Gisli Frimannsson, pointed out that his account can also be found in a book by Hafsteinn Björnsson: "Sögur ur safni Hafsteins midils" (Stories from the collection of Hafsteinn the medium which was published by Skuggsja in 1972)

### Moment in the morning

One morning I could feel that my mother was with me. I could not see her but I strongly felt that she was there. It only lasted a short moment. A few hours later I was told that she had died. She died shortly before I had felt that she was with me. I had not expected her death. (5070)

### The loss of a son

After I lost my boy he came to me one night and I saw him, his face and all. I saw him beside me in the bed and it was as if someone would go through my body. My heart was pounding. I woke up my wife and we got out of the room. When I stood by his picture I collapsed. It was as if my feet were swept from under me. I said to my wife that something terrible was happening and I ran into the room to check the children but they were asleep. When I was again at ease I went back to bed but then I felt it coming over me again and I started to pray... (7512)

The man's wife confirmed this account. She remembered the incident well. They had discussed the matter over a cup of coffee. Their son died in a shipwreck that same night, at the same time as when the father had his experience. Only two years had passed since the incident when the couple told us about this.

### Walked by a window

I was sitting in the kitchen in my aunt's farmhouse and was chatting with her after dinner as she was in the room adjacent to the kitchen. Then I saw a man pass by the window and I said to my sister that we had company. I went to the front door but no one was there. She said that I must have been mistaken, but when I described the man I had seen, she said:"Why, that is Eggert". Eggert was an old friend of ours since childhood. He was living in Vik when this happened. Later that day a guest arrived and brought us news of Eggert's death. He had passed away suddenly earlier that day. (403)

## Incidents that happened some time after the moment of death but within twenty four hours

### In the fishing town of Sandgerdi

I lived in Sandgerdi where we had just bought a house two months ago. I was alone in the house. My husband was out working. Suddenly I saw a man enter through the front door and go to the kitchen. This happened suddenly and was over. I then felt a strong smell of liquor. I never use alcohol. Then my husband came home and he said, "Who has been here?" No one, I told him. "Oh, there is such a strong smell of liquor." Yes, I said, but nobody has been here.... The next day my husband came home for supper and said, 'No wonder there was a liquor smell here yesterday.... Erlingur from whom we bought the house was missing in Siglufjord yesterday." He had been quite drunk and it was feared that he had fallen into the harbour and drowned. Two weeks later his body was found floating in the harbour. When this incident occurred, we had no idea about what had happened. My husband is now deceased. (2116)

### Deceased lady friend

I once saw a friend of mine but I did not know until later, that she had been ill down south in Reykjavík. I was living out west in Skardsstrond. I was standing at the stove and there was a room adjacent to the kitchen. By the window in that room I saw her standing when I looked up from the stove. I saw her whole body from the side. Shortly afterwards her husband came to my house with my husband. They were coming from Stykkishólm and told me that she had died. (2078).

## By Blanda

I was out in the country and going to visit my grandfather. I was having a pleasant trip, stayed at the village of Blanda for two nights, or rather, was going to. I was not in any hurry. All of a sudden I sensed my grandfather right there with me. I instantly knew that he had passed away, went to the post office and called. It was confirmed that he had died the day before. (2015)

## The sailor suit

When I was a kid I was always afraid of a particular boy who was always teasing me. I had to run errands and I hated to have to go past the house where he lived. One time I was running an errand. I was ten years old. I passed this house and the boy was sitting there on the steps or on the threshold. The house was called Billiards because billiards was played there. The boy sat there on the threshold all dressed up, wearing a sailor's suit and a white scarf. I will never forget this, it was so odd. He was just sitting there whistling. I thought to myself that it was odd that he should leave me alone. I hurried passed him and went about my business. When I came home I told my foster mother about this and she said: "Do not be silly child, he died last night." He had caught pneumonia and died the night before. (2019)

## A knock on the bathroom wall

I was working in the country during the winter. One morning in spring when it was already light I was awakened along with the rest of the household in the living room by a loud knock on the living room wall, on the side where I was sleeping. The head of the household slept on the same side and woke up too. On the other side of the wall an old man was sleeping who had been bedridden for a few days and was expected to die. When the old man was attended to he was found dead. The masters of the house reckoned that the old man was letting himself be known. (521)

**Accounts where the participant knew that the perceived person was ill and death was expected, but did not know that that person had already died when the experience occurred**

### The father-in-law

My father-in-law was very sick, and my husband stayed at his deathbed the last nights. The night he died I woke up at five o'clock and had the feeling that the old man was coming down the hall into the apartment. Although I did not see this I could feel it, and this feeling was accompanied by a sense of warmth and comfort. I knew he was visiting me. Later that morning when my husband came home from his father's deathbed I said to him, before he said anything to me, 'Your father is dead'. When we compared notes we found out that his death occurred around the time of my experience. (2028A)

### Arndis

My friend had been in hospital since the fall and we knew that she was going to die. I woke up one morning between 5 and 6 and felt that she was in my room, standing by my bed. I felt that she was dead and was letting me know. When I came down the following morning, my brother-in-law had just got up and he said that somebody had called. I said, 'Yes, they must have been calling to say that Arndis has died". Then they called shortly after and we were told that she had died between 5 and 6 that morning. (5006)

### In Kopavogshæli

My mother was in hospital and when she died I was working at the Kopavogshæli sanatorium. I saw her there walking down the hall. I was a bit startled but understood it immediately that she was saying goodbye. I was not thinking of her, was just there busy with my work. An hour later my sisters came over to tell me that she was gone. She had passed away about the same time I saw her. (5020)

### In Vifilsstadir

It was evening. I was washing the floors in the day room at the Vifilsstadir hospital when I saw a man come in. He was wearing pyjamas. I knew immediately who it was; a patient in the hospital about thirty years old who had been seriously ill. He disappeared very suddenly. Then I heard that he had been dying at about that same time. Soon after the incident I was scared and I can still remember it very vividly. (602)

**A school mate**

I was at sea and in my bunk when an old mate from school came through the door. I knew before I went to sea that he had cancer and was waiting to die. I was surprised and said to him: "How are you?" and he said: "Yes, now it's all finished, all over and I feel just fine but there is a lot of work to do. Yes, I need to visit more places, I just wanted to say goodbye to you, be well and blessed." And he disintegrated and vanished in front of me, not like he came; he entered through the door. I felt this was a bit strange. I had to pinch myself to see if I was really awake or in a sleepy state. As far as I could tell I was awake. Then about noon the announcement came on the radio that he had died. I realised later that we had not really talked, we had communicated through the mind. I was not aware of the fact that one can communicate in that way; it felt like I was talking to him. (7012)

In some accounts the experience is indirect. After having received news of a death, a strange experience which had happened around the moment of death becomes associated with a certain person. It becomes understood as the deceased person drawing attention to themselves.

**Slippery**

This happened a long time ago. I was a teenager at a farm up in the country. I saw something come up the road towards the farm but no one came. I was then saying it must have been a wild horse. But someone said that no horse without iron hoofs would walk across the sand spits out there because it was so slippery from ice. The next day we learnt about a shipwreck. The men aboard had stayed at this farm on their way to sea to work on that boat. I felt I had seen them. I thought I had heard crunching sounds of somebody walking on the icy snow. (2031)

**Three phantoms**

This happened when I was eight years old. I was sitting in a pile of snow and was building a snow house beside the shops in the village of Saudarkrok. On the steps of the house was standing a grown up man that I knew. We both saw three men go by as fast as lightning, or we sensed them as men. I remember him saying: "They certainly are in a hurry those three." The next day I heard that three men had died at sea by Skagi. I associated the experience with them and

48

that, at least, their minds were going home. It happened at about the same time as they drowned. I remember that this was rather unclear but I did see these three men. I did not really think much about but I have always remembered it. (5016)

## On Stjarna RE3

I was at sea on the boat Stjarna RE3 and was lying on a bench in the cabin. It was during the morning and the only light in the cabin came from the window beside the stairs. I saw a man come down the stairs turning his back to me. I thought to myself that is must be the cook. When the man got down the stairs and turned around I recognised that he was not a member of the crew. This man was wearing a dark blue shirt with light shining buttons. I could not see his face in the dark but I felt I recognised him although I could not remember who he was at the time. I was going to say something but then he disappeared. I was very startled. I went upstairs and told the cook about it and we wrote down the time when it happened. When I went back ashore I was told that my grandfather's brother had died at the same time. I always connected his death with my experience. (7010A)

## At Basar

My grandmother used to soak socks in a bucket full of water and would sometimes then get us kids to stir them around to make it easier for her to wash them. She had put a bucket with socks in the hall outside our kitchen door and asked me to wash them out a bit. I was not really that fond of this job and the hallway was cold so I tried to get out of doing what she asked me. She was persistent so I finally obeyed her. The bucket was on top of a stool in the middle of the hall and there was a lot of space all around the bucket. I had been thinking about something else while doing my job when I heard someone start walking around me. I could hear footsteps just like when old people are walking; they drag their feet a little. I could hear that the person was wearing shoes with leather soles. I listened for a while then ran inside to my grandmother and told her I had quit, because I did not want to be in the hall when somebody was walking around me. She told me to stop complaining; she knew full well that I was just lazy and did not want to do the job. Finally I went back into the hall and started again but was always listening. Before long it started again and I could hear it very clearly. When it went between me and the doorway I got scared and as soon as it had passed I ran in to my grandmother crying and told her that somebody was really walking around me. She realised that this was something real and let me stop. A short while later my grandfather came home to Basar from the south. He brought the news that old Sigrid had just passed away that morning. As soon as he said that, I realised that the footsteps I had heard were hers. It was just like what I had heard lots of times before. I felt that she walked just like she had all those years that I had known her. I can remember this incident as clearly as if it occurred a short while ago. (7034) (see 6014)

### A friend of the station manager

I was learning to be an electrician here at the electric station on the Westman Islands. In the evening the station manager went to visit a man who was very ill, called Gudni Johnsen. They were good friends and the man had asked the manager to come and see him. I did my duty, looked at the engines and then came into the manager's house and washed my hands. Then the door opened and I could see a man's hand holding the door handle and the hand was pulled back. I guessed it might be a lady who sometimes brought clothes to one of the employees. She was sometimes there in the evening. I kept washing my hands and then I went into the hall. Nobody was there. I went all around the station but the outside door was locked and it was not possible to get in without keys. So I guessed that it was the ghost of Gudni Johnsen. When the station manager and his brother came back, I could sense that something has happened. I asked him whether Gudni had already passed away when they got there and they said yes. "You must have been about half way there when he died", I said. The station manager guessed I was right. So this had happened at about the same time as Gudni died. His friend the station manager did not get there in time before he died. (7558)

It was in the second group of interviews (1980-1981) that we asked exactly how long after the moment of death the deceased person was perceived. In total we collected 349 accounts - about as many as the days in the year. If these cases are spread around the year by pure chance one of these incidents should have occurred on the day that the perceived person died. However, in this study, 38 of the 349 cases happened on the day the person passed away. Indeed, experiences of the deceased often happen at around the time of death. A study conducted by British researchers over a century ago also suggested that visions of the dead are especially likely to occur at around the moment of death (Gurney, Myers and Podmore, 1886).

It is noteworthy that in 84 percent of the incidents that occurred at the time of death, the perceiver did not know that the perceived person had died. In some cases the participant knew that the deceased person had been ill but in others they believed that they were in normal health. We did not ask whether the perceived person's death had been expected, so we cannot go into more detail on this matter. Nevertheless, through reading the accounts it appears that in most cases death was not expected.

In some of these incidents another person witnessed the encounter. In addition, there were a few accounts where the perceiver told another person about the experience before they came to know about the perceived person's death. We will discuss these accounts in more detail in another chapter.

## Deceased persons appear shortly after the participant has been told of their death

### The seamstress

I was at work as a seamstress in Isafjord and heard the door to the room open. I thought the manager was coming in to talk to me so I turned around, but it was a deceased friend of mine. I had just heard of her death that morning. She died only 21 years old. She had just got engaged and had a bright future. She looked serious, walked up to me and said that everything was all right and she would come to me soon. A few years later I had a child who was named after this friend of mine. (2098A)

### At the loss of a mother

I was ten years old when this happened and had lost my mother earlier that same day. She died quite suddenly from tuberculosis. A few hours after her death I saw my mother walk past a window where I was sitting. It may have been my imagination. More likely it was controlled by my mother's thoughts which at that time were most important to me. I had often seen her walk past this window on her way to visit her friend who lived in the next house. (2007)

### An orderly grandmother

My grandmother's name was Gudlaug Palsdottir. She was always very orderly and always knew where everything was. She spent a lot of time at my home when I was young. If I needed something, like a missing mitten, I would ask my grandmother where it was and she would always know where to find it. Then she died at old age in a hospital. The day after she died I was at home alone. The radio was not on and it was very quiet. I was in the kitchen looking for a pair of scissors, but did not find them. As I went into the bedroom to look for them I heard the scissors drop loudly right behind me. I turned around and saw them lying in the window in the hall I was passing through. But there was nothing there they could have made them fall off. At the same time I distinctly felt my grandmothers' presence and was very happy. It was so much like her to know where to find the scissors. (7009)

# 8

## How Soon After Death Were the Deceased Encountered?

I T has already been mentioned that every ninth encounter with the deceased occurred on the day that he or she passed away. What about the other incidents? How soon after death did the encounters take place? The timing varied greatly, as would be expected.

We have a rough estimate of the time that had passed since the encountered person died in 337 accounts. About half the incidents happened within a year, about a fifth happened in the next four years and the rest later. For more details see table 2.

| Table 2. How soon after death were the dead encountered? Results from all 449 accounts. | | | |
|---|---|---|---|
| | **Frequency** | **Percentages** | |
| | | | **In total** |
| **Within a year** | 168 | 50 | 50 |
| **Within 1-4 years** | 75 | 22 | 72 |
| **Within 5-10 years** | 34 | 10 | 82 |
| **Later than 10 years** | 60 | 18 | 100 |
| **Unknown** | 112 | - | - |
| **Total** | 449 | | |

For the larger of our two samples (349 participants) we have more detailed information on the cases that happened within a year. Of the incidents where the timing is available, 7 percent occurred at the moment of death, 14 percent occurred within 24 hours and 22 percent happened within a week. Almost a third of the incidents occurred within a month of death. Around half of the accounts in this sample occurred within a year, which is similar to the percentage found when both samples are examined together. In 77 out of 349 incidents the deceased person was not identified or it was not known when he/ she had passed away. These results are shown in Table 3.

**Table 3. How soon after death were the dead encountered? Results from the second survey (349 cases)**

| | Frequency | Percentage | |
|---|---|---|---|
| | | | In total |
| **Within an hour** | 19 | 7.0 | 7.0 |
| **Within 24 hours** | 19 | 7.0 | 14.0 |
| **Within a week** | 23 | 8.4 | 22.4 |
| **Within a month** | 24 | 8.8 | 31.2 |
| **Within a year** | 56 | 20.6 | 51.8 |
| **Within 5 years** | 57 | 20.9 | 72.8 |
| **Within 10 years** | 25 | 9.2 | 82 |
| **After 10 years** | 49 | 18.0 | 100 |
| **Unknown** | 77 | - | - |

In the former survey (100 cases), people were asked in what year the incident had occurred. The informants seemed to remember the year quite well, unless many years had passed since they had their experience. We also asked for the name of the deceased person and the age at death. With the help of official records (mainly *Islendingabok* and the websites of cemetaries) it was possible to discover the exact age at death. This information could then be used to calculate how many years had passed since the encountered person had died. If it had happened within a year we had no way of knowing whether it had happened within 24 hours, a week or a month as we could in the later survey. Most of the accounts in the former survey occurred within a year (24 cases) or between 1-4 years after death (18 cases). Only nine accounts happened 5-10 years after death and ten incidents occurred more than 10 years after death. A few of the incidents happened decades after the encountered dead person had passed away, with 30 years being the longest time that had passed.

## How much time had passed from the encounters with the dead until we were told about them?

33 incidents had happened within a year of when the interviews took place. Many of the examples should therefore have been fresh in the mind of the informants. A quarter of the accounts happened within 5 years, one half within 14 years and the rest happened later. On average, the incidents were reported to us 14 years after occurred.

## In what years did the incidents happen?

To answer the question: 'In what year did the incidents happen?' the reader must keep in mind that the interviews were taken at two different points in time. The first 100 participants were interviewed in 1976, 183 were interviewed in 1980, 161 in 1981 and five in 1986.

The oldest case (6000) probably happened before or around the year 1900. A woman who was born in 1884 told us about her encounter which she had when she was a child. This account can be found in chapter *Is Someone Watching Over Us?* The next incident happened in 1900. These two cases are by far the oldest accounts in our collection.

Eirikur Kristófersson, who was a captain in the Icelandic Coast Guard in the Cod War, told us of the second incident. Gunnar M. Magnus includes the account in his biography of Eirikur Kristofersson: *Captain Eiríkur* (1967). Here is his acccount:

### Captain Eiríkur

When I was 7 or 8 years old a girl died on the farm next to us; the fields of the farms met. She was the farmer's wife's sister. She was quite boistrous and people felt that she made quite a racket after she died. This was during the spring. At one time we were going to the cowshed to milk the cows; it was a rather long walk. The girl had only recently died. There was my mother and at least one of the maids and a few of us kids. Then we met the deceased on the path. It looked just as if she was a living person. Just before we met her she walked off the path, walked around us and kept walking up the path. All of us saw her...

At that time people used to sit with the dead people's bodies. At our house there was an old lady who was not scared of the dark at all. They got her to sit with the girl's body. After the funeral the farmer's wife wanted to thank the lady for her help and gave her a knitted top that had belonged to the girl who had passed away. The old lady put the top in the box where she kept her finer clothes, the ones she seldom used. After that the girl started haunting the old lady. This old lady always did the job of closing up the outside door in the evening. But then she could not do it anymore. We kids were scared but not that much since we used to watch her trying to close the door. We could see that the old lady was trying to close the door by putting her back to it but it did not work. It was always about a width of a hand away from closing. She could never get it any further unless some of the kids were standing outside the door, then she and anybody else could close the door.

My mother now asked the old lady to give back the woollen top but she said she would not, whatever this deceased girl would do. Finally, no one would go and close the door with her and she used to take a light with her to close the door. Next time she came back running, threw away the lamp and said she was never going to try to close the outside door again. In the end she gave back the knitten top and after that there was no trouble at all. (2056)

Eirik suggested that we speak to his sister Johanna, who was then 96 years old. She said she remembered the old lady and the jumper and how difficult it was for the old woman to close the doors to the house. She says she was not present when they saw the dead girl and could not remember if she had heard of the incident. Johanna told us of another case which is included in the chapter *Is Someone Watching Over Us?*

The youngest accounts happened in 1981, the year when the interviews took place. This is one of them:

### In the flicker

We were going on a visit in town one Thursday night. That is when I saw my grandfather, my father's father, as if flickering light behind my father. It was as clear picture of him. My father was going out, was about to go out of sight when the man I am named after appeared. He appeared in the flicker. He was dressed up, that was very obvious. (7548)

Our informant said he told his father immediately what he had seen. We contacted his father after the interview. The father said he had been told of the incident but only after he came back from the visit he had been setting off for. The informant said he had been in full health at the time of his experience, even if other people may not have been of the same opinion. He added that people did not always take him seriously. The informant had had a good relationship with his grandfather until he died after a long illness. The grandfather died seven years before the occurrence. The informant said his grandfather had looked good-natured and peaceful when he appeared suddenly that evening. Our informant did not know of any other relatives who had seen his dead grandfather before and this was the only time he perceived his grandfather after he died. The experience had been a positive one. He often read books about the supernatural and believed in the afterlife. He also said he did not feel the experience had changed these beliefs in any way.

The incidents are spread over a long time. This is not surprising since some of them occurred in the childhood of old participants. Just as many cases occurred before 1966 as after that year. 150 occurred 1971-81, 106 in the years 1961-70, 63 from, 1951-60, 44 in 1941-50, 46 in 1931-40, 22 in 1921-30, six in 1913-20, one in 1900 and one possibly a little before 1990.

**At what time of the year did the incidents occur?**

The incidents happened in all four seasons of the year. This question was not asked in the first survey. In the second survey, 316 informants remembered what time of year they had occurred: 22 percent of the incidents happened during the summer, 23 percent during the winter, 11 percent during spring and 15 percent during the autumn. (See table 4.)

**At what time of day?**

About an equal amount of incidents happened during the day (29 percent) and in the evening (30 percent), 13 percent in the morning and 21 percent at night. There are also a few incidents, such as sounds, that occurred more than once and at different times (5 percent). The majority of our participants (443) remembered at what time of day the incident had occurred. Details are shown in table 4.

**Table 4. Time of the year and time of day that the 449 incidents occurred (percentages).**

| Time of day | | Time of year | |
|---|---|---|---|
| Morning | 13 | Spring | 14 |
| Day | 29 | Summer | 28 |
| Evening | 30 | Autumn | 19 |
| Night | 21 | Winter | 30 |
| Different times | 5 | Different times | 3 |
| Uncertain | 1 | Uncertain | 6 |

## How light was it when the encounters took place?

It is appropriate to treat visions seperately from perceptions where sight is not involved at all, such as sound, smell, touch and sense of a presence. This can be seen in table 5.

Half of the participants (52 percent) reported that their experience occurred in full daylight or electric light. These results do not support the widespread belief that encounters with the deceased usually take place in darkness. Further details in table 5.

**Table 5. Degree of light when the incidents happened. The percentages are based on 425 cases, 300 visions and 125 cases in which other senses were involved or presence was felt.**

| | Visions | Other perception | Total |
|---|---|---|---|
| Darkness | 9 | 14 | 10,4 |
| Dusk | 35 | 22 | 31,3 |
| Electric light | 16 | 16 | 15,8 |
| Full daylight | 36 | 38 | 36,2 |
| Other/ changeable | 5 | 10 | 6,4 |

# 9

## WHO WERE THE
## DECEASED PERSONS?

THE answer to this question reveals some interesting facts about the deceased who appear to the living. We already know that many of them died in accidents or suffered a violent death. What else is typical of the encountered dead? Are certain groups or types more common than others?

Around 449 deceased persons are mentioned in our collection. There are a few more because some of the accounts mention more than one deceased person. However, this is not important, since most of the informants mention only one person and that person is the centre of our attention in the interviews. In 302 of the accounts, the informants were able to give details about that person (name, age, year of birth and/or year of death) that sufficed for identification. Therefore it was possible to test whether these people had existed by comparing the given information with official documents. In 147 cases the deceased people were unnamed or only known by first name and there was no way to identify them. Only a few informants thought they had recognised the dead person but could not give enough information for us to find out who he/she had been.

**What was the relationship between the informant and the deceased person?**

About half of the apparitions were relatives of the informants (51 percent), others were acquaintances (12 percent), friends (9 percent) or colleagues (3 percent). Then there are strangers (26 percent), who were almost unknown or completely unknown by the informants until after the experience. It is surprising how big this category is. See further details in table 6.

**Table 6. Nature and strength of the relationship between the informants and the dead peesons.**

| Nature of relationship | | | Strength of the relationship | | |
|---|---|---|---|---|---|
| | **Frequency** | **%** | | **Frequency** | **%** |
| Family member | 214 | 51 | Very close | 115 | 33 |
| Friendship | 38 | 9 | Quite close | 67 | 19 |
| Colleague | 11 | 3 | Not very close | 39 | 11 |
| Acquaintance | 51 | 11 | Not close | 128 | 37 |
| Stranger | 109 | 24 | | | |
| Unknown | 26 | 6 | | | |

Let us look more closely at the group where the informants and the deceased had been related. It is most common to have perceived fathers (43); followed by mothers (22), grandfathers (21) and grandmothers (16). In eighteen examples, deceased husbands appeared to their living wives, and in nine accounts deceased wives appeared to their living husbands. Sons were perceived in sixteen accounts, mostly by their mothers. Encounters are much less common with siblings, cousins, aunts and uncles or in-laws. On the whole, it is more common for male relations to appear (139) than females (76). We will later discuss gender differences as well as how common it is for widows and widowers to perceive their deceased partners (27 examples in our collection). Those who have lost their life partners probably have more contact with the dead than any other group.

### How close were the informants to the perceived dead person?

In 349 cases we have information on the relationship between the informants and the perceived dead persons. In 115 cases the relationship was very close; in 67 there was some relationship; in 39 cases there was very little relationship and in 128 cases there was no relationship at all between the informant and the perceived dead person. Of course, the nature of these relationships varies greatly.

**Gender and age; why a great gender difference?**

What about the gender of the dead? The strange thing is that two thirds of the dead are men and less than a third are women. Men appeared in 305 of our accounts but women appeared in only 130 incidents. In 14 cases the gender was unknown or people of both genders appeared. This percentage is almost the same, regardless of whether the informant was male or female. 67 percent of those perceived by men are male and 69 percent of those perceived by women are male. There is no significant difference. Someone has asked whether this pattern meant that the world on the other side was also male dominated. We will soon explore a more obvious explanation.

As can be seen in table 7, we know the exact age at death of 302 of the perceived dead people but in 147 cases there was not enough information for comparison with official records. (See table 7.) We do know the rough estimate of the age of a few of the dead people because sometimes they are described as being young or old. Nevertheless, these examples will not be included since the information is not deemed accurate enough.

It is obvious that the deceased as a whole must have died at a younger age than people generally do since many of them suffered a violent death. This was indeed found to be the case. The mean age at death of the perceived dead is much lower than the average age of Icelanders when they die. The perceived men died at a mean age of 52 years and the women at 58 years, although the age at death varied greatly from just having been born to 99 years old. Those who had died of an illness died on average at 66 years of age whereas those who suffered a violent death only lived to be 35 years old on average. Combined, these numbers give an age of death at 55 years.

| Table. 7. Age and gender of the deceased. | | | |
|---|---|---|---|
| **Age** | **Male** | **Female** | **Total** |
| **0-10** | 6 | 2 | 8 |
| **11-20** | 11 | 6 | 17 |
| **21-30** | 22 | 7 | 29 |
| **31-40** | 18 | 8 | 26 |
| **41-50** | 31 | 11 | 42 |
| **51-60** | 31 | 11 | 42 |
| **61-70** | 35 | 22 | 57 |
| **71-80** | 31 | 13 | 44 |
| **81 and older** | 15 | 22 | 37 |
| **Total** | 200 | 102 | 302 |

## How did the perceived people die?

It is surprising how common it is for the perceived dead to have suffered violent deaths, such as in accidents, by suicide or manslaughter. We obtained reliable information from official records on the cause of death of 346 of the perceived dead. 74 percent of them had died of illness and 28 percent had suffered a violent death. This is far more than the actual percentage of the population who suffer violent deaths.

Let us have a look at the population records of the National Registry of Iceland. The years 1941-70 were chosen for comparison since roughly half of the perceived dead died in those years (164). 76 died before 1941 and 64 died after 1970. In the years 1941-1970, 94 percent of all deaths were caused by an illness (33.924) and 7.86 percent suffered violent deaths (2.894). Of those who suffered violent deaths, 6.69 percent died in accidents, 1.12 percent committed suicide and 0.05 percent were murdered.

Not only is our group of the perceived dead who suffered violent death unusually large, but it has also a great gender difference. See table 8 where the number of men and women are listed according to cause of death. There it is obvious that men are much more likely to have suffered violent deaths (91 percent) than women (9 percent). However, there is much less difference between the sexes when death of an illness is considered (60 percent of men and 40 percent of women).

**Table 8. Number of perceived men and women categorised by mode of death.**

| Cause of death | Frequency | Gender of the perceived | | | |
|---|---|---|---|---|---|
| | | Male | | Female | |
| | | Frequency | % | Frequency | % |
| Illness | 248 | 148 | 60 | 100 | 40 |
| Accident, suicide, manslaughter | 98 | 89 | 91 | 9 | 9 |
| Unknown | 103 | 68 | 76 | 21 | 21 |
| | | | | | |
| **Total** | **449** | **305** | | **130** | |
| | | **(Gender of 14 is unknown)** | | | |

According to the National Icelandic Registry, 12.02 percent of all men (2.308) suffered violent deaths but only 3.33 percent of women (586). This means that 3.94 times more men suffer violent deaths than women. This may explain in part why more men appear than women. However, this cannot be the whole explanation because in the case of encountered dead who suffer violent deaths, men are not only four times more likely to appear than women as they appear nine times more often than women.

How do we explain the fact that people who suffer a violent death appear more frequently than those who die of natural causes? This depends on whether we think the root of the experience lies with the deceased person or the perceiver. If the gender difference is explained by the first theory, one might argue that men have more strength and will to appear to the living than women and that sudden and unexpected violent death increases the motivation to contact the living.

If the experience has its root in the mind of the perceiver it might be argued that dead men are stronger in the minds of the living than women; or that the living have a greater need for contact with deceased men than women.

## A more detailed categorization of violent causes of death

We have information on the causes of death of 277 of the participants who were contacted around the year 1980. This concerns not only whether they suffered violent deaths but also whether it was by accident, suicide or manslaughter. Of these 277 individuals, 70.4 percent died of illnesses and 29.6 percent suffered violent deaths. Most of those who suffered violent deaths died in accidents (23.5 percent), some committed suicide (5.0 percent) and a few were murdered (1.1 percent). The percentages of those who died in accidents, suicide and manslaughter in the years 1941-70 can be found in table 9. When the first 100 accounts were collected in 1976, this information was not obtained but later we managed to gain information on whether the encountered dead had suffered violent deaths but not as to whether it was by accident, suicide or murder.

As mentioned earlier, it is noteworthy that the number of encountered dead who suffered violent deaths is much greater proportionately than the percentage of the population who suffered violent deaths in the same time period, regardless of the year being compared. This applies to deaths because of accidents, suicide and manslaughter.

| | | | Died in 1941-70 |
|---|---|---|---|
| Cause of death | Frequency | % of 277 | % |
| | | | |
| Illness | 195 | 70.4 | 92.14 |
| Accident | 65 | 23.5 | 6.69 |
| Suicide | 14 | 5.0 | 1.12 |
| Manslaughter | 3 | 1.1 | 0.05 |
| Unknown | 72 | - | |

Table 9. The cause of death of 277 individuals who appear in our encounters and the causes of death for the population Iceland in the years 1941-1970.

## Relationships and cause of death

Most of those who were physically related to or had some other relationship with the informants, died of illness ( 82 percent). This number is relatively close to the 92 percent of Icelanders who actually died of an illness in the period that the deceased people appeared. If the cause of death had no influence on which dead people appear to the living, around 8 percent of the dead should have suffered violent deaths. But they are 28 percent - or 3.5 times more likely to appear. Why? Is this a result of a statistical measurement error? The following suggests that this is not the case.

If the cause of death of the encountered stranger is considered, this difference is even greater. Instead of 92 percent of the encountered dead strangers having died of an illness and 8 percent having suffered violent deaths, a great majority actually suffered violent deaths (63 percent) and only 37 percent died of an illness. Such a striking difference can also be found among those who appeared to their colleagues and acquaintances. In total, these results are far from what would be found if it was purely up to chance. See more details in table 10.

**Table 10. The dead categorized by their relationships with the informant and the cause of death.**

| | Frequency | Illness | Accident, suicide or murder | Unknown |
|---|---|---|---|---|
| Family | 214 | 172 (82%) | 38 (18%) | 4 |
| Friendship | 38 | 28 (76%) | 9 (24%) | 1 |
| Co-worker | 11 | 5 (50%) | 5 (50%) | 1 |
| Acquaintance | 51 | 26 (57%) | 20 (43%) | 5 |
| Stranger | 109 | 15 (37%) | 25 (63%) | 69 |
| Unknown | 26 | - | - | 26 |
| Total | 446 | 246 (72%) | 97 (28%) | 106 |

The cause of death seems to effect who appears. According to these figures, it is much more likely for dead people to appear to the living if they had suffered violent deaths. One might affirm that people who suffered violent deaths have more strength and motivation to appear than those who died of an illness since they do not only manage to appear to those who were close to them but also to people who hardly knew them or did not know at all.

Could there be a hidden error in this estimate? It seems to be quite unlikely. This is one of the puzzles of apparitions which is hard to explain unless you assume that some power is hidden in those who are dead, in such a way that their image appears in the minds and in the world of the living.

# 10

## Who or What is the Source of the Apparitional Experience?

WE have mentioned two possible explanations for apparitions. Either encounters with the dead are created by the minds of the perceivers, or the dead are making us aware of them by creating a sensory image in the mind of the living observers. The initiating source is different.

If the latter theory/explanation is true, namely that the dead person is making the perceiver aware of them, it is easiest to imagine that the deceased person creates a perception in the mind of the perceiver. We find a similar phenomena in hypnotism with highly hypnotizable persons. In both instancs the perception can be so real that the perceiver experiences it as an outer physical stimulus. Regarding appartions of the dead, it is obvious that at the time of their appearance - in most instances - the body of the dead person does no longer exist in a physical form like the vision that is seen. The body has in most instances been buried or cremated etc. and may no longer exist. There can hence only be a cognitive or telepathic connection between the living and the dead. The deceased person moulds the perception in the mind of the living person. It appears that such a perception can range from sensing an invisible presence, to images rising in the mind, to the perception of an outer physical reality just as with any other sensory perception we know of.

Now the author would like to make an exception to the rule of only giving examples from his collection of cases. The following account is taken from the autobiography of the famous psychiatrist Carl Gustav Jung, *Memories, Dreams, Reflections*. The book reads;

One night I lay awake thinking of a sudden death of a friend whose funeral had taken place the day before. I was deeply concerned. Suddenly I felt that he was in the room. It seemed to me that he stood at the foot of my bed and was asking me to go with him. I did not have the feeling of an apparition; rather it was an inner visual image of him, which I explained to myself as a fantasy. But in all honesty I had to ask myself, 'Do I have any proof that this is a fantasy? Suppose it is not a fantasy, suppose my friend is really here and I decided it was only a fantasy – would that not be abominable of me?" Yet I had equally little proof that he stood before me as an apparition. Then I said to myself, 'Proof is neither here or there! Instead of explaining him away as fantasy, I might just as well give him the benefit of the doubt and for experiment's sake credit him with reality." The moment I had that thought, he went to the door and beckoned me to follow him! That was something I had not bargained for. I had to repeat my argument to myself once more. Only then did I follow him in my imagination.

He led me out of the house, into the garden, out to the road and finally to his house. (In reality it was several hundred yards away from mine.) I went in, and he conducted me into his study. He climbed on a stool and showed me the second of five books with red bindings which stood on the second shelf from the top. Then the vision broke off. I was not acquainted with his library and did not know what books he owned. Certainly I could never have made out from below the titles of the books he had pointed out to me on the second shelf from the top.

This experience seemed to me so curious that the next morning I went to his widow and asked wheather I could look up something in my friend's library. Sure enough, there was a stool standing under the bookcase I had seen in my vision, and even before I came closer I could see the five books with red binding. I stepped up on the stool so as to be able to read the titles. They were translations of the novels of Emile Zola. The title of the second volume read: *The Legacy of the Dead*. The contents seemed to me of no interest. Only the title was extremely significant in connection with this experience. (Jung, 1995, 343-344).

In Jung's mind, this was a mental vision. We could also call the experience an imagination, but the name does not matter. The interesting thing is that his friend led him to a shelf in his library that Jung did not know and the next day he could prove that on the second to the top shelf were indeed five books bound in red. And when he examines the second book, it had the interesting title: *The Legacy of the Dead.* The author has investigated one similar case; The Iyengar-Kirti case (Haraldsson, 1987).

Later it surfaced that this friend was the physicist W. Pauli with whom Jung wrote "Naturerklärung und Psyche" (Rascher Verlag, 1952).

A third possible explanation is the theory that the experience is not only cognitive in nature but rather that the deceased person creates or materialises in some inexplicable way a physical form for short period of time. This theory is closer to the popular understanding people tend to have on this subject and can be found in folklore in Iceland and in other countries. According to this theory, the experience is not hallucination (namely perception without appropriate physical stimuli), but a normal perception of a physical reality which exists for a brief period of time, a few second or minutes.

Is there any support for this theory? Phenomena which were experienced and reported at the heyday of the spiritistic movement in the latter part of the nineteenth and early twentieth century can be presented as examples. Two prominent men of the time: Sir William Crookes (1972) and the Earl of Dunraven (1924) did a great deal of research on the most famous medium of all time: Daniel Dunglas Home (1883-1886). They, as well as many others, witnessed material phenomenon, apparitions and touches, as if they were part of the physical reality – and then simply dissolved and disappeared (even through walls) after quite a short time. Some of these phenomena were measured and examined with various instruments, as if they were physically real.

The same could be said about Indridi Indridason (1883-1912), by far the greatest medium in Iceland (Gissurarson and Haraldsson 1989, 1995). He became the subject of critical and vigorous research by Gudmundur Hannesson (1924), professor of medicine at the University of Iceland; by Haraldur Nielsson (1924), professor of theology, Einar Kvaran and others. At the séances of Daniel Dunglas Home and Indridi Indridason, deceased people often appeared, and appeared very briefly to take on a physical form.

It must be added that such material phenomenon have rarely been seen around mediums since then. Therefore, their existence has been disputed, on the one hand because they cannot be reconciled with the world view of modern science; and on the other hand because later some unscrupulous men managed to produce what appeared to be similar perceptions with tricks alone.

If this third theory/explanation has some validity it would follow that perceptions of the dead are like any other perceptions and not hallucinations in the normal sense of the word. It is wise not to make strong statements about the nature of these phenomena and remember the limits of our knowledge on this subject. Also, different explanations may apply for different incidents.

# 11

## ACCIDENTS AND VIOLENT DEATHS: SAILORS AND DEATH BY DROWNING

L ET us turn to encounters with those who died in accidents. They are prominent in our case collection, for there are 98 such accounts, as almost a quarter of the total sample died in accidents. This is strikingly high and way above the 7 percent of the population who actually die in this tragic way. These incidents varied greatly and took place both at sea and on land, indoors and outdoors and involve women as well as men, young and old.

Fishing in the rough seas of the North Atlantic has been a major source of living in Iceland through the centuries. Drowning is the most common accident found in our accounts. At the time these people died, drowning was the most common type of violent death in the country.

### A man in his fifties from Reykjavík

I was suddenly awakened from sleep one night by what I thought was a man entering the appartment, walking past the bedroom and into the bathroom. The feeling for this man was so strong that I became wide awake. I was so startled by this that I could not go to sleep again. The day after a friend of mine was reported missing. Later the name was publicly announced and still later he was found; he had drowned. He was 36 years old. We had known each other since childhood and worked together as carpenters for many years. The day he set out to sea he called me and urged me to settle some unfinished business with purchases of appartments that we had built with two others about which there had been some dispute. (143)

### A fisherman from Olafsvik

I was on a boat fishing with a Danish seine and we brought in a dead man. He had fallen in the water and drowned about six weeks earlier. I had to open the bag and by mistake I touched the man's head. Old men used to make the sign of a cross if they came close to a dead body but one of my shipmates (he has since passed away) did not do that. In the autumn I saw him and the dead man followed him. Three of us saw him. These friends of mine have all passed away now. They died a year later. We had heard on the radio that this man had fallen in the sea and drowned and my skipper immediately said: "We'll probably get him in our nets." (816)

### A nationally known fisherman and former member of parliament, now deceased

My father died in the last days of November in 1940. He was in a shipwreck along with six shipmates. At the beginning of the new year, a year later, I was hired to work on my father's brother's boat, to bring in some money for the home. I never dreamt about my father and there is no prologue to what I am going to tell you. We woke up early in the morning, I was ashore, landman as we called it, one of seven. The weather had been wonderful, sunny every single day and we had gone out every day and as a boy of fifteen I was still quite unused to so much hard work. My mother watched over me and made sure I was up at the right time, about four or five in the morning. One morning it felt as if somebody had given me a nudge and told me: "Now you are late lad", just as my father used to talk to me. I jumped up. I slept on the top floor and ran into my mother's room but she was asleep. I said: "I was woken up". I sat down on the bench and got dressed and she came over and asked who had woken me up. "I do not know", I said. But we were both sure who it had been. Then she went to warm up some cocoa for me or something like that and I sat down and started talking to dad. I was not sure whether I was quite awake or half asleep. I felt like I was talking to him as if he was there, that he was beside me and I talked to him until my mother brought my cocoa. At that point a man came round outside the house, it was an old house with corrugated iron and in those days they used to bang a wooden stick along the iron

72

to wake people up. One of my colleagues from the boat said he had been told to wake us up. My mother was a bit angry, opened the window and said: "You do not have to wake him up so often and make such a noise." When she came back from talking to the man I was still talking to my father, or so I felt... (7632)

### A fisherman in his thirties

There was a man working on our boat. He quit but then he was going to come back to our boat but he died on the boat he was working on in between. He was 32 years old. I always felt I could see him in my room but I was not sure... This did not happen now, it happened last winter. When I was in my bunk I felt as if I could see him to the side of me, see him move, he moved fast. I could see him from the neck down to the waist. (7622)

### A nationally known man, a successful ship owner who lived in Reykjavík

A ship owner in Hrisey had a motorboat which he had bought from Akranes. The boat was haunted to such a degree that both people who had the special gift to see the deceased, and those who had no such gift, could see it. I was 16 years old when I was on that boat along with my father. Once I was sent to warm up the engine before we set off in the evening. This was in the month of September and we were rowing from Hrisey. When I got in the boat I lit the gaslamp and was holding it in my hands. I heard that somebody was in the engine room and guessed that another shipmate was on the boat. I walked backwards down the stairs sure of this fact, holding the lamp. When I got downstairs there was a man standing about two feet away from my head. Of course I was really scared, threw away the lamp and hurried up to the deck. The boat caught fire but it did not take long to put it out. That was the first time I saw him so clearly and he looked just like everybody had described him, wearing a black jumper which was cut at the sleeves, a red scarf around his neck and an english hat. I thought the man looked quite normal. Still, after this incident I was always really scared when I was on my own in the engine room or the wheelhouse.

Then there was that other time. We had had to stay awake a lot and the boat was half full of fish. The foreman called me and asked me to go downstairs to make some coffee, as we had almost finished pulling in the line. It was bright and sunny and the middle of the day. I was washing the blood off my hands on the deck and looked towards the cabin door. Then he is standing there up to his waist in the doorway. More of the men saw him, the engineer as well, who was standing by the door holding the line. We watched the man's head disappear into the cabin. This engineer saw the man most often and especially when there was something wrong with the engine. He was not scared of him. He was my brother-in-law... but now nobody wanted to go in the cabin... But soon after, the man at the wheel fell asleep and the boat stranded east of Hrisey.

The last incident I want to tell you about happened on a Sunday. The house we were living in was right by the sea in Hrísey. Several people lived there, about twenty. The boats were anchored close to land as there were no piers at that time. We were sitting on a concrete surface drinking our Sunday afternoon coffee. The boat was about 40-50 metres away from us. Then everybody saw some man walking from the cabin door and back to the wheelhouse. All of us had just come ashore and no one was the boat.

I later found out from Haraldur Böðvarsson in Akranes who had owned the boat before, that this man had been engineer on the boat before. He was crushed under the boat as it was pushed down the shore to sea. He was so badly hurt that he died of his wounds. (2128)

### A captain in his forties from Akranes

This happened during the summer of 1966. I was somewhere between sleeping and waking, when I became wide awake. I saw a man at the stove of the cabin, a young man who was stooping over it. He was doing something. I recognized that this man was not a member of the crew. I was going to check this further but then he disappeared. Later I came to know that he had some time ago got burnt inside the cabin. He did not get burnt to death, he suffocated in smoke. I remember so clearly that he was wearing a blue sweater and a scarf around his neck. My description fitted what I later learnt about him. (7018)

### Captain on a boat from Akranes

I was captain on a boat from Akranes. I had a steersman who had had a disagreement with another shipmate and he insisted that I fire this shipmate. I refused to do so, as first I wanted to try and settle their dispute. The next thing that happened was that the steersman got drunk and again he was insistent. I had convinced the shipmate to go and apologize to the steersman and was going to go with him. That was not enough and the steersman left.

The following winter, the steersman fell in the sea off a trawler south of the coast. He disappeared in the sea. That same fishing season I was lying in my bunk and was awakened by a shove. This man was standing at my bunk. I reacted rather angrily and addressed him. I said that since he had not stayed with me when he should have, he should leave me in peace now, whereby he left. I have not seen him since or been aware of him. (7022)

### Fisherman, now a goldsmith in Reykjavík

Ever since I was a child I have seen deceased people. My aunt's husband drowned abroad in England. He was almost always with me, I saw him like any other person. The case I will describe now is special because it was the first time I noticed a deceased person dressed according to the weather. It was surprising because one often sees them differently dressed, but that is not like it was in this case.

I was at sea during the war. We were often alone on duty, and he was always with me. Actually he had been a steersman on this ship when he lost his life. I remember one time when we were in Hrutafjord during the winter in a bad snowstorm. When I went up to the bridge to relieve one of my collegues on duty he was standing there. I greeted him...spoke with him. "Hello" I said to him and he answered. This was just as clear as speaking to a living person. On the same shift I remember he pushed me to make me alert. The weather was clearing up by then. That made me go below deck to let the steersman know. (2158)

### Fifty year old man from Grindavík

I worked on the trawler Isborg, which was built in 1948. On that ship I saw a man twice. The first time we were by the shores of England and the second time we were coming from Germany. At this time, after the war, it was common to find stow-aways on board. I saw the same man on both occasions, he was a bit fat and was wearing a blue overall. I told the men about this and after the later incident they started looking around the ship to find if anyone was hiding in the lifeboats or somewhere else, but no one was found. The radio telegraphist on board Olafur Björnsson was good in English and very much into the spiritual matters and believed in them. The other men on the ship thought of this as nonsense. Olafur found out that the man I saw had died on bord in an accident when the ship was being built. (7506)

We contacted Olafur who said he used to be radio operator on Isborg. He recalled the man who told the story but said he could not remember the event.

These are only a few of the many accounts in our collection of incidents involving fishermen. The rest can be found in different places in the book.

### Sixty year old man from Hunavatnssysla tells of his experience:

It was dark, I looked out of the window and saw a man standing there, who had died a few months ago in his thirties. He was standing still outside the window and had two horses. I knew him because he had been engaged to a girl who lived in the same house as me. I looked away and went outside to have a look but could not see anything. Another person was in the room with me but she did not see anything. Other people had seen him before, in the same way I saw him. (838A)

### Forty year old lady from Sudurnes

I often saw my grandfather, who drowned when I was a child. In 1970 I had a child who died in birth and they often talked about burying it with somebody else. Those days I often saw two men, my father and my uncle, standing by me and they kept telling me to wait to bury the child. I had never seen them in real life since they had both passed away when I was born. I could see them very clearly and they spoke to me normally and were very calm. At the time, three old people were waiting to die in hospital. (152)

### A restauranteur in his forties in Reykjavík

One winter when I was a little boy, I was repeatedly visited by three men who had drowned, their boat sank somewhere out there... I was so young at the time that somehow I did not understand what was going on. I was a little frightened by this and it kept me awake. I did not get much sleep because of this. The experience ceased after I had been prayed for.

This boat had been wrecked off the south coast and one of the men had never been recovered; his name had been Hermann. He was the only one I had ever seen and the only one I recognized. I felt as if Hermann was trying to make it clear to me that he was in some cove, on the Vatnsleysuströnd-shore or somewhere near there. (2026)

### Teacher in his seventies, living in Reykjavík

At home I had dozed off in a chair and was woken up when a man was standing in the door holding the door open stiffly with his arm. He was wearing his fine clothes and looked alive. I knew the man immediately and knew who he was and looked at him. He had died, he had drowned... This lasted only for a moment (5031)

### From a lady in the North of Iceland

I had just been told of my brother´s death. He had been out riding and had drowned. This was late at night, though not past bedtime. I was naturally shocked, because this had been an accident not a disease. I went to bed though, and tried to sleep but I kept thinking about it. I think I did not fall asleep and I was startled when I heard horses riding past my window, making quite a noise. I got out of bed and went to the window but of cousrse no one was out there. I did not think more about this and a few years went by. Then I met a young man who had been a friend of my brother´s when they were 14 or 15 years old. When the accident happened he was a grown man working on a boat. He told me he had dreamt about my brother that same night and he had found it strange that my brother asked him for help. I realized immediately, although I said nothing, that my brother had been riding to the shore that night on his horse that also drowned. (7514)

### Woman in her fifties from the West Fjords

I woke up in the middle of the night and saw him walking to my bed and back again. It was my half- brother, who had drowned some time before that. I felt he looked younger than when he died. I felt I saw him wearing clothes he usually wore when he was alive. Perhaps I was thinking about him. The day before we were talking about accidents and my brother was discussed. (495)

### Engineer in his fifties living in Reykjavík

When the ship Godafoss, owned by the company Eimskip, was shot down here in the Faxabay during the second World War, a friend of mine from school was onboard the ship. He was the third engineer. At that time I was working as an engineer for the energy company in Reykjar. We worked shifts and I was sleeping when the ship went down. I woke to find somebody in my room; there was no doubt about it even though I could not see anything but once before I had been in a similar state... I was neither awake nor asleep... I could not see him, I knew of him, I could not hear him but the connection between us was so strong and powerful that I did not doubt it a bit when I woke up, what had happened...

I went to my wife and told her that this man was dead and I could describe exactly what he had been wearing. He was wearing a white overall, with a white tie around his neck, a small hat on his head, there was a bit of shopcloth sticking out of his pocket and he was wearing clogs on his feet... This picture came to mind without me seeing or hearing anything to explain it... According to information from those I knew who were on the ship and survived, he had been on a shift and was dressed exactly like that. And I was aware of it just as it happened... (7584)

### Seventy year old lady in the North of Iceland

I am not quite sure whether it happened while I was awake or asleep. A man who lived in my house drowned and I often thought of him. One night after he died I saw him, his face or head. And then it disappeared into smoke or steam in circles upwards. I know my aunt has also seen him... (762A)

### Sixty year old lady from Eskifjord

I woke up one night and saw an old acquaintance of my husband standing over my bed, as if bending over me. His face was soft and he was calm. He was wearing a seaman's jacket but it was not wet. He went backwards out of the room and in some way evaporated and I could feel a slight wind as he disappeared. I later found out that this man had died on a boat from Stokkseyri one or two days earlier. (880A)

### Housewife in her thirties in Reykjavík

A man came into my apartment, that is, he was there when I got home. He was dripping wet. It took me a while to realise who he was and I did not like this at all. But it was as if he was in a joking mood because he walked through the curtains a lot as if he enjoyed doing that and kept walking into me and sort of running around the apartment. He was so happy and it was as if he was teasing me. He drowned at the age of 24 on a boat steaming from Stykkisholm to Akranes. We were friends and I named one of my children after him... (7586)

## Forty year old lady in Reykjavík

I have once seen an apparition of a deceased man who had drowned three years earlier. I was at home alone in the living-room and was not thinking of him in particular. He suddenly appeared and seemed very much alive. He was very gay and smiling, like he was feeling well. He seemed to be wearing clothes just like the ones I remember him wearing. There was nothing negative about this. The only explanation I can give is that he was feeling fine. I have not told about this before... (2036)

## A teacher in his sixties, living in the North of Iceland

When I was 14 years old a maid by the name of Maria was working for my parents. The house is so arranged that the kitchen leads to the cellar. We were sitting in the kitchen. She had her son in her arms and was giving me coffee. Suddenly the door to the cellar opened. Up came this being that was visible down to its knees. I call it a being and not a man because what I saw looked like a solid shadow. I said to the woman: "Maria, what is it?" She said : " It's my deceased boyfriend. He drowned." Then this being disappeared. I saw it as clearly as if it had been made of black stone. (2053)

## A carpenter's story

It was probably in the year 1965, when I was working in Laugalækja school. There was a storm blowing from the north or the north east. I had to go outside the house to get some wood and when I came around the corner something strange happened to me. I started thinking about my friend from Hvamstangi, who had been to sea with me. I thought I saw him and I started talking to him, felt like he was asking me about something that had happened a few years earlier. I did not think about it a lot at the time and did not associate it with anything. Then I heard on the radio an announcement about a search for a small fishing boat. On the second day it was announced I realised that this was the boat owned by that friend of mine. The boat went under somewhere out on Breidafjord and then I started thinking about the incident and how I could have seen him. It happened on the same day that he drowned and probably at about the same time as he died. What happened to me in a crazy storm that night was a little like when you are about to fall asleep and consciousness starts to roam... (5055)

### Lady in her eighties in Reykjavík

We were drinking coffee on our coffee break where I work. I saw my son as if in a mist or haze but I could not see his feet. He had drowned a year ago. This lasted only for a moment and no more. Perhaps it was my imagination but I felt it, as if he had passed me by... He was 42 when he drowned but in my mind he looked as he did when he looked his best. (2102)

### Sixty year old housewife from the West of the country

I was at Patreksfjord and it was shortly before the Vardar accident. My brother-in-law was on the ship as a first engineer. He was not the dreaming type but very intelligent and a lovely man. Two days before he went to sea he said to me: 'My dear H, you are so spiritual, I have to tell you something. I dreamt of my mother and she was coming to fetch me. I am not ready to leave. I am not ready to prepare for the move." And I said to him: "No, my dear, we really cannot control it, each of us has to leave when the call comes".

Then one morning I woke up at 6 o'clock and I saw him and all of those who were shipwrecked with him. My brother-in-law and uncle came first, then all of the others. I felt they were wet and all of them were really sad. When I was up, a close friend came over and was very sad. I told him: "You do not have to tell me anything. I am on my way to my sister (the drowned man's wife). Were there not five of them?" And I counted the men for him. "Yes, how did you know?" he said. He kept going because he was bringing the news to the families... (7604)

### Fisherman on the bridge

This was in the autumn. I was foreman on one of two fishing boats in the village and we noticed that there was quite a racket at night on the seashore. It seemed as if barrels were being tossed around making a very loud noise. Most of the men were spooked and were afraid to be there alone in the dark. One night I was leaving home at 5 o'clock to bait. I was walking down a hill to a bridge over a river, when I saw a man who had just crossed the bridge. There was a lamppost by the bridge so I saw the man quite clearly in the light. I saw how he was dressed, but I did not recognize him as one of my men. I thought I should catch up with him. When I had seen him he was walking quite slowly, so I should have been able to catch up with him on the shore. But I never saw the man again. I asked the men on the boats if they had seen anyone, but no one had and no one was missing. Shortly afterwards the other boat went down; it sank in the harbour here. Later I was telling the father of one of the drowned men about the man I had seen and I described him. He recognized the man I described as being a good friend of his son who had also drowned at sea before this incident. The racket we heard on the shore persisted after this. (7524)

# 12

# ACCIDENTAL DEATHS ON LAND

WE find no indications that the mode of accidental death has any influence on the way in which the appearences or encounters take place. Or perhaps it does and the reader may notice some difference.

**Thirty year old lady from Reykjavik**

I was busy in the kitchen when I felt that a man had entered the apartment. I looked up and saw that a man walk passed the kitchen-door and I felt as if he went into the bedroom. I went into the bedroom but no one was there.

I told my mother-in-law about this incident and from my description of the man she thought it was her half-brother who had died at the age of thirty in an accident. (454)

**Woman from Husavik**

I was coming home. When I came in I saw my neighbour sitting there who had died in an accident. He seemed to be in a very normal state compared to what he was like when living. Shortly after this two lads drowned here and somehow I associate the vision with that. I later felt the presence of both young men. (453)

**Sixty year old lady living in Reykjavík**

When I was twenty I moved to town from the country. I rented a room and was a student. I did not know many people and I was terribly bored. On one occasion, I was feeling very bad, I was bored stiff. Then suddenly I felt the presence of my father, who had died when I was six. He was with me in my room and touched me. I had not been thinking about him and I remembered so little of him. I was not bored anymore, I felt surrounded with peace, warmth and love. I felt as if it were being pressed into me that it was my father and that he wanted me to know that he was there with me. After this I felt much better... I was more content with being alone... (2040)

**Woman in her fifties, living in Reykjavík**

My son died at 16 years old in the month of September. He rode a motorcycle. The night before January fourth, a year later, I could not sleep. I lay awake until I heard the clock strike six; that is the last thing I remember. Then I woke up, just as if someone had woken me up. My bedroom door is opposite the door to another room. I sat up in bed and leaned forward to look into the other room and there I saw my son. I saw his back. I looked at him and thought: it cannot be. I closed my eyes and opened them again. I watched him turn around, it was very hard for him and then he was standing in front of me. His head was drooping, his chin was to his chest, I did not see his face. He seemed to be much taller than he was and he had more hair, though he always had a lot of hair. Then he floated backwards away from me... I fell asleep immediately after this and slept for a few hours. My daughter who is living in Norway was staying with me but she was leaving later that day. I told my daughter about this, then my daughter said: Oh that's right mother, I had a dream about him last night, not exactly in the night but after 6 o'clock this morning.. I felt like he was saying goodbye to me." Really, what did he look like?" I asked. "He was much taller than he used to be and he had so much hair," my daughter said. Her description was the same and the timing was the same and I told her what I had seen.

I went to a seance with Hafsteinn the medium. I think it was in the middle of February, and I asked the boy: "Did I see you?" and he answered:"Yes mother, I came to say goodbye to my sister..." (2076)

### Woman in Reykjavík, in her thirties

My husband´s grandfather is always with him. My husband works irregular shifts and sometimes comes home during the night. When that happens I am often aware of his grandfather just before my husband appears. I also see him beside him. He always wears dark clothes and I see him appear for a short while. Once I saw him walk past the kitchen door which was open and into the living room and there I heard him sit down. My mother, who was with me at the time also heard him that time. (2084)

### Roughly forty year old lady from Reykjavík

I lost my daughter in an accident. I was mostly aware of her the first half year after she passed away. I may have been a little more open than normal and perhaps I was even waiting for it for I was glad if I felt she had given me some attention. I tried to make up my mind that this was not wishful thinking.

My daughter was 17 years old when she died and a very active teenager who had a lot going on when she left this world. We had always helped each other out when I got home from work and she got back, like doing the dishes. After she left it happened so often that I was aware of somebody helping me with the dishes. That is, I could not see anything but I could hear the sounds and could feel I was being helped. She loved toast and I often heard bread being toasted, the toaster made that sound. She also loved roses and used to buy a rose when she had some money and give to me or keep in her own room. Often after her death when I came back home tired I could feel this strong scent of roses. It really reminded me of her. (2114)

### Worker in his forties, living in Suðurnes

I lost my son when he was 17 years old. A week after he died he appeared before me in a snow-white gown down to his toes, just like when he was confirmed. I saw him wide awake – well maybe one could not say I was fully awake because I was lying in bed but had not fallen asleep. He stood behind the bed in the white gown... I have never seen him looking so handsome... I fully understood how he felt. It was like he was telling me that he had not quite oriented himself but he was calm... I felt as though his mind was inside my mind. (2206)

**Doctor, roughly forty years old**

There is this one occasion that is so memorable to me because it was so vivid. It actually happened in Germany, we were staying with some relatives, an Icelander who lives there with a German wife. We were having lunch and suddenly a man was standing in the middle of the room. I looked at him for a while and immediately could see that he was a family member. He looked so much like my friend's wife, obviously family. I thought that he might be her father who had died during the war. I had only seen a picture of him. It was as if he was standing there alive, it was so clear. He looked very healthy, his hair was well brushed and he was very neat as if he was wearing his best suit. The wife's mother was also there and he walked towards her. It was so strange that although I looked down I could still see him. I looked down and kept eating but I could still see him... He was there for quite a while and then he disappeared... I talked to my wife about it and she had also seen him. (2154)

The wife of the informant adds:

It was quite a young man or in his thirties, wearing grey clothes. His hair was divided in the middle and he was very clean cut. Obviously the lady of the house was related to him for he looked so very much like her. I could clearly see his aura and the connection... He walked back and forth and was acting very loving towards his wife, daughter and grandchildren. (2154)

**Man in his seventies tells of an incident which happened when he was about twenty**

I was in a country home om Mosfellssveit. I was in the cowshed and saw there a man by the manger where they kept bad hay from the cows. He was half bent over the manger so I could not see the face and did not think about it as I thought it was the farmer. But then the farmer appeared yawning and said he had overslept.

Then we received a phone call and heard that a man from Mosfellssveit had been on his way by horse into Kjos to stay for a week. He never arrived in Kjos and people started searching for him. That same day his two horses arrived back home, one had the saddle under his stomach. The man had fallen to his death on the way. We expected he had been fetching hay for his horses... (5014)

The informant told his master immediately about his experience but he had passed away so it was not possible to contact him. The informant also said that a female worker at the farm later saw the same man.

### Housewife in her forties, working as a teacher in Reykjavík

This only happened that one time. I really do not believe in these sorts of things. My brother had just died at 54 years of age and I had been invited to visit his family. I was wondering whether he was there. And then I saw him in the lounge. First it was as if I had seen him out of the corner of my eye and only the lower part of him. Then I looked right at him and saw all of him but only for a moment. Nobody else in the living room had seen him and I did not tell anybody about it. Shortly after, I dreamt about my brother and he told me that there he was able to show me that he was among us. He knew I was skeptical about an afterlife... (5050)

### Roughly thirty year old woman

My friend died a few years ago 16 years old. I was at work one evening and was walking along the hallway. Then I heard somebody call me. I looked around but there was nobody in the hall. I recognised the voice but did not hear anything more. I think my friend was letting me know that she was there... (5088)

### A seventy year old lady tells of an incident which happened five years earlier

I lost my son when he was almost 32 years old. He died in a car accident in the West Fjords. We did not know about his death until it was announced to me by a visit the following morning. Then we all met up at his house. He was married and had a step-daughter and a three month old daughter. They were there and his siblings, and I had an older son and a younger daughter. I am sitting there near a window. Of course we were all very silent and we did not talk much. Suddenly I saw him through the window come running towards the front door dressed just as he had been... He had a sad but warm looking face and seemed to be upset. This was a very clear image in my mind, yes, as if I had been shown it. I instinctively looked away because I knew it must be a figment of my own imagination... (5092)

### On the road to Keflavík

I was at home, in peace and quiet, when a man appeared there and pushed some papers at me. I felt he was trying to get a message across but I was not sure what he meant. There was a sort of light around him but not in himself. He seemed to hang in the air and he calmly walked away. Since then I have seen him often. He died when he was 25; he had just got married and had a baby. He had also just bought himself a boat and an apartment. I told my husband about this. This man had been a friend of his and died in a car crash on the road to Keflavik. (5036)

### Sixty year old man from Hveragerdi

There was said to be a ghost called the Hellisheidi ghost. Many think they have sensed this being. This being is supposed to be a man that got lost on the Hellisheidi moor before the turn of the century. A middle aged boat builder from Eyrabakki. His bones were found in 1930 and were identified by the money and the tools he carried. I often travel by route of Hellisheidi because I go to work in Reykjavik. It was especially during one winter that I felt this being and it was as if it was in my car every time I crossed the moor. This was very uncomfortable for the first few times but the discomfort gradually decreased and it felt like friendship in the end. Now I hardly ever feel the presence of this being but just last night I felt its presence on my way home. (7508)

### Fisherman from the east coast of Iceland

My son died in an accident. A few days later I lay down on a couch in my living room. Then, after lying on the couch for a while, I saw him sitting at a table up against a wall just as if he were alive. He looked at me with a serious face and did not say anything. This lasted for a little while and then he disappeared... There were two of us in the room, my wife and I, but she did not notice anything. (7536)

The fisherman's wife remembered the incident. She also had an encounter with her son a few months later. This is her story:

I was at home on my own. My husband had gone south to take our younger son to the doctor. Our older son had died in an accident some time before that. I sometimes had a hard time sleeping. Once I was going from the bedroom down to the lounge and I felt somebody supporting me and through my mind flies the thought:

"Now my Hannes is leading me." Just then somebody put their arms around me and supported me down the stairs and into the living room... I felt it was him giving me a hand. (6016)

**Farmer in his sixties:**

I lived on a farm in the south of the country near the coast. One day a man from the next farm went to the village of Stokkseyri and did not come back in the evening. The morning after I was taking milk to another farm and had to go past the farm that he used to work at. I used also to take milk from this farm and he used to bring it to me. We used horse-drawn wagons then. This time I had to go up to the farm and there I met the farmer who told me the man had gone to Stokkseyri and not returned. I was not surprised because the man was fond of drink and so I said: "Well, he must have gone on a bout of drinking and is somewhere either drunk or passed out, somewhere heading towards home".

Then I went to Loftsstadir and I was looking towards Stokkseyri to see if I could see the horse with this man – it might be there somewhere. Then I did see the horse coming from the east. It is going very slowly, looking around. The horse was about two kilometres away when I first saw it. I saw a man with the horse. Then the horse got to where I was and I managed to reach it. The horse was not in a good mood and had the saddle under the stomach. I looked around, sure that the man had passed out somewhere close by. I wanted to help him get back. I fixed the saddle and rode back where he had come from for about two kilometres but could not find anybody. I thought this was strange because I was sure I had seen a man beside the horse and was sure it was him. I turned back. A few hours after I got back home I was given the message that the man had been found dead east of Stokkseyri. I was not surprised.

This man used to spend a lot of time in my home and he had borrowed a book from my grandmother. The brother of the farmer who the man had been working for was very spiritual and had the gift of second sight. He was a well-known tailor in Reykjavik. He visited the farm a little later and was in the kitchen drinking coffee. Then he saw this man come in and the man asked him to return the book for him. (7572)

According to popular folk belief, those who suffer violent deaths are more likely to appear than those who die of an illness. The question is whether this belief exists because experience has shown that people who suffer violent deaths are actually more likely to appear or if it is because people believe that those who die violently are more likely to appear and hence experience more? This study appears to support the former theory rather than the latter. That is, this folk belief is probably based on experience, although folk beliefs surely also have an influence on how people interpret their experiences.

# 13

## SUICIDE

IN thirteen cases the deceased person had committed suicide. That constitutes just below 5 percent of the accounts where the cause of death is known. This number may be a little higher since in two accounts it is not known whether the deceased had committed suicide or died in an accident. According to official records, 1.5 percent of all deaths in Iceland are suicides. If the number of suicides in our data were to match this percentage, the incidents should have been four, not thirteen. Only three of our cases concern persons who were murdered. Murders have been rare in Iceland. First we report a very remarkable case.

### Lady who worked for years at a sanatorium

Jacob was a patient in a sanatorium where I worked. He was sometimes depressed and I tried to brighten his stay with a bit of humour. One day I had told Jacob that he should visit us because he came from the same village as my husband and they would enjoy talking about the people from there. He said 'yes' to that, was glad and I said to him: "You promise to come tomorrow." "Yes, yes, I promise," he said. During the night, I woke up, and all strength was like taken away from me. I was unable to move. Suddenly I saw the bedroom door opened and on the threshold stood Jacob, with his face all covered with blood. I looked at this for a good while unable to speak or move. Then he disappeared and I felt as if he closed the door behind him. I became my normal self, woke up my husband and told him about the incident: "I can swear that something has happened at the sanatorium." I telephoned in the morning and asked if everything was all right with Jacob. "No", said the nurse, "he committed suicide last night." (5076)

We interviewed the husband after the first interview with the informant. He said he remembered the incident well. His wife woke him up in the night and told him about what she had seen. That was before they knew about what had happened to Jacob in the night.

The informant whom we interviewed in 1982 did not remember Jacob's surname. Through further inquiries in 2002, we were at last able to fully identify Jacob with certainty and know more about the circumstances of this incident. On the morning of October 8, 1962 Jacob was missing from his room. The police were called and a few hours later he was found drowned some hundred yards downstream from a walking bridge over a river close to the sanatorium. The postmortem report declared the cause of death as "suicidum submergio," that is, suicide by drowning. In the report, it is written that he was seriously injured, with "two large cuts on the head and the scull is very badly broken". "These injuries probably occurred at the fall when the man threw himself in the river, although it is hard to imagine how such great and many injuries can have occurred in a single fall".

This fits the percipient's description that she saw Jacob "with his face all covered with blood." The river is rather shallow, but it flows over sharp rocks of lava that must have caused the severe head injuries. A girl working in the sanatorium and returning home from a dance in the middle of the night had briefly met Jacob. He told her that he had climbed out of his window. As he disappeared into the darkness, he asked the girl to tell his wife he loved her and disappeared into the night.

It should be added that the informant never saw the body of Jacob. The nurse she had spoken to on the phone that morning had passed away when we conducted our interviews.

### Man in his fifties, from Reykjavík

I was 15 or 16 years old and was working in a big company. I saw a man walk from the end of the machine I was working on and towards the wall and the same way back. He was blonde and was wearing brown clothes. I went to see who was there but did not find anybody. When I told my co-workers about it they thought it was a ghost who had been seen by several other people. It was the ghost of one of the former directors of the company who had committed suicide. (822)

### Woman in her forties in Hveragerði

I have often been aware of the presence of deceased people, especially when I was younger. I lived in the countryside and once I was in the fields raking hay. I looked up and saw a man standing at a place we called the doors to the shed. I only saw him for a moment. I knew him from descriptions but had never met him when he was alive. He was wearing a cap and light coloured clothes. I saw him one other time but then he was on horseback. This man had lived on the farm where my parents were living and he had died where I saw him. That was a few years before I was born. (426)

### Thirty year old man from Reykjavík tells of his dead friend

I once had a friend called Kjartan. He committed suicide. I perceived him several times over the course of a year. I saw him very clearly beside me, sometimes very small and sometimes large... I was always aware of him, kept feeling his presence, saw him very vividly; it was constant. I never heard him but could feel him and see him... He kept coming to me; sometimes he was very jolly and sometimes he was feeling really bad. I was aware of him beside me and it was very strange that he should appear so small so often. It was as if I perceived him in that way. I really do not know how. He was not full size, far from it, sometimes he came closer and then it was as if he was full size... really seldom in full size. He felt bad because he was trying to get alcohol; he was a drunk when he was alive. I remember one incident especially. Then he was in a really bad shape and he was all torn and ragged and had a very bad time as if he was fighting a storm or something like that. He appeared to me as if in a picture beside me. (2144)

### Man from Mosfellsbær tells of an incident

It was up north where my parents-in-law live. My wife and I saw a man who had recently died. It was around the time of the sheep round-up and he always used to take part. He seemed calm and normal. He was walking in front of me. My wife knew him much better than I did and we both saw him. His friends had supposedly also seen him on the mountains during the sheep round-up. (759)

This man's wife described the occurrence with the following words:

The incident happened at a farm in the north where I was born and raised. I was there during the sheep gathering with my husband. We had just come from the sheep gathering and were standing by the cowshed. Then we saw a man walking along a path between the cowshed and the farm. The man then walked to the shed but walked above it. When we came back to the farm we asked who the man had been and found that it had not been anybody from the farm. The description fitted a man from the country who had recently died. He had walked along this same path the year before. This happened in 1996 and the man had just died. (6022A)

### Attacks reported by a woman in Reykjavik

This is about a woman who committed suicide. I was given a closet she had used. At first I knew nothing about this person and did not know that she was deceased. She appeared to be quite real. She was very violent, came in and slammed doors so I never had any peace, night or day. I could hardly move about because of her. She thrashed about and was very mean. This was accompanied by a drop in temperature. She was threatening and I thought she was seeking revenge on something. I felt her touch me; she hit my hands and back. This went on for about four months. A medium was brought in and he informed us what this was all about. After we had taken these steps the woman was not revengeful anymore and I saw her in a great light. (2022)

### A quiet and unsociable man observed by a middle-aged woman

When I was between 11 and 12 years old a man came regularly to our house for meals. He suddenly stopped coming and was later found dead in the harbour. Naturally I did not know that then; I only knew he was dead. Then one time I was alone at home and was waking up; I happened to look out the window and I saw this man. He looked like he was wearing a coat and a hat, just the way I remembered him from when he was alive. This seemed normal to me until he appeared transparent and I could see a big boulder in the garden right through him. Then I came to realize something was not right and was frightened... This man had been very quiet and not very sociable and later I knew he had had problems in his private life. I did not learn about his death until after this had happened... (2048)

### By the river

I have once seen a deceased person. I was only 12 years old at the time. Two brothers of a friend of my parents came to inform us of her death. She had drowned herself. The brothers had come by car and parked it by the stream that flows nearby. When they walked back to the car we saw the woman getting out of it, walk down to the stream and disappear into it. The three of us watched this, my mother who was clairvoyant, my brother and me. Both of them are deceased now. (2064)

### Lady in her forties in Garðabær

I often feel something around me. But that time I woke up, and felt I had been woken up quite suddenly. A name came into my mind without me thinking of him in the least. I did not see him but I knew he was standing there in the bedroom door. And I could speak to him in some way; I cannot explain it any other way. This man had committed suicide a few years earlier and was asking me to help him... (2100)

### Forty year old worker from Reykjavík tells a story:

I have often seen apparitions of people I do not know. It is somewhat like on a television screen, good and clear pictures, but usually only down to the chest and it is like they appear in the mind. I have only once seen a person that I knew, my grandmother and I saw her as a bust. There were other persons with her. I was in bed resting. She did not look the same as when she died for there was no sign of her illness. My grandmother died at the age of 78. (2018A)

This account is reminiscent of hypnagogic images which appear in the minds of some people just as they are about to fall asleep. Such images are usually of strangers and seem to slide along as if on a screen.

### Steersman around fifty smells alcohol

This has to do with a friend of mine who was a heavy drinker; we were often together out at sea back in the old days. Then he drowned, or rather it was thought he drowned himself. After this I began smelling alcohol and I was put in connection to my friend.

He was trying to indicate something in this way. He was always so 'down to earth'. (2059)

This steersman told us that he used to have lucid and prophetic dreams; "Without fail, if I dreamt of a certain woman, the weather would always turn out to be dreadful".

### Seventy year old man from Reykjavík

An acquaintance of mine lived in the next apartment from me and my wife when he was middle aged and had been dead for about 4-5 months when this happened. I started smelling this strange smell in our lounge that I believed came from this man. It was the smell of cats, which had been with him when he was alive. It happened a few times during a certain time period and especially during the evening – but also during the day and weekends. He used to take a lot of medication and had a hard time coming off them. He came over most evenings and often at weekends and he always smelt of cats. This went on for about 3-4 months. He apparently wanted to keep up our friendship. (5040)

The informant added that he often smelt the man before he visited when he was alive. He said his wife had also perceived the smell but when we asked her, she said she had forgotten about it and would not discuss it. This incident had happened about twenty years earlier.

### Old electrician in Reykjavík

I had bought a house on Odinsgata where a man had committed suicide. They thought he was moving about for people had seen him. For example, there was a girl who saw him when she woke up in one of the rooms in the house. But before that, I was aware of him myself. I felt somebody's presence, it was an uncanny experience. I associated it with him. The feeling was as if I was aware of him when I woke up, some sort of energy which I associated with the presence of that man. It was an uncomfortable feeling for he was in that sort of mood or the effect was at least like that (7046)

# 14

# Murder or Manslaughter

Finally, here are the three accounts in which the deceased person was killed or murdered.

**Woman in her sixties**

Many years ago I woke up during the middle of the night and saw some sort of mist appear in front of me and change into a person in armour. I thought to myself that it was strange that it was a person wearing a suit of armour and still it was not a man. A few years later I went to France and I lived in a hotel called the House of the Virgin of Orleans. There was a statue in the garden of Jeanne D'Arc and I saw another in a church and I thought to myself: "That is it". (5005)

This is the only incident in our collection which involves a historical person from a distant past. The informant interpreted this as an encounter with the dead so the account is included. However, the experience should probably rather have been considered as a sign for the informant of what she was later going to meet with.

**Seventy-year old lady tells of a strange incident**

I was in the basement finishing my washing and was washing up the boiling pot. I heard somebody walking into the basement but did not check. Then I heard somebody walk down the hall towards the door. I looked to the door but did not see anybody so I just kept on with my work. Then I looked towards the washing machine which was on my right hand side. I saw a man standing there; I could see his feet first. He was wearing boots, leather boots up to the thigh and wearing black trousers. I did not recognise the clothing but it was from an older time. The cut of the trousers and the back pockets had a cover, buttoned from the outside like they used to. I looked very carefully up the man with my eyes. He was wearing a blue sweater, like the seamen used to wear and may still wear. I kept looking up towards the shoulders, then he disappeared, in front of my eyes. I did not get to see the head. I started wondering why he was contacting me and expected it must be a premonition for somebody's death. I recalled that I knew two people who owned such jumpers but it was neither of them.

The morning after I went into the basement. I did not perceive anybody but I heard somebody say behind my shoulder: "I am Thorbjorg's husband, I was here yesterday." And that was all. After a while my daughter's son came over and said: "My great grandmother died last night." His great grandmother was Thorbjörg, her husband was called Thordur and he died in England when he was in his prime. He is supposed to have been murdered. I did not recognise him; I had never seen him or spoken to him. (7550)

Here we may add that the informant told us that she had told her son of the incident in the evening of the first day. The son confirmed to us that she had told him of the incident on the first night, just as it is described here. This happened about a year before the account was related to us.

### Woman in her fifties tells of an incident which happened 8-10 years earlier

A murder took place here a few years ago. The murdered man was a taxi driver who was an acquaintance of mine. He kept very close to me for two weeks following the murder. I was just lying down when this man appeared. I saw him, spoke to him and he put his hand on my shoulder. He was white in the face like a deceased man, must have been about fifty when he died. I felt this man was asking me to help him. He showed me pictures of two men. He thought they had caused his death and wanted me to get a message to the police... I did not like this at all and I told a clergyman about it... (7580)

# 15

## CIRCUMSTANCES, STATE OF MIND AND CONSEQUENCES

I N what circumstances did the encounters with deceased appear? We have already mentioned that at least half the visions happened in daylight or with electric lights turned on. The incidents happened all year around and no more during the winter than in the summer. Furthermore, the dead have been perceived at all hours, although it is less common for these encounters to happen at night. Several other factors can be looked at.

**What were the perceivers doing and in what state of mind were they at the time of the encounter?**

It is natural to question whether the informants were in some special state of mind when they had their experience. What were they doing when they had the encounter? This is often clear in the accounts and we made a point of asking about it specifically. One of the reasons is that some theories have suggested that experiences such as the ones we have been discussing usually happen when the mind is not active or is in a resting state. According to this theory it should be easier for these images/hallucinations to appear when the mind is in a resting state or not occupied by some other task (Gurney, Myers and Podmore, 1886).

| Table 11. What were the perceivers doing at the time of their encounter? | | |
|---|---|---|
| | **Freqency** | **%** |
| Working | 206 | 47 |
| Resting | 99 | 22 |
| Just before sleep | 30 | 7 |
| Just after waking | 74 | 17 |
| Uncertain whether sleeping or awake | 32 | 7 |
| Unreliable or missing information | 8 | - |

The answers show that in almost half of the cases (46%) the informants were fully awake, at work or engaged in some activity at the time of the encounter. It was also common for the perceivers to be resting (22 percent), and several had their experience shortly after waking up (17 percent). Some of the informants encountered the deceased just before they fell asleep (7 percent). Therefore, one could say that half of our informants were awake, about a quarter was awake and resting and the remaining quarter was wake but close to sleep when the incident occurred.

On the whole, our data do not support the theory of the resting state of the mind although it could apply to a considerable number of the accounts. Let us have a look at a few interesting examples where the experience occurs at the moment of waking up.

### Uninvited guest

At night I always locked the door to the room I had rented. I do not remember what time it was, it must have been around five o'clock in the morning, when I woke up. I was suddenly wide awake and my eyes were wide open; I had not even moved in my bed. There was a man sitting beside me on my bed. He had on maroon-coloured woolen underwear, no shirt, no jacket, just the maroon underwear, the oldfashioned kind. He was a small man and thin, and was sort of muttering and I was startled. At the same time I thought: "Good God! I forgot to lock the door!" I rushed out of bed but the door was locked tight. The man disappeared as soon I got up. (5056)

### Burdened with sin

My father-in-law died at 56 years of age. I dreamt a very vivid dream. I felt he came to me and was alive and said this exact sentence:

"I have had to pay for my sins but now I feel well." Then he went pale and passed out in front of me. I woke up and felt as if he was standing by my bed, stretching out his hand over me. I looked at him and he pretty much evaporated as he disappeared out of the room. I did not perceive him as a living man. The event gave me a fright and I was left sitting up shaking in my bed... (7620)

## On Flateyjardalsheidi

We were staying in one of the bothies in the mountains on Flateyjardalsheidi. I woke up in the morning to find a woman standing on the floor. I stared at her for a long time and saw that she was wearing clothes similar to what women wore at the turn of the century. She was accompanied by a smell of burned peat and brushwood and coffee that is cooked on an old stove. She said to me in a very direct manner: "Is it not about time to wake up?" Then she walked right across the floor and through the wall beside the door. She was tall and strongly built but not fat. I did not know who she was... but I felt quite good after the incident. (7006)

## At Breidafjord

This happened four years ago. I was pregnant, carrying my son and we were living in the country. We were considering moving down to the small town of Stykkisholm. I wanted to stay in the countryside but my husband wanted to move to town. Then one night I woke up to see two rather small women and a man who was taller; these were elderly people. They started talking to my husband who answered them in his sleep. I do not remember what they said but I clearly remember my husband saying: "No." And they walked away. Later I was told who these people were. They had lived there before my parents. They had been dead for a long time when I lived there. (7538)

## Father makes an appearance

My father had recently died. I woke up one night and felt somebody touch my arm and somebody is lying very close beside me. I sat up and saw my father, just as he used to be. I saw him, as if he was sitting up in the bed, wearing his pyjamas. (7570)

## Bearded old man

I was five years old and slept in a room to the side of the lounge that had a slanting roof. Suddenly I woke up. I do not know what time it was. It was not late because the radio was on. There was a small dresser opposite the bed I was sleeping in and I saw a man sitting on it, and it felt as if he did not touch the floor with his feet. He had a long beard and was wearing thick knitted clothes. He sat with his legs crossed and had a stick between his legs. He just sat and looked at me. I stared at him for a long time and of course I was scared. I did not expect anybody there. My mother was awake in the living room with my sister... My mother told me that the description fitted my grandfather very well who had died before I was born. I cannot remember if I described him in detail at that time but I can remember this as clearly as if it happened yesterday. (7628)

And finally two accounts where the informant is not sure whether the incident happened while he was awake or asleep, and another where the message is unclear.

### I am lonely

I am still not sure whether I was awake or asleep. It was early in the morning when the man appeared to me. I did not know him personally but knew of him and knew him well in sight. He appeared to me as if in a mist or some sort of whiff of smoke and said: "I am lonely." That is what he said, nothing else, and then disappeared. (5086)

### At Gamli Gardur

I was living in Gamli Gardur, the old student hostel at the university, when this happened. One night I woke up, or was suddenly woken up when a cold and uncomfortable breeze came up my legs. I got up bewildered and saw a being as if it came across the end of the bed, by my feet. I quickly realised who it was. She had died a few months earlier from childbirth, roughly twenty years of age. She was in such a hurry or seemed to have some important business with me. She called me by name and said: "Gudmund, you have to help Bardur, who is being tortured." I remember it so vividly. I was a bit scared or confused and must have looked away. Then the bad feeling went away. I looked up and saw the girl standing at the foot of my bed as if she was alive... I was wide awake and saw her for a moment but after a short while she disappeared. She had died a few months ago. We were cousins... (2164)

Bardur, who was mentioned by the woman, was not known by the informant but he thought that a man by that name had been missing at about the time he had his experience. He was not sure and had never met the man.

The last few examples were at the time when the person woke up. We asked about the health of the informants in when they had their encounter. Most of them (94 percent) were in normal good health, 12 (3 percent) were sick in bed or had a fever; 7 were under the influence of medical or recreational drugs, and 5 were in hospital. Most informants were in a normal state of mind (84 percent). Some were in a depressed (7 percent) or sad (6 percent) mood. These informants were often widows or widowers or others who had recently lost a loved one.

### The impact of the experience

For three quarters of those interviewed their encounter made a strong impact (43 percent) or had some impact (33 percent) on them. The fact that four out of ten participants thought that they might possibly have had such an experience before the incident occurred, shows that many were open to the possibility of having an encounter with someone who had died. 133 informants (38 percent) had not expected that this could happen to them, and for 69 informants (20 percent) this experience changed the way they thought about encounters with the dead. For 40 percent of the informants the incident increased their belief in life after death.

A great majority felt that the encounter had been a positive experience (69 percent), for only 6 percent was it a negative experience, while 17 percent felt it was neither positive nor negative. A few could not make up their mind about this.

**Table 12. Positive or negative feelings about the experience and the informants' relationship with the deceased.**

| Relationship: | Positive | Neutral | Negative | Do not know | Total |
|---|---|---|---|---|---|
| Family | 133 (83%) | 13 (8%) | 7 (4%) | 8 (5%) | 161 |
| Friendship | 25 (89%) | 3 (11%) | 0 | 0 | 28 |
| Coworker | 6 (67%) | 2 (22%) | 1 (11%) | 0 | 9 |
| Acquaintance | 23 (49%) | 9 (19%) | 3 (6%) | 12 (26%) | 47 |
| Stranger | 52 (50%) | 33 (32%) | 9 (9%) | 9 (9%) | 103 |

The informants were more likely to rate the experience as positive if the deceased person had a close relationship with them. If the deceased person had been a friend or a relative, 84 percent of the informants found the incident a positive experience. On the other hand, only 50 percent of those who had encountered acquaintances or strangers felt the incident had been a positive experience. See table 12.

It also made a difference if the deceased person suffered a violent death or died naturally. See table 13.

| Table 13. Cause of death and positive or negative feelings about the encounter. | | | | | |
|---|---|---|---|---|---|
| Cause of death | Positive | Neutral | Negative | Do not know | Total |
| Illness | 155 (80%) | 18 (9%) | 9 (5%) | 12 (6%) | 194 |
| Violent | 48 (58%) | 21 (26%) | 5 (6%) | 8 (10%) | 82 |
| Unknown | 36 (50%) | 21 (29%) | 6 (8%) | 9 (13%) | 72 |

It is therefore a fact that the great majority felt that their encounter with the dead was a positive experience. This is in opposition to the terror which is commonly believed to be associated with experiences of apparitions and ghosts. Here is such an account:

### On Christmas Eve

It started on Christmas Eve. I was waiting for my brother when suddenly I saw my mother, who died many years ago, appear before me. She was dressed in clothes that I remembered very well. This was the first time I saw her after her death. I was filled with a joyous feeling, I was very happy... (2082)

We did not ask how often our participants had encountered deceased people but clearly it was quite common - if not very common - for such an incident to have happened more than once. Nevertheless, we asked about other supernatural or paranormal experiences, without defining what that experience could be. Two thirds answered 'yes' to that question, which is a similar percentage to that found in the survey from 1975. In this older survey, 64 percent of participants had experienced some psychic or supernatural incidents. Two thirds perceived the deceased person only once but a third of informants more often. 47 percent said that a close relative had also had such an encounter with the dead.

# 16

# WIDOWS AND WIDOWERS

W E have eighteen incidents in our collection where a widow experienced her deceased husband and in nine cases widowers had encounters with their wives. We must keep in mind that there are many more widows than widowers since women tend to live a few years longer than men. Widows and widowers are more likely to have encounters with the dead than any other group. According to our data, about a third of those who perceive their dead partners only encounter them once; around a fifth have had two to three such experiences; but around half perceive their dead partners four or more times. Generally you could say that around half of all widows and widowers perceive their dead partners so strongly that they believe that they have a real connection with the deceased. Or shall we say the living deceased?

Below are examples of incidents where widows and widowers talk about their relationship with their deceased partners. More cases can be found elsewhere in the book.

### The Joker

My husband died at 46 years of age. He collapsed at work. He was a big man, tall and stout, good-humoured and quite a joker actually but deep down he was a serious and very dependable man. I have often sensed his presence and seen his apparition. Sometimes he seems to appear in a natural way, like he had entered the apartment in a normal fashion, or had come from another bedroom, shutting his eyes slowly. I have also often smelled his aftershave after 5 o'clock in the afternoon or about the same time as he used to shave. My two daughters have also smelled it. I have also smelled his body odour. He often teased us about things. He wanted his presence to be known. I have seen him at various hours and at various intervals - sometimes days or even weeks apart. This had a rather pleasant effect on me. I felt as if an eye was kept on me and I was being helped. (682)

**Fisherman and engineer in his nineties told of his frequent encounters with his wife who had died 15 years earlier:**

I have been touched by my wife who passed away. I feel a sort of flutter or a vibration, especially in my back. It usually happens when I think of my wife and this has happened several times... (2106)

**A lady around fifty tells of an incident which happened when she was 35 years old and her husband had just died:**

My husband drowned about eighteen years ago but I am often aware of him. I was pregnant when he died, had three months left and of course it was very difficult for a certain time period. Then he came even more often and spoke to me and said he would have to stop coming if I could not stay strong. His body was found three weeks after he drowned. One night, the memorial was over, I cannot quite say I saw him but I was awake and he lit the lamp on my bedside table... I have also often perceived him while driving a car and when I have been to séances I have always been told that he is with me. (2055)

**Woman describes a memorable incident.**

In the same year I lost my 53 year old husband and my apartment burned down in a fire. Of course I was very upset and was staying with my brother. One night, when I was not quite asleep, the bedcover was pushed aside and I was moved in the bed. It was so strange but I was not scared at all. Of course I perceived my husband. I knew it could not be anybody else. This or a similar thing happened to me three times... I know he came to comfort me... (7568)

**Widow of a clergyman tells of an incident that happened 12 years earlier.**

The night after my husband died I could not sleep and was at home in my bed and very lonely. Suddenly I sensed him standing by my bed. He seemed to be covered in a mist. I saw him and felt his hand as he stroked my head and recited part of a well-known poem that was about how good it was to rest and then wake up one day surrounded by eternal joy. I felt quite differently after this. (2090)

## Radio mechanic tells of his regular contact with his deceased wife

This has happened so many times... that I feel my wife is with me... We had been together for 40 years... When I lie down and am about to go to sleep, then it is as if I am somehow disconnected, as if some force comes up through the small of my neck. I am awake and I can sense what is happening. I know my wife is beside me and can feel her hand. I cannot see her but I feel her touch. I cannot explain it but it is as if some strong power goes through my head and when she becomes more distant it disappears.

Shortly after my wife died I got very drunk. Then I could hear her and she asked me if I was actually going to do that. I stopped immediately. That was all it took. I can still feel her presence today, after seven years. Usually this happens between 12 and 3 at night when I am lying in my bed. Sometimes I hear her voice just as when she was alive; I can perceive her and the movement in her hands and the hand says so much... (2122)

## Strong handshake

I lost my husband in the year 1950. It was as it usually is - quite tough. A week later his sister died. She had been a patient for a long time. I went east with the body, to Arnessysla. The weather was awful, very windy and the funeral took a long time and I was very cold. The night I came back west I put my clothes on and lay down on the bench and he appeared and held me so tight... I could not see him but I could feel it was his embrace... This was about half a month after he was buried. I felt he had come to comfort me and give me strength. (2124)

## A man who took fright

I lost my wife and really grieved for her, was a broken man after she died. I will not say for sure, but I woke up and saw a white being come towards my bed. I took fright and then she moved aside and disappeared. I associate the event with my wife but most memorable is how scared I was... (2132)

**Like a mild electric shock**

For about two years I was aware of my wife every so often after she died. I was between being awake and asleep and a strange feeling came over me, like a mild electric shock. I was aware of her in my bed, I opened my eyes and saw her hair and when I was going to give it a better look of course it disappeared. Then there was the thing with the name. They were going to name a child after her but decided not to. She appeared at around that time so I had that decision changed. Then she came back the following night and seemed to be relieved... (7598)

The incidents described above show the warm and intimate relationship which can exist between couples after one of them has passes away. How this happens, what is perceived and how it is perceived is extremely variable. It is noteworthy that touch is felt in 29 percent of these cases, whereas touch is only felt in 11 percent of the other accounts in our collection. This seems best explained by the intimate relationship formed between couples.

Another thing which is usually apparent in these accounts is that most of these perceptions are experienced with positive feelings. The accounts include descriptive words like: comforting, happiness, help and strength. Fear is very seldom mentioned and terror is only mentioned in one account.

The first large scale study of widows and widowers was conducted in Britain by a physician, W. Dewi Rees. His research was published in 1971 and was based on his thesis at the University of London. Rees contacted everyone who had lost a partner in a particular area of Wales and interviewed a total of 293 widows and widowers (81 percent of those in the area). Some were not included for reasons such as ill health or for other valid reasons. Rees managed to speak to 94 percent of the remaining widows and widowers as only a few declined to take part in the study.

Rees called his article "Hallucinations of widowhood". He had very strict requirements for what he called a hallucination. For example, he did not include accounts where people had perceived their partners as if in their mind's eye; or if the experience happened in bed at night (unless the persons were preparing themselves for sleep) or if the person was in any way uncertain about whether the incident had been real.

47 percent of the widows and widowers in Rees' study had perceived their partners after they had passed away. There was no difference

between the percentages of men and women who perceived their partners. 50 percent of the widowers and 47 percent of the widows reported such incidents. It was most common for them to sense a presence (39 percent). Others saw (14 percent), heard (13 percent) and felt the touch of their deceased partners (3 percent). Several participants said they spoke to their dead partners (12 percent). One in every nine widows/ widowers felt that they had a constant relationship with their deceased partners.

Sometimes these perceptions appeared on and off over a long period but they were most common during the first ten years after the partner passed away. The likelihood of such occurrences increased the longer the couple had been together and the happier they had been. Only 28 percent had told others of their experience. More widows had talked about their experience than widowers. Only one had told a priest and none of them had told their doctor. Half of the informants gave no reason for this but some said they were afraid they would be laughed at and others felt that the experience was too personal. It made no difference whether these people lived alone or with others as to whether they told other people about their experience. Such an experience was less common when the couple had no children. Rees came to the conclusion that hallucinations of this sort are not indicators of ill health but rather a natural consequence of sorrow and loss.

Similar results have been found in America. The researchers Olsen, Suddeth, Peterson and Egelhoff (1985) interviewed 46 widows. Of these, 28 (61 percent) had perceived their deceased husbands. A great majority described their experiences as having been positive and helpful. Roughly half had never told anyone about their experiences before the interviews. According to books and articles on the loss of a partner, such hallucinations are now thought to be a natural response to sorrow and a consequence of losing a loved one.

In our survey on psychic experiences in 1975, we received answers from 902 individuals who were part of a randomly chosen sample. When their marriage status was considered, it became clear that 43 of the participants were widows and 6 were widowers. 23 of these (47 percent) gave an affirmative answer to the question of whether they had "sensed the presence of a dead person". According to the results of the sample as a whole, only 35 percent should have answered "yes" to the question (based on the high number of women in this group).

A slightly higher percentage was found in a survey conducted by the American sociologist Andrew M. Greely (1987) who used a representative sample of two thousand participants. In this study, 53 percent of widows and widowers reported that they had perceived the dead which is a significantly greater percentage than the 41 percent found in the total sample.

There follow more examples of how people who have lost their life partners have perceived or sensed their deceased spouses.

### I sometimes feel a stroke on my cheek

I sometimes sense my deceased husband, who died at 74 years of age as well as my mother. I do not see them but I can hear them and feel their touch. I sometimes feel a stroke on my cheek and then I think of the dead. They also come to me when I am thinking strongly of them and if I need them. This is normal to me and I am never scared. I feel peaceful. (707A)

### Good vibrations

My husband died seven months ago and I have sensed his presence. I get good vibrations from him and I can see him looking happy and content. I know he is feeling very well. I have seen him; I feel him and know he is there. It is hard to describe but this is very dear to me. He was an invalid before he died and often he did not know what was going on. He died here at home with me. I sat with him when he died and was holding him and it is my belief that I saw ectoplasm coming out of him. Death is always cold and I was not sure if I had been kind enough to him. I thought earlier I might not have anything to do with him anymore even if I believed he was alive, but now things are quite different after I saw him. I have never heard the deceased speak, but it is like their thoughts are being pressed into me. (2045)

### Mother, did you hear that?

I had sensed my husband many times before. Shortly after he died one of my daughters was staying with me. We had a glass to drink before we went to bed. We had lain down and were just about to fall asleep when we heard someone enter the house and go straight into the kitchen. The glass I had been drinking from was lifted and placed on a barrel; this made quite a loud noise. I did not say anything because I thought my daughter was asleep but then she said: "Mother, did you hear that?" I asked her to come with me to check what was going on otherwise I would not be able to sleep. We both went into the kitchen and saw that my glass had been moved from the table and into the sink. (2058)

## I am coming

This was shortly after my husband passed away. I have sometimes dreamt of him but this has only happened once. I lay in bed on my room one afternoon. I was feeling a bit tired and I was home alone. I was just lying there. The window was above the bed head and I felt him come in through the window and I clearly heard his voice saying: "I am coming darling." There was just that one sentence. Then I felt him lying next to me, to my left, like he used to, and he touched my armpit. I opened my eyes and felt the touch of someone leaving... I felt very good... (2066)

## He wanted us to get going

It was the day of the viewing of my husband, Hafsteinn the medium. I lay down for a nap and I felt as if he had come to see me and that I could see him. He wanted us to set off for the viewing. He had been a very punctual man. I am not sure whether I was awake or asleep. My mind was always with him. He went so suddenly... (5048A)

## He was looking at me with his eyes sparkling

I lost my husband during the summer. He had been a clergyman. I have never been very sensitive. One night I was ill and not feeling very well and of course I missed him. Suddenly I saw him standing by the bench I was resting on in the lounge and he was looking at me with his eyes sparkling. I was just very happy. I do not know for how long or short a time he was there. I cannot remember whether I saw more than the face but I distinctly remember the face and the sparkling eyes. He had such beautiful eyes. I was most definitely not asleep, that is a fact. (5051)

## I felt his touch very well

My husband died at 42 years of age. One evening I was sitting on my sofa. I was alone in a big house. I was sitting in front of my television and suddenly I felt my husband sit close beside me and say: "Ruth!" I was bewildered and a bit beside myself. I felt his touch very well. This has happened twice. (5110)

### "You should think of your child"

This was a few years after my wife died. I was on the Canary Islands for Christmas. The Icelanders had a joint Christmas gathering on the 24th of December. I was sitting at a table with some friends. We were waiting for our food when I suddenly get a strong feeling for my wife's presence. I could sense her, could not see her with my eyes but felt very strongly that she was there beside me. And I felt her saying to me: "You should think of your child. They are thinking of you ". I had a daughter who was staying with her grandparents in Akranes. We usually spent Christmas there. (5042)

### Scent of perfume

I was getting out of bed and then smelled a particular perfume that my wife always used. She had died some time back and this smell had no normal cause or explanation that I was aware of. My wife was making me aware of her to comfort me. (6001)

### Should we not have him between us?

I went to a séance with Hafsteinn the medium after I lost my wife. There she told me that she came to me during the evenings after I was asleep and in the morning before I woke up. Then during the winter in 1980 I woke up one night. I had gone to bed early. I got out of bed and went to the toilet. When I came back into the bedroom and was about to lie down in bed, I was so lucky as to see my wife lying in the bed she had occupied since we got married, with a boy that we had lost when he was three years old. I saw my wife lying in bed and the boy in front of her. When I saw it I said: "Should we not have him between us?" And he came like a spirit and lay between us. It was a good moment. Then I said to my wife: "Are you not both well?" Then she disappeared along with the boy and did not say a word. And I saw some sort of trail of thin smoke after them. (7032A)

We finish this chapter with an account from one of our informants, Johann Kuld, who was a well-known writer in his time and wrote many books - especially about life in the country and at sea. He died in 1986. In an interview with us, he read the following account from his book: In the swirling seas of life (*Í lífsins ólgusjó*, 1979).

### Johann Kuld's account

We were both patients. She was very ill and was not expected to get better. But she was very brave although she could feel that her bodily strength was faltering, like a bird with a broken wing. But nevertheless we were happy. We had been married for seven years at this time and we had had a boy and a girl but our girl had died... During the autumn, in October, she had an operation on her lungs at the Landspitali hospital. She lived through the operation and I came to her and spoke to her for the next few days. We said goodbye and I told her I would be back very soon. I went with high hopes and bright spirits back to Reykjahæli where I lived.

Two days passed. I got a phone call from Landspítalinn very late in the evening and I was told that my wife had suddenly got much worse and that she did not have long to live. When I got to hospital she had high fever and was delusional. I sat with her this last night and watched life battle with death. But early the next morning the fight was over, my wife was dead. I walked out of the house sad and lonely...

After roughly a week I dreamt of her and she told me that she was alive although her body was dead. After this I could feel her presence, even though I could not see her...

One day in January about three in the afternoon I was sitting on a bench in my room. Suddenly I saw the door to the room open and my wife came in through the door. She was smiling and walked right up to me where I was sitting. I stared at her as if I was hypnotised and could not say anything. When she came close to me she put out her hand and said: "Do not be scared, I am alive." I took her hand and felt that she was not cold, she felt normal to the touch. Then I dared to ask: "Where have you been, what has happened?"

"Soon after I died in the hospital they let me stay there to look after a woman who was very ill. Since then I have been to many places. Now this time is over, I am leaving. I have come to say goodbye." Then she said: "Take off your shoes and lie in the bed, I am going to lie down in front of you." I did as she asked. She stroked my cheek and whispered beautiful things to me. And I was filled with a feeling of joy. Then I was filled with calm and I was surrounded with a sense of peace that cannot be described with words. I could feel that she still held my hand and stroked my cheek and I fell asleep. When I awoke a few minutes later I was alone. The space in the bed where she had been was empty. She was gone but I knew that she had been there, spoken to me, had stroked my cheek and my skin. In that way she said goodbye and thanked me for our time together.

This incident is still so vivid in my mind. It does not get old or fade with the years that have passed since then. I have often asked myself: "Could I have dreamt it all?" But my answer to that is definite: "No." This was reality as far as there is a reality, unusual and unforgettable at the same time. However, it is beyond me to understand how it could happen. But it did... (7016) (Kuld, 1979, 132-135)

# 17

## How Did the Phenomena Appear and Disappear and How Long Did it Last?

We asked our participants how the phenomena appeared and disappeared and how long they lasted. In 27 percent of the accounts, the phenomena appeared suddenly but 17 percent of the incidents did so gradually. It was most common for the phenomena to already have appeared when the informant paid attention to them (56 percent). Or they appeared quite naturally just as when a person appears in the flesh, either because they were standing there when noticed or they came walking around the corner or into a room. In roughly a third of cases the vision gradually disappears quite slowly and naturally. In these examples, the deceased person walks out of the room or simply disappears out of sight. However, it is more common for the dead to suddenly disappear (40 percent) than to suddenly appear. The reader may already be aware of this after reading several accounts of these encounters.

### In the lounge

I came home one morning at seven and was going into the kitchen when I decided to open the door to the living room. I do not know why, I just did. Then my mother-in-law was sitting there in my chair. She disappeared quite suddenly. She had died four years earlier at 91 years of age... (2166)

This is one of the many examples where the dead person suddenly disappeared. It may be added that the wife of the informant of this case remembered him telling her of his experience and could describe what the woman had been wearing. It was relatively common for people to have looked away from the deceased person and when they looked again, the person had disappeared (22 percent). One example:

### A bright summer night

I was 10 or 11 years old. It was dark in the living-room but outside it was a bright summer's night. I was awakened by a man who was walking in the living-room and stopped by the spinning-wheel and leaned against it. I closed my eyes and the visitor was gone when I looked again. The next evening we had a guest from the next farm, and the housewife thought, judging from my description, that it was his father I saw. And I recognized his gait from the night before. This experience freed me of fear of the dark when I thought about it a few years later. Maybe it did so right away. (889)

When informants were asked whether they felt that the vision had disappeared naturally, almost a third said 'yes' but two thirds said it had been strange how the vision had disappeared. Examples:

### On Snæfell

I was a skipper on the old Snæfell from Akureyri and we were about to set off on a fishing trip. This was shortly after my father's funeral. My cabin was underneath the wheelhouse and there was always a light under the bridge wing so it was bright enough to read in my cabin. I heard somebody turn the door handle and the door was opened. I thought it would be the deck officer, who would need to contact me. But then I saw the old man, my father, come down the stairs and stop on a small landing by the last step. He was jollier and healthier looking than he had been before he died. I was going to speak to him but then it was as if he had evaporated... (7000)

### A knock on the door

I was a child at home and we had been making such a racket my brothers and sisters and me. Then there was a knock at the door and a very loud knock indeed. I went to answer to the door and there stood a man in a coat, with a hat, well-to-do. I bid him good evening but as I spoke he disappeared. I was sure my mother had also seen him... (932)

## The clergyman

When I was working in the Landspital and looked after a clergyman who died there. He was quite an old man. After he died I saw him, the upper part of him, heard him and felt him. He passed me a sort of grail to sip from and said three sentences that I cannot remember. When he gave me a drink from the grail he touched me and it was as if a cold storm had rushed through me. I felt he was like he used to always be but he disappeared unnaturally, much too quickly, not like a normal person could have. (166)

## A motherly look

I was putting one of my children to sleep and not thinking about anything in particular except for the song I was humming. I glanced over by the bed and I saw a woman sitting on a box for a vacuum cleaner that stood there. I had never seen this woman. For a moment I was scared, I stared at the woman; saw her head and her face but the rest of her was hazy. She had a kind and motherly look and sort of dissolved. I told my parents about this and described the woman. They said it had been my father's first wife who died long before I was born. This is the only time I have seen a deceased person but I have sensed them in other ways, e.g. experienced their odour or their touch. (2032)

The following account probably has the best description of the appearance and disappearance of the apparition:

## Wish for forgiveness

It was about 20 years ago. I was very attached to a woman whom I called my grandmother. I was raised by her. She was one of the family members in my home. Well, she died in Isafjord. I had her moved here to the south at her own wish. But this caused some arguments here in the south. There was a gathering after the funeral and when people start drinking alcohol they change. One of her sons pretty much lost control of himself. He claimed that it had been my personal decision to bring her south, that I had only done it for me. I was not living here in Reykjavík at the time so that did not even make any sense. I went back west and the first evening I went to sleep at about 12 o'clock. At three in the morning I woke up quite suddenly, or rather was woken up. I felt strange, I was not quite sure and I thought: "What is wrong with me, I thought I was perfectly well when I went to sleep but now I feel strangely ill." I started checking but no, my forehead is not warm at all and I am not feeling hot. Then I looked towards the door and saw that in the middle of it there is a colour that is not usually there. Gradually it became more, became a mist and it got thicker and thicker until the old lady appears right there. I saw her clearly and she was trying to speak to me. Then I realised that it would not help to try speaking, I could just as well think. This did not take long but long enough for me to understand that she was there to tell me that she did not approve of the arguments that happened in the south and asked if I could forgive her son, which I did. This vision then gradually disappeared in exactly the same way as it appeared. I did not hear any words exactly but I contacted her with my thoughts and perceived her in the same way. (5100)

When you compare how the apparitions appear and disappear, it is clear that they are much more likely to disappear unnaturally than to appear unnaturally. Sometimes the person is said to have been unnatural in that they were transparent or "it was as if you were looking through glass".

### The carpenter

Twice I have seen a deceased man, a carpenter I knew quite well. It was a little after his death with about a month passing between the two encounters. He was my brother-in-law and was 74 or 75 years old when he died. This was during the middle of the day and I was coming in. He was sitting in the chair that he used to sit in at the dinner table in the dining room of his house in Kopavog. He looked very similar to what he was like from the time I got to know him. He seemed to have no special reason for being there and was transparent but slowly evaporated. Soon after he died, it was common to hear the sounds of hammering, especially during the day and the evening. (7036)

### The mother-in-law

I clearly remember this incident that occurred in the hospital not so many years ago. I sensed my mother-in-law with me in my hospital bed. She had died about two days earlier. I lay sick and sadly could not be at her burial. She sat there by my side on the bed and held my shoulders in her arms. This was very clear. On the other hand this 'vision' was in fact transparent as if it was seen through glass. She did not look so real that one could think that her body was made of flesh and blood... I felt completely awake. (2212)

It is typical for these perceptions to last only very briefly. In half of the accounts, the perception lasted only for a moment or a few seconds. In almost half the incidents it lasted for a few minutes and in a few cases it lasted a little longer. It may be added that people tend not to be very exact at judging the length of time for such short time periods particularly when it happened years ago. There are also some examples where people perceived the phenomenon many times for a short time period each time or even often over a longer time period, even for weeks. This is particularly common among widows and widowers.

It is interesting to examine how close to or how far from the perceiver the phenomena tend to occur. Concerning the visions, it appears that in almost half of these cases the deceased person appears within reach (47 percent) and in about a third of the incidents the dead person is further away and inside. Finally, there were 39 accounts in which the perceived deceased person appeared at quite some distance and outside (16 incidents). It was more common for the vision to be moving (59 percent) but often it was still (40 percent). Usually the phenomenon appeared in front of the informant (76 percent) but it was also common for it to be seen to the side of the perceiver (22 percent).

How often did the informants perceive the deceased person? Only once in 66 percent of the cases, in 17 percent it was two to three times, in 15 percent more often and some could not remember how often.

# 18

## How physically Real Was the Experience?

WHEN it comes to the visions – how physically real were they? Almost three quarters of our informants said the deceased person had been physically present until he or she disappeared (73 percent), which could be understood to mean that they felt as if the person was there in the flesh. In 15 percent of the accounts the deceased person was only perceived to be physically present in part, that is, they were transparent, or only a part of the person could be seen. In almost as many incidents (13 percent) the dead person was not perceived to be physically present.

Were there any cases where material objects were perceived along with the experience? This was rare. In five cases objects moved in an unusual manner. Three examples include strange responses from animals and there are also a few other unclear incidents. Let us have a look at three accounts with unusual movements of objects and one case where the informant claims that a child was lifted off the ground without the touch of a human hand.

### The assault

I had just moved into a house on the west side of town when some disturbances and discomfort began to bother me at night. They increased steadily and became clearer and more rhythmic. For some weeks I either could not sleep or I was awakened from 2 to 4 in the morning and it felt as if I were being pushed or downright beaten.

Never did any of the others in the bedroom wake up but I often thought they did not sleep well the time I was awake. My wife slept in the room as well as my two grown up daughters and my young son. One night I saw my younger daughter levitate from the bed, two meters into the air and then she slowly went down again. The beatings became more intense but there were never any marks on my body. (57)

### In the hallway

I lived with my parents on a remote farm. I was once walking down the hall in the wintertime in the dark when I heard a door open at the end of the hall. It was a door that closed automatically. Afterwards I heard footsteps approach and felt I was being stroked lightly over the chest. Then the footsteps slowly faded away. When I came into the living-room I asked if anyone had gone out, but no one had. This startled me. I felt convinced that it must have been my brother who died a few years earlier. A few years later my father saw him in the same place and under the same circumstances. (2033)

### Smell of whisky

It has happened more than once that I have felt a man close to me since I moved into this house. He lived here before me and was my husband's brother. I have felt that he was here and he always moved fast with a breeze. On occasion he used to drink alcohol and when he was accompanied by the breeze I also smelled whisky. This has happened several times. In the morning when I wake up, or if I wake up during the night, I feel he is saying something or calling but it has never been clear enough for me to understand. Once I was here in the kitchen putting the dishes away into a cabinet. I could feel him behind me. He was angry and suddenly the plates started flying out of my hands all over the place... I had no control over it whatsoever. (5000)

There are two examples where the informant is convinced of the physical reality of what he sees and grabs for it but there is nothing there.

### In Eidar school

I was in school at Eidar. Two friends of mine and I had broken school regulations. We had stayed out later than was allowed in one of our friends rooms. We were sneaking in the hall back to our rooms and were going to stop at the toilets on our way to bed. We were walking one after another and I was up front. Then I meet a man I thought was my school friend and I grabbed his arm but there was nothing to grab, so my hand went through his arm. At the same time he grabbed me in the same manner, lifted me up, and threw me back at my friends so we all tumbled down the hall. This was quite physical, very remarkable and an unforgettable experience. I saw the man open the door to the next room, where there were two girls, enter and leave the door open. My friends did not see him. We went to the bathroom in quite a state of terror. When we returned the girls were in the hallway and scolded us for being so rude, for opening the door to their room and leaving it open so late at night... (2146)

We were able to contact one of the boys who were with the informant when he had the experience and asked about the incident. He vaguely remembered that something happened to them and said he had thought that it had been a prank, but "that was clearly not the case". One of the girls remembered that she and her girlfriends had scolded the boys. She also said that they had sensed someone opening the door and entering the room but they had not seen anything.

The next example is from a fisherman.

### On the boat Faxi

I was once on the boat Faxi. We were transporting goods off the east coast and there were four of us on the boat. I had just come on duty and was in the wheelhouse when I saw a man walking on the deck. I imagined it was one of my mates off duty. We had barrels on the deck and I saw the man get on top of them and walk on them past the wheelhouse. I went to the side window and said: "Give me a cigarette." He kept walking so I opened the door on the back of the wheelhouse and saw him standing by the hauling rope. I repeated: 'Would you give me a cigarette." Then I saw he was holding onto the hauling rope and was about to fall overboard. I threw myself at the boom and caught him by the waist but there was nothing there. Just in case, I went to the stern and they were all sleeping there apart from the man who was on duty with me who was in the engine room. So we were all aboard. It was said that this man had once sailed on this boat and while he was at sea his bankbook went missing or was stolen. He later died on a trawler but was said to be on the boat. (2007)

# 19

# WAS THE WHOLE BODY VISIBLE?

IN some accounts the informant mentions only seeing a part of the deceased person's body, although it is much more common for the whole body to have been perceived (roughly 78 percent of incidents). It is in about a fifth of the accounts that only a part of the body is seen, mostly the face and the upper part of the body. In a few accounts, other body parts were seen, as in the example here below.

### Feet and trousers

I can hardly say that I have been aware of the dead – only once. It was in an apartment that I once lived in. I felt it was a man. I could see his feet and trousers but nothing more. I saw it from the corner of my eye – always the feet first and then up the trousers. He wore black shoes and brown trousers - sort of grey brown. My son must have often been there at the same time. He was just a small child of four to five years. He often talked about the man that he saw in the evening when he was going to bed but never seemed to realise that there was anything unusual about it.

I never told anybody else about it – not that I can remember. I had no idea who it could be. It usually happened that way - that suddenly he was standing there or was walking and if I looked around there was nothing to see. I was always most aware of him in the kitchen and in the hall and in my son's bedroom. I also had feelings about him being there. It was a good feeling – it was somehow good to know of him. He made me feel safe. And that was without knowing who he was. I have never perceived anything like that either before or since and I usually do not believe in this sort of things. I did not feel that this man wanted to talk to me but it made me feel comfortable. The perception probably lasted for less than a second each time. It happened often with a short time interval in between. This happened all the time while I was living in that apartment - not every day but mostly when it was quiet, especially in the evening. I worked every day and was not at home except during the evening. It never happened if there were other people there. When it was calm and peaceful and I was reading or just relaxing I was most aware of it. It was a few steps away from me and to my side, usually when there was an electric light. It disappeared very suddenly but somehow I felt that he could have been there for a long time when I noticed his legs. They did not just suddenly appear.

I do not know who it could have been and I never talked about it with the people I was renting the flat from. I did not ask anybody about it. I may have spoken to my father about it sometime or just told him that I had perceived it and it made me feel good – but that's all. I did not try to find out anything about it. Perhaps I did not really believe it. I was very scared of the dark as a child but I grew out of it. It is more interesting that I was never frightened – did not feel scared at all. The feelings were more of protection. My moods are quite changeable but I cannot remember it having anything to do with my moods. I rented the flat out a few times but nobody ever mentioned anything – I did not either. (630)

The accounts often include descriptions of how the deceased person had died – and this question was also asked in the interviews. It is, however, very uncommon for the dead person to show symptoms of their illness or the way they died. It only happened in about 3 percent of incidents. Memorable is the sentence from a case which is reported in the chapter about suicide (5076): "Suddenly I see the bedroom door opened and on the threshold stands Jacob, with his face all covered with blood."

In a few incidents a smell is mentioned, sometimes a bad smell accompanying the disease which led to the person's death. In a few incidents fishermen who drowned are reported to have appeared wet from the sea.

# 20

# UNUSUAL BEHAVIOUR OF ANIMALS

ANIMALS sometimes show behaviour which is interpreted as a response to an invisible presence. In some cases there may be a reason to wonder whether the animal is simply responding to humans around it as when dogs perk up their ears because they know that they are listening for something. In three cases that follow we let the participant be the judge.

### The year before the volcano erupted

It was the year before the volcano erupted. I was standing here in the field with a dog and heard the voice of an acquaintance of mine who had died. This has happened a few times. Once it was just like the dog had also heard the voice because he perked up his ears and I am sure he heard the voice as well and recognised it because the dog used to belong to the owner of the voice. He was an extremely good man. (2047)

### Little sister

My little sister died long before I was born. My mother later told me that she had washed her with soap. One autumn, when I was nine years old, we were letting the horses out and there was suddenly this strong smell of soap, just out of the blue. I also felt the dogs had become aware of something. I told my mother about it and then she told me how she had prepared my sister for burial and that other people had told her they smelled soap before she arrived, especially the people on the next farm... Now my daughter is named after this sister of mine. I felt I was very aware of her after my daughter was born. (5104)

We contacted the people on the next farm who had this to say: A woman at the farm said she could not remember the sister who had passed away but said she always smelled the scent of perfume before the participant's mother came to visit. She said it always happened but she was never given any explanation for that scent. A man at the farm said "yes, yes, always the smell of perfume... that was before anybody visited from that farm... It did not matter who it was... without fail, if there was a smell of perfume, somebody was about to visit from the farm".

**Go to God**

I saw him more often than once and others also perceived him. He just appeared, came to the farm and then wandered away. He often pointed west, to where his mother lived. She was to die of tuberculosis later that winter. This was usually just outside the farm. There was a silage pit there and he used to walk backwards towards it, then seemed to realise where he was, set off sideways and then evaporated into a mist. That is what usually happened. I can well remember a clearer example. It was during the winter and the sheep were grazing all over the valley and I had to gather them together. I had brought them all back and was getting them into the house. But then the sheep would not enter one of the spaces no matter what I tried to do. They just jumped away. So I had to go and see what the bother was and found the man standing in the doorway leading into the barn. I told him off and told him to go to God and stop hanging around here on earth. He left and I got the sheep in and everything was fine... (6026) (see also 7616)

**In Korpulfsstadir**

I was a helper on the large Korpulfsstadir farm. The workers there were always afraid of the dark for the place was supposed to be haunted. Once I offered to take horses to Gufunes which is not far away. The horses were owned by the owner of the farm. But one of the cows was missing; she had not come back to the barn. When I got to the gate where I was supposed to let the horses out, all the horses started shaking and became wild. I let them through and they ran for it. I knew something must be wrong since the horses were so scared. Then I saw the missing cow lying there and was going to take her home but I got scared and let her be. I walked home calmly, saying all the hymns to myself that I knew. I told the man in charge that I had seen the cow but that I had been frightened. I used to sleep alone in a small outbuilding but all the other men slept up at Lágafell farm. Then the man in charge came to get me; I was no longer allowed to sleep there because of an oppressive presence... (5029A)

# 21

# MEANING AND MESSAGES

WE have already shown several examples where the deceased appear to interfere in passing events or their presence has a meaning in some way. Typical for this group is the experience of widows and widowers, where the deceased partner returns to give peace and consolation to the grieving spouse. Another common example is the experience of seamen who were given warning of dangers and saved from drowning. We will come back to this later.

We wanted to know how common it was for the deceased person to pass on a message. The majority of our informants (65 percent) did not feel that the dead person was trying to communicate a message, whereas 25 percent did believe the apparition was communicating a message and 9 percent were unsure. Could the deceased be trying to convey a message by simply appearing? Yes, 32 per cen were sure that was the case and 10 percent of the informants were uncertain. In most cases the informants were sure that the deceased person was not trying to reveal a specific purpose by appearing. If there was a meaning or a message, it was usually given in words (58 percent), by facial expression (2 percent) or in other ways (39 percent). Here we are reminded of an account given by a former member of parliament, whose colleague had appeared to him and said: "You were lucky, you fared well" (7030). The man who appeared had died of a heart attack but the informant had recently survived a heart attack. Below are some more examples where the informant felt that the deceased person was trying to convey a message by appearing:

### This is the man you shall marry

My fiancé and I were talking but I was not sure if I should marry him. Then I felt my father's presence as if he were whispering to me: "This is the man whom you should wed" My father drowned when he was 42 years old. I was his only child. This experience made me happy. (517)

### My grandfather's fish

Shortly after my father died my son fell ill. I sat with him a lot and once I perceived this strong presence of my father. I felt I saw his face and he showed me with a smile that I could be calm. I was very happy to see him... and I felt sure that my son would get better. When the boy awoke, the first words he spoke were: "My grandfather gave me a fish.." (64)

### In the hospital

I have twice seen my deceased father, and especially clearly after an operation in the hospital. He sat in a natural pose on a chair by the bed and was wearing ordinary clothes and was looking well. I closed my eyes to see if I was dreaming. I have always been surprised how little I dream of him. This was between six and seven o'clock in the morning in absolute peace and quiet and it was fully bright. He died in his seventies was religious in his own way but was ashamed to admit it publicly. He was a courageous man, very tough, never believed things that were not possible. He had a big temper, was easily angered but quickly simmered down. It felt as if he had come to let me know that my illness was over. The effect of this experience was very good. (961)

### Tend to the sheep

I sat working at my desk when I looked up and saw a man in front of me who had recently died. He had owned a sheepshed close to my workplace and he often visited me. He was dressed as usual. He died at sixty years of age but he had a strong longing to live. We were acquaintances. I think he was telling me of one of his sheep who always had problems when she had her lambs... (798A)

In several of our accounts the informants felt that they had received guidance from the dead. This is demonstrated with the following examples:

### Good advice

I have had all sorts of psychic experiences. When I was 22 years old I had a big problem and then a woman came to me and gave me good advice. My relatives reckoned by my description that this had been my great grandmother. I acted upon her advice and it proved helpful. I saw her entering the room, she moved easily about and all her movements were quick. It felt as if it was brighter in the room while she was there. It was as if she spoke to me in words and it felt as if she was physically present, until she disappeared. I do not quite know how she disappeared..... This had a great impact on me and I am very grateful for it. It has been very positive and useful for me. (82)

### The new farm

I was out in the country where I was building a new farm and I was thinking about how much land I should fence and cultivate. Then I felt as if my father and my brother, who both were dead, were sitting on each side of me. They suggested I should fence a four times larger space than I had planned. But I answered them: "You are both dead and I will not listen to you". A few years later it was evident that they had been right. (234a)

### The debt

Once a man came a long way to me to collect a debt. I did not know how to explain to him that I could not pay him. Then my deceased father appeared to me and he showed me a written board saying: 'Do not worry, you can settle this with the man tonight." And that proved to be the case. (234)

### You knew it

A friend of mine appeared to me more than once. Five to ten days after he passed away he appeared in my room and I could feel him saying: "You knew it." And I could feel myself thinking to him: "It is going to happen to all of us." I felt he was telling me that I had been right about the afterlife... (5068)

### On the steamer Gullfoss

I was in Copenhagen working on the steamer Gullfoss that sailed between Reykjavik and Copenhagen. My sister was expecting a child back home. I had fallen asleep in one of the bunks and woke up to find a woman standing in front of my bed and she said to me: "Your sister has had the child." First I thought it was somebody on board the ship but saw her go through the door and then I realised that she was dead. It was as if she was surrounded with a white light. First I did not recognise her but I guessed it was one of my sisters who had passed away. I was young when she died and felt at that time that it was strange that she had disappeared. When I came back home my mother told me that my sister had had the baby and I was not surprised. (6008)

**Father and son**

I was sitting in the living room at home and had a vision of my father and grandfather who had both passed away some time ago. Half an hour later there was a phone call and I was told that my grandmother, the wife of the grandfather I had seen, had died. She had died at the same time as I had the vision.

When interviewed, the informant's wife said she remembered her husband's experience quite well. (7008)

It is a part of Icelandic folklore that the dead can appear to remind others of them for the purpose of giving their name to an unnamed infant or to give permission for an unnamed infant or an unborn child to bear their name. Three such accounts can be found in our collection.

**Grandfather appears to give his name**

This happened when I was eleven years old. One morning I woke up with my family. We were sleeping in the living room and it was getting light by the early morning sun. Then I saw the back of a man who is standing there stooping with one foot on something as if he were tying his shoelaces. At first I thought this was my father because he usually put his shoes on in this way. I sat up in the bed as I often did in the morning and then I saw that the man had his arms extended over my mother's bed. She was pregnant and gave birth to a son later that month. Then it looked as if the man slides over the bed and disappears into the wall. I was startled by this and woke up my father and then the rest of the family and told them what had happened. I had seen very clearly what the man was wearing and I could describe him. By this description the members of the family were sure this had been my grandfather who died when I was four years old, and that he had appeared in the hope that they might give the unborn son his name. (15)

### Father-in-law appears because of his name

When my father-in-law died I had a newborn son who had not been baptised and I was wondering whether I should name him after my father-in-law. I went to another part of the country to be at the funeral and left my son at home, unbaptised but was very worried about it. A week later I was back home. One day I was about to go into the kitchen but I felt he was there and I could not get in. The kitchen was quite small but the man had been very fat. I could not see him but I felt and knew that he was there and was giving me permission to name the child after him. (356)

### Aunt appears because of her name

When I was pregnant with my first child I usually had a nap every afternoon. Once when I woke up I saw and felt that my aunt was sitting on my bed and then I saw her disappear. She was thirteen when she died, was the daughter of my father's brother and I had decided to name my child after her. I knew her as soon as she came to me. I think she appeared because of the name... (7578)

Sometimes the message, words or thoughts between the deceased and the living are said to be of a mental or cognitive nature. The next account is such an example.

### Flow of energy

I was in bed and my girl was beside me. Suddenly we both saw the door open with a bang. It was not really that unusual for the door to blow open but then we could both sense someone walking in across the floor. Then I sat up and spoke to the person, not with my mouth but with my mind and the answers were very good and clear. It was my girl's relative who was passing on a message to her. It is a shame that I cannot remember what the message was or what we talked about. I spoke to him through my mind, words were not necessary. It was more like when you think - you create whole ideas. It was like a flow of energy. I could physically feel the presence of someone in front of me and then the conversation that took place was just like when you think... (2190)

# 22

# EXPERIENCES FROM CHILDHOOD

S EVERAL informants tell of experiences that they had when they were children. Therefore, such incidents happened many years ago.

**Engineer remembers an incident from childhood:**
I was following ducks with four or five of my friends on the beach in Keflavik. The ducks were running away from the rocks we were throwing at them, towards the sea. Then one of the group shouted and said something like: "Look!" We all looked up to see a man standing about 50-60 metres away. The man had died during the winter but this happened in the following spring. He was the father of one of the boys in the group and had always been kind to us. The sight gave us a scare and we turned around and fled. When we looked back we could not see anything. I think the man wanted to point out with his presence that we should not throw stones at the ducks. (5022)

**A woman around twenty living in Reykjavík**
I was 13 years old when I perceived a man and I especially remember how noisy he was. I heard footsteps but did not see anything. I had just woken up. First I thought I was dreaming but I was not. I was wide awake. I started telling people about this and found that more people had perceived this man. It happened twice with about

a week passing in between the incidents. It happened in a house just outside Egilsstadir. The man had died in a car accident. He was going to a dance with a few friends and there had been two or three who died in that accident. Hafsteinn the medium was there, I think he said that the man was earthbound because he did not know he was dead - he had died so suddenly... (5030)

## Eighty year old man from Reykjavík

As a boy, before I was confirmed, I used to live in Kalfafellsstadir in Sudursveit. The window in my bedroom faced west and there was a table fastened below it which had a chest for a seat. I woke up one night and there was a man sitting at the desk. A happy looking man wearing striped clothes. I thought to myself that I should not look away from him. I spoke to him until he started to tremble and got smaller. Then he changed into a blue smoke and left through the keyhole. I tend to think that this was Vigfus Sigurdsson, a man who went to Hornafjord and drowned there in his thirties. He was my sister's brother-in-law. (7590)

## My father

My father drowned when he was 42 years old. I was 5 or 6 at the time. He had anticipated his death and 'was ready". Shortly after he died I saw him. It was on a Sunday and mother was dressing me up. He walked around me from left to right, then he walked behind me and disappeared. I was a little frightened of him, kept this a secret. I did not even tell my mother about this. (2020A)

## In the stable

I was an energetic and disobedient teenager but I was fond of animals. I was in my eighth or ninth year, had gone out to my father's stable to have some fun with the horses as I often did. When I was leaving the stable I saw an arm that blocked the exit. I saw the arm all the way up to the shoulder. Twice I tried to get out, but could not, the arm was outside in front of the door. I took a horse and led it out in front of me, then it disappeared. I did not like this, my fear of the dark increased. Still, I have always felt as if I were being accompanied through my life. I have been woken up and warned in some other ways on my adventurous journeys. (721)

### The man in the cloak

I was nine years old, had been picking berries and was running home. I looked over my shoulder and saw a man behind me wearing a cloak. He had an ordinary appearance. I was startled but kept going, but when I looked back he was gone, then I became a little frightened... (775)

### Before and after death

When I was at the age of 8 to 13 I saw my mother come and sit at my bedside with me, though at the time she was a patient in hospital and still alive. It often happened, especially when I had to make important decisions. It was always dark above and behind her when I saw her while she was alive. After she died this continued, but after her death it was always brighter all around her. She always came walking and sat down, but I never saw her stand up. I waited for her and I was always ready to receive her. She was very determined and strong-willed. She warned me of many things, sometimes having a warning expression on her face. She was always as thin as ever, wearing a grey coat with a black belt and a big buckle - always well groomed. (404) (see 5023)

### Out in the street

My father drowned at the age of 38, when I was 11 years old. I was out in the street with my girlfriend. The ground was covered with snow and it was very bright. Suddenly I saw my father coming towards us, and I ran to him but then he disappeared. He had on his best cap, had his hands in his pockets and looked very calm. This had a great impact on me, although it made me sad. All the same, this has had the positive effect of making me realize that the deceased are not gone forever. (344)

### The strange horseman

I was ten years old, was feeding the sheep and heard someone on horseback come riding up to the stable. I thought it odd that someone would come up to the stable. The temperature was well below zero and there was no snow. I finished what I was doing and went outside and saw a man riding away taking a course up the field. There was no path there and no gate and the rider disappeared into the night... I told my mother about this, she thought this had been my nanny's father. He was the provincial manager and inspected the fodder supply. This came as a surprise to me - I have often thought about this but never come to a conclusion... (689)

## My Grandfather

I was ten years old and was coming home in the evening as the work was over. An old farm house was being torn down where I lived. Its framework was still standing. When I arrived at the site I saw an old man with a beard standing inside the framework where the foyer had been. He stood still for almost half a minute like he was looking things over. I was going to approach him but then he disappeared. From my description of him people concluded it was my grandfather, Kristjan Sigurdsson. I did not know him, but I had wanted to see him. I had heard so much about him. I was both surprised and pleased to have seen him. (671)

Here is a similar case, although it did not happen when the informant was a child.

## Lady wearing a dress of two colours

I arrived at the front of the farm where I was living. When I stepped out of the car I saw a person very clearly in the window of an old house that stood beside the new house. The old house was going to be demolished. This only lasted for a few seconds but the person seemed very clear and vivid. It was a lady wearing a dress of two colours. She seemed scared, waved her arms and looked as if she was in a hurry. Since then I have seen this lady in passing but never as clearly as that first time. I still do not know who she might have been. (629A)

## The son of the widow by the river

I lived in the country. In the livingroom there was a small window and outside there was a path. I sat by the window and was looking out as children do. I was six or seven years old. I remember this quite well as if it were happening now. It became so fixed in my mind. I saw a man walking passed the window. It was an old man. He was stooping, had a grey beard and a grey hat on his head and wore a coat and his grey trousers were tucked into his socks. I called to my mother and told her there was a man coming. It was quite an event in the country when a guest came to visit. We went outside the house and no one was there. Then I was asked to describe the man and my description was so accurate that there was no doubt about it - it had been an old farmer from the next farm who had died about the time I was born.

This man's name was Kristjan, though I do not recall his last name. He was the son of the woman about whom the famous poet Gudmund Fridjonsson wrote the poem "The widow by the river". He was one of her children. What he was doing here out west I do not know. He had had a difficult life, lived in poverty, never had much... His three sons who were daily guests at our home came right after this happened. A short while later one of them drowned. This might have been some kind of an indication of that. (2012)

## The lady next door

I was probably eleven years old. I was going home and saw a woman, our neighbour. I felt it was her, here in front of our house. I said good evening to her but she did not answer me. I looked at her more closely and then I saw that it was a lady who had recently passed away. I stood staring at her as she just stood in front of me, very clear and vivid. Then she got fainter and disappeared... (5010)

## Rose

It happened when I was a young boy. I ran into my grandmother's room. There was a woman sitting in a chair and I felt that she was speaking to my grandmother. I felt that she was wearing a dress that she often wore when she visited my grandmother. She was sitting in a large bolstered chair and I was almost beside her. She had her back to the door. The lady was called Rose. I was a little shy as a boy, turned around and my mother said: "Why do you not go in to see your grandmother?" I told her that there was a lady in the room with my grandmother. Then I found out that the woman had died a few days earlier but I had not known anything about that. (5080)

## In the garden

When I was twelve years old I was sent to stay in the country-side in Gardur with my foster grandmother who was confined to bed and was in a lot of pain. If she needed attending to she would knock on the wall and make sounds of being in pain. I often went to help her when she made those signs. My grandmother died and about a week later and I had pretty much stopped thinking about her. We were never that close. One day I was going into the basement to fetch something and was standing in the stairway when I heard that knock and the sounds my grandmother used to make. I ran into her room and was going to help her as I had done countless other times before. When I got there I realised that she was dead. I got scared and ran back down the stairs to one of the maids who should have been able to hear the sounds just as I had. But she had not heard anything... (7594A)

## Fetching the matches

I was seven years old when I first saw a deceased person. It was in the countryside and everybody was in the main room, my father was reading to us, not religious texts but stories. He read to the people in the evening as was common in those days before we had radio.. He needed a match to light his pipe. He was sitting in the doorway between the main room and my parents´ bedroom and further in was a room they called the lounge. That is where the matches were, on a table. He sent me in to fetch the matches. I was a little scared of the dark. This was during the winter, everything was dark and only one light in the main room over the book my father was reading but a small light shone into the room from this light when the door was opened. I got my younger brother to come with me. I fetched the matchbox and we left the lounge but in doing so I looked at the bench that was situated along the wall with the door. A man was lying there with his hand supporting his head... When I came back to the main room, I did not dare run or make a noise and I gave the matches to my father. A little later he asked me: "My dear Gusti, what is wrong, are you ill, you are so pale.?" I did not dare tell them what I had seen.

Two years later I passed a winter in the countryside in Borgarfjord. For Christmas I was given something that had the size of a matchbox and could be used to examine photographic films. I used to enjoy it and to look at pictures. But one of the pictures was of that same man I had seen, in the same position he had been lying in two years earlier. It gave me such a fright that I lost all longing to look at the pictures.. My grandfather and his father had been brothers. (2184)

## The father

I was with my mother and foster father and slept in the same room as them. I was 14 years old. In the middle of the night I woke up and sat up in bed. I saw a man standing by their bed on my mother's side. He held his hand straight out over her head. He was quite pale and wore a suit and a tie. I was not scared that time and I just looked at him. Then I lay down and felt it was all right. I never saw him disappear... In the morning I told my mother about it and described him in detail. She said it was my father... (5090)

## The sister

I had not yet been confirmed. I believed that I had seen my sister who died when she was a few months old. I felt it was her. She came into the room where I was sleeping, opened the door and came in. The picture I saw of her was as if she were of the age she would have been had she lived. This lasted for some time... It was during the night but there was some light in the room so I could see her very clearly. She was surrounded by whiteness and was brighter than her surroundings. (7562)

## In a strange place

I was 14 years old and was babysitting in a house I had not been in before. There are so many incidents like this, but now I remember one in particular. I was not afraid of the dark. This was back in those days when there were plays on the radio on Saturdays which were often full of suspense and I was listening to one of them. Then I became aware that I was not alone in the living room and saw what looked like a man standing in a doorway. There seemed to be an open door on the wall and the man was leaning easily up against the doorpost. He was not looking at me or anything else in particular - he was rather pleasant. He was dressed for cold weather, wearing a woollen sweater. He looked to me like a sailor. I knew there was not a door there, so I was a bit frightened. The couple I was baby-sitting for would not admit that anyone could have been standing there, because it was a solid wall. The next day when this was checked a door was found in the wall that had been filled up before the couple had moved in. (7001)

# 23

# LOCALIZED APPARITIONS

I T is an old folk belief that some apparitions of the deceased are tied to specific locations which were important to them when they were alive. This has also been found in other countries, such as in Britain, where research on people's sightings of apparitions was first conducted in the latter part of the nineteenth century (Gurney, Myers & Podmore, 1886; Gurney& Myers 1887-88). When these accounts were examined and grouped according to their characteristic features it became evident that it was rather common for the same apparition to be seen more than once and often, in the same location. These apparitions were therefore called localized apparitions. Accounts of such encounters can also be found in our collection. Here are some examples:

### The being in Hvitarnes

We were taking part in the autumn sheep roundup and were in the house belonging to the Travel Association at Hvitarvatn. I was watering the horses with another man who has now passed away. The weather was lovely. Two people were in the bothy but they were going to bring a light to the stable as it was starting to get dark. We saw a man come walking from the bothy. He walked past us but dissappeared and when we went to check on it both of the men inside the house were still there and neither of them had left the house. I cannot say for sure whether this was a woman or a man that we saw or how the being was dressed. (407)

### The white lady

I guess I must have been about twelve or thirteen years old. It was at the school for farmers in Holar in the north of the country. I was looking at pictures of former pupils and looked up suddenly as I was going to walk over to the light switch and switch on the light; it was getting quite dark. Then I saw a woman, I saw her back, it was very clear but not like usual; it was a bit hazy. When I switched on the light she was gone. I thought she had gone behind the door, I felt it was so normal but when I looked there was no woman... I was staying with my aunt and told her about it. She was the clergyman's wife and she told me that there was a lady. She was always called the white lady because so many people had seen her... (2140)

### The chief carpenter

I was the tour leader for a large group of women on the house-wives' vacation. We stayed in Laugagerdis school during the month of August. I had to sleep downstairs in an empty classroom. I have often done that but the women were sleeping in another hall. When I was going to sleep that evening I was very tired but did not get enough peace to fall asleep. It was always as if a man came to me and lay down next to me or bent over me and felt I could hear his breathing, whether it was my imagination or not. I felt it was a man, tall and skinny; an older man. But I could not see anything. This went on all night and even though I was very tired and do not usually find it hard to fall sleep I did not fall asleep at all.

In the morning I met the woman in charge who knew the place. I told her that I could not sleep. She said: "I'm not surprised, if you are trying to sleep there." Then she told me that the head carpenter, who had passed away, was the one I had been aware of. A clergyman who lived not far away later told me that the work on the basement of the school had gone wrong and especially under that classroom. Therefore they sued the carpenter, who was very distressed about the whole thing. It turned out quite badly and the carpenter died while the lawsuit was still going on. (5001)

### The old man

I lived in Siglufjord. It was the first summer we lived there and during the middle of the day. I was going back home for some coffee. This was in the house of a doctor. I had to walk up some stairs with no window and it was quite dark. There was a man there and

I walked right into him. I told him I was sorry and moved to the side. But still the man was in my way and the third time I tried I realised that there was something unnatural about it... and I ran back into the kitchen in a fit. Those sitting there had not seen anything. I saw the man very well. He was between seventy and eighty years of age, with grey hair, a dark hat and staff - a very nice looking old man. I was told that the house had always been haunted but I do not know what to believe on that matter. I was nineteen when it happened. (17)

**In the front room**

During the war years I sometimes spent time in Siglufjord. Once I was there and was going to stay with some acquaintances. It was about an hour after midnight and I thought they had gone to sleep. When I got to the house I saw a man in the front room. He was pacing back and forth. I knocked in the hope that the man would open the door for me but however much I knocked and called to him he did not seem to notice anything. In the end I went and stayed with some other people I knew.

Shortly after this I was in a hotel in Siglufjord and was talking to some girls about the house where my acquaintances lived. They asked me whether I had seen the ghost that lives there. I told them I had not and told them about the man that had not noticed me that night. Then one of the girls brought me a picture of her cousin who she said had died when they built the house. He had been working on it. It was a picture of the man I had seen in the front room. I was told that the man had often been seen in the house. (5013A)

**On Stapi**

I was a passenger in a car driving from Keflavík to Reykjavík and it was just getting dark. When we got a few metres from Stapi a man ran in front of the car. I did not understand why the driver did not stop the car but when the lights lit up the man he seemed to evaporate. I felt there was something unnatural about it and it gave me a fright. I froze, as they say, and did not get a word out until we got to Straumsvik. Then I said what I had seen. (5039)

**Cutting the grass**

I was born in Nordfjord and moved away when I was two years old but went there every summer until I was 14 years old. There was a house there owned by my godmother and my real grandmother lived a little further east. I used to walk between the two houses during the evening, spent my time equally in both places. Once I was walking from one house to the other quite late in the evening and saw a man cutting the grass. He had a dog with him. I thought it was a bit strange but did not really think that much about it. I told people about it and they said many people had seen the man before. (5012) (see also 6006)

Here is another case strikingly similar to the account above:

I came back home and heard a sound. I looked up and saw a man cutting the grass and there was a dog beside him in the grass. I spoke to my mother-in-law about it and she told me who the man was and that he was dead. He looked about sixty... (6006) (see also 5012)

## Lady from Sweden

I was on a boat that was built in Sweden and a few times I became aware of a girl who seemed to be watching us; she stood at the window and looked out. This girl was wearing a grey dress with a wide red belt. I told the other men about this who had been abroad when the ship was in construction. They said that others had also seen her. They even saw her in the same clothes as I did. This girl had taken part in the construction work in Sweden but died shortly before the boat sailed to Iceland. (7026)

## The grandmother

I was pregnant and was staying with my parents in Siglufjord. I had so much heartburn that I sometimes got up during the night when I could not sleep, to have a tablet which I drank with water. There was a lamppost outside the kitchen window so I did not switch on the light because I did not want to wake up my parents who were sleeping two rooms away for they always left their door open. One night I was standing by the window where the light shone in from the lamppost waiting for the tablet to dissolve in the water. Suddenly I was aware of a person in white coming out of the bedroom. I thought it was my mother and said: "I thought you were asleep." I saw her out of the corner of my eye. Then I heard my mother call me from her room asking whether I was out there and if I was ill. At that point I realised that what I saw was not my mother. At the same time this being evaporated as if into cotton and just gradually disappeared. I walked into my mother's room and she asked who I had been speaking to. I told her I had thought I was speaking to her and told her what I had seen. She said I should not be scared, so many people had felt they had seen my grandmother here. She had passed away many years before. She died before I was born. (7040)

The mother of the informant told us that she remembered her daughter telling her about this.

### In the fish factory

It was a man who was born here, called Andres and he was over eighty years old. Two of us came up to the house which was a fish factory that was no longer in operation. We had to get into the house and we looked in through a window. We did not expect anybody to be in the house but then I saw a man. When I looked more closely I knew who it was, especially from the way he moved. He opened the door in a very special way, nobody did it like that. He put up his arm at the same time and supported the door with it, quite high up. He seemed to be wearing the same clothes that he usually had on when he was living. He had always worked there and this was his last working place. I could see the side of his face and then the back and knew the man, both from the way he walked and the way he opened the door... Then he just disappeared through the door... I told the man I was with about this but he could not see anything. (7042)

### The herring factory

I owned a fishing boat and went in the autumn to work in a herring factory in the north of the country. My stepfather was working there that summer. Late in the autumn I was going to go to Reykjavík and I went to ask him to give me something to put my things in, mainly dirty clothes and so he did. Then I went back to the hut where we stayed which was partitioned and had a mess in both ends of the hut. On the side of the hut that overlooked the mountain there was an entrance and a stairway leading to the second floor. When I came up the stairs and opened the door to the hall, which was always lit, I saw a man standing at the door to our room. He was wearing a hat and maroon pants spun from wool. They were buttoned as was the fashion then, the pants reaching just below the knee where they were buttoned. I looked at him for a while and did not find this peculiar.

I thought it was just someone I did not know. I closed the door and glanced away from him, but when I looked up again he had disappeared. Things had sometimes been stolen in the hut so I thought: "I see, he is one of the thiefs." I raced to the door but it was locked tight. Four of us shared this room and we always locked it when we went out. I tried all the doors in the hallway but they were all locked except for the door to the kitchen. I went in and looked around, checked the closets because I was sure the man was there. I stopped to think: I had definitely seen a man, there was no doubt about that. Then I felt the presence of someone and was quite startled but I left the kitchen anyway and went to our room and put the bag on my bed. My stepfather was in the room sleeping but I did not wake him. Then I locked the room and went out to the factory again to work with my mates, the three of them were there. Then one of them said to me: "What a sight you are, why are you so pale, are you sick?" I said I was not sick, but that something had happened that I could not accept or explain and I told them about it. Then two of them started laughing, but the third, an elderly man from Keflavík, did not say a word until we had stopped talking about it. Then he said this had happened to him three times but he experienced it differently. When he was leaving the room the man stood outside the door and he was dressed just as I had described. The others stopped making fun.

The rumour of this story reached the man who had given me the bag. He asked me to describe the man I had seen and so I did. He chuckled and said: "Is he still there the poor man". He told us that in the first year the factory operated, a man from Fljotum came to work at the factory. He had put his bag in his room and was on his way out again and as he walked out the door he fell down dead. So there was the explanation. (7502)

### The Norwegian

I work on the Akraborg ferry and straight away on the first day I perceived a man who had passed away and every day for the first three days, then every so often for about three years but he has gone now... I always saw him just above the floor. I knew he was Norwegian and always knew what he looked like, could describe him. I once asked one of the crew without meaning to: "Who was the man who died on board?" Nobody knew anything about this man but the ferry was bought from Norway. I felt I knew him like a living person. I always saw him very clearly but he has gone now... (7564)

### Localized vision

I have often seen deceased people. For example I have seen a man a few times who died when I was two years old. He always appeared to me in the place that he died. I used to live there for a while but since I've moved I have not seen him. (258)

### The old family ring

I wear an old ring that I inherited and was once my grandfather's. Lately I have often felt his presence. For example at work, I feel as if someone is next to me, especially if I am alone. I somehow see this right next to me. I do not see his face. I sense that I am not alone, but if I look up it is gone. (7500)

### The main road

I work on the west side of Reykjavik but I live in nearby Kopavog. I have my own car and always drive the same route to work. For two years, a few times each winter, I saw a man walk straight across one of the main roads near the old Teachers College. This was four years ago and during the darkest days of winter. He walked right in front of the car. Once I had to jam on the brakes so as not to drive into the man and the car went spinning for it was very slippery. I saw the man in profile walk across the street. This was an elderly man, seemed a bit deranged, walked stooped wearing a grey-green jacket with a hood. I thought it very peculiar that he should be walking from the town and into the marsh.

Then I mentioned this man where I work. One of my collegues said: "Was he dead or alive?" I also described this man to a woman who works with me. She said that others had seen him in the same place. She even told me his name which I no longer remember. I thought about this and when I went home I looked things over and saw that there is a wire fence along this road so the man could not possibly have walked there into the marsh.

This happened only if I was exceptionally early on the road, before or around 7 o'clock - then he was there but not if I was late... and I only saw him during dark winter mornings. I have not seen him since I realized he could not be a living man. Later I learnt that this man died of an injury after an accident he had at this spot on the road, early in a dark winter's morning. (2034A)

**Gratitude**

I rented a room here in Reykjavík when I was a young girl. The room had been used to keep firewood and nobody had lived in it before. Quite soon I felt that there was somebody in the room. I am not psychic but it gradually got clearer and I felt it was a friendly person and that it was a man. As the winter passed I was gradually able to describe what the man looked like. It got clearer and clearer, did not all happen at once... The man was friendly and I always felt like he was asking my forgiveness.

Then one cold night I had switched off the light and turned towards the wall in bed, ready to go to sleep. I sometimes spread a blanket over my duvet but now I clearly felt somebody spread something over me, like a mother tucks in her child. The man was looking after me but he always seemed to be asking me to pray for him. I could not hear any words but it was as if it was being pressed into me, the understanding came through that way, there was no hearing or sight, I just perceived it somehow, I do not know how to describe it, I understood it without words...

Once, when we were paying the rent the landlord asked in a joking manner whether I ever perceived anything in the room. We went silent and his wife told him off for asking about things like that. I thought to myself that I should tell them the truth and let them laugh at me and said: "Yes, there is a man in the room but he is friendly towards me." The man was surprised and he said: "Why do you say that?" "Well, I am not sure... but he is friendly and looks after me rather than anything else. There is nothing bad between us." Then he asked me to describe the man, which I did. He was a little unusual, his hair was curly and he had some features that not everybody has, nothing big but which he could be defined by. The man was very surprised and was one big question mark as they say. He asked whether I knew what had happened in the room. I told him I did not and asked if the room had not been used to keep firewood. "Yes, but a man committed suicide in there a long time ago and your description fits him perfectly." It all fits with what the man had been told when he bought the house. I never felt any bad feelings but I felt that he was friendly, pleasant and was thankful for the prayers I said for him... (2118)

# 24

# Person-Centered Apparitions

I n the accounts in our collection we found a few examples where living people are 'followed' by deceased people. Other people can become aware of the dead person around the living person. This is why we have named these visions person-centered apparitions. Such accounts can also be found in collections of incidents from other countries like Britain.

### In the doorway to the barn

I was staying with my fosterparents in the country and was about twelve years old. One evening about 10 o'clock I went outside to urinate. This was late in the summer. About 200 meters away there was a barn. It was open and I saw a man walking towards its opening. The man looked at me but I did not recognize him. I thought this a bit strange but thought people from the farms nearby might be about. I went back inside and told the household what I had seen. I was then told to go to bed. Among the household there were two brothers who had lost their brother a few years earlier. It was said that the brothers were accompanied by their deceased brother, and my description of the man I saw seemed to fit the deceased brother. (7014)

### In the hallway

I have seen deceased people walking, heard knocks on doors and very clearly saw a man walk past my window here before a certain man who came shortly after. We believe it was his father Sveinn. He walked past the window like normal but I could not see all of him. I saw him from the basement. I never saw him when he was alive but judging from descriptions that I have been given it could have been him. Sveinn died about 30-35 years ago, an old man who had always lived in poverty. (540)

In the following two accounts, the informants cannot properly identify the dead women who appear although they associated the apparitions with specific people.

### Deceased fiancée

I was 13 years old and lived on a farm. One day we went to an old empty house rather far away that was owned by my mother. I had to do some work on it. I went there in the morning and spent the day there and went back later in the day and stopped at another farm on the way. Then I saw that they were placing peat on a truck. The peat had been put in a bag and the opening had been sewn together. The car looked full. There were very few cars travelling this road and I did not expect another chance at getting a lift back. That is why I ran towards the car when I saw they were about to set off. The truck was of the smaller kind so there was only space for one passenger. I ran to the front of the car and saw a young woman sitting in the front seat. She had black hair and was pale. She was very clear, looked just like any other person. I asked the driver whether I could sit on the back of the truck. "You do not need to, you can sit in the front with me", he said. I paused but did not say anything about having seen a girl there. I took another look; there was nobody there. I was so surprised that I started looking around to see where she could have gone. There were no trees or hills in the surroundings so I was wondering whether what I had seen might not be of this world. I entered the car and sat in the seat where she had been sitting. I got a ride back home. I thought about what I had seen but decided it might not be very sensible to talk to the driver about it. Later I heard that the driver, who was married, had once had another fiancée but she had died very suddenly. I never saw that lady so I cannot say whether the vision is related to her or not. (5106)

### The prettiest girl

I was seventeen or eighteen and lived in Akranes. I was coming home from a dance late at night and went into the kitchen and heated myself coffee on an oil-stove. I was going to wait for my two brothers whom I thought would be coming home shortly. I waited for a while, but when they did not show up I decided to go to bed. I opened my bedroom door, which I usually kept open and saw a fair girl, very beautiful with long hair that she wore loose and it was all the way down her back. The girl smiled at me. I was startled by this and then the girl evaporated. I did not know her but I imagine she was accompanying one of my brothers. (5027)

### Follower

I was awake in bed and suddenly I saw a man in my room. He was walking around me and bending over me and a child of mine. I knew it was not a real man because I only saw his face as if in a fog, not clearly, there was always some mist over it. Later that morning, when I was up, a man who I had not expected came to visit me. I was later told that somebody always came ahead of him if he did not call before he visited or let you know. After this he did not come without me knowing so it would not happen again. He had heard of it from other people, another woman who was always aware of the man. According to the description it was the same man that had been seen by both of them. (7576)

Steinunn, the sister of the informant, said she remembered her sister telling her about the incident. She said she herself had been aware of the man but never saw him. "He always sat in a special chair in the living room and soon afterwards I would be visited by a certain man. This always happened if he had not contacted me before visiting".

### God bless you

I was cleaning a large room in a business where I had recently started to work and was alone as far as I knew. Suddenly the door is opened and I hear 'God bless you'. I turn around and see a large woman walking into the room. I was sort of hypnotized and could not move because of fright. She stopped at a machine that was out of order and disappeared. She was in a long dress with a shawl over her shoulders and had grey hair. As she disappears the director enters and walks the same way as the woman. I heard it much later that she had been the mother of the director. (5060)

The two accounts above are reminiscent of the Icelandic folk belief in something called *fylgjur* in Icelandic (fetchers/ followers/ doppelgangers). According to this belief, *fylgjur* are mostly connected with people coming and going and the arrival of guests. In the survey we conducted in 1975, every sixth person said they had at some time been aware of a fylgja. This happens equally often among men and women. This is interesting since more women than men have encounters with the dead. In the classic book by Jónas Jónasson from Hrafnagil (1856-1918) called *Icelandic National Customs* (Íslenskir Þjóðhættir), it says that according to the *fylgjur* belief, *fylgjur* are either something which follow a man and jog along before him or fylgjur are some sort of awakenings (corpses which have been brought back to life, cf. zombies) which follow families (1961, p.224). The accounts given by our informants do not include information on whether the fylgjur have also been seen with other family members, dead or living and we did not ask about it.

# 25

# WARNINGS AND RESCUE AT SEA

I<small>T</small> was quite common for our informants to believe that they had been warned about approaching danger or even that they had been rescued from mortal danger. Here are five accounts from men at sea. The first informant is well known in Iceland as a leader of the labour union of fishermen, and was a member of parliament for a long time.

### The old lady we had teased

When I was a boy in Keflavik an old woman was living in an old house where my parents had lived before building our new house. My mother had allowed the old woman to live there. She was under her protection, was good to her, gave her food and to stay without paying rent. Her name was Kolfinna and many found her a bit peculiar. My older brother and I sometimes teased her. She would then stamp down with one foot and pretend she was going to run after us and catch us, and we would run away.

I was on the Icelandic trawler Tryggvi gamli (Old Tryggvi) steaming with a cargo of fish to England. It was wintertime shortly after World War II. We had exceedingly bad weather on the way and were far behind normal schedule. North of the Orkney Islands we had to stop, and hove towards the wind. The weather was so bad that the stoker dared not go on deck to hiss up the ashes in buckets which had to be thrown overboard at the end of each watch. Therefore we who were on the navigational watch did it for them, for we had our sea garments with us on the bridge. I was out on deck and had begun pulling up the buckets. They were heavy and full of ash and tephra. Then I looked back on the deck and saw the old woman coming towards me and shouting forcefully 'Now I will get you'. Instinctively I let the bucket fall and ran towards the starboardside of the bridge and into the wheelhouse where the skipper, the mate and a deckhand was. At the same moment an enormous wave fell over the ship. The trawler got emerged in the sea, the wheelhouse became half full of sea as a window got broken, either by the first or second wave, and the skipper got a bleeding wound on his face. Everything loose got washed out of the wheelhouse.

If I had been on deck then I would not be here to tell about this. That I saw the old woman and was terrified and ran away as we did as children - that obviously saved my life. (7592, see also 5028)

### Good guidance reported by a seaman in his forties from Isafjord

I was with another man on a small boat and we were going to cross the Faxabay to Arnarstapi. When we were out on the bay we suddenly had stormy weather and it became hopeless for us to find our way because we had no equipment of any sort and the boat was filled time and again with water. My partner was exhausted and lay down and I was of course dreadfully tired and sleepy. Then a man appeared at the stern of the boat. I remember to this day how he was dressed. He wore jeans and a green checkered shirt and had grey hair. I did not recognize him, I did not know him. I was tired and drowsy and thought it was quite normal for him to be there. I did not think it unusual until we came ashore, but I did find it strange how courageous he was to be standing there in the wild storm as the waves broke on the boat. He spoke to me but I could not hear a word. He became very angry when he saw I was about to give up. Each time I was about to fall asleep he took out a key and held it to my face and pointed in the direction I should steer. I did as the man told me and of course did not realize what was really happening. The remarkable thing was that I landed in Arnarstapi, passed the reefs and landed at the dock. And it was all the doing of this man... The voyage across Faxabay lasted for about 24 hours.

I told my mother about how odd this had been. She told me that this man had been an engineer, a friend of my father and that he was dead...Oh, of course I had seen him before, I just did not remember him at the time.

G. Sigurjonsson, the friend who was with the informant on the voyage, said he remembered him telling him about the incident when they reached the shore. He added that when they came ashore they met a man who asked them where they had come from. When they said they had sailed from Reykjavík the man walked away from them because he did not believe them.

### Seaman in his seventies from Isafjord

My grandmother has saved me several times. Johanna was her name, she was my father's mother. I had a motorboat that bore her name. We were on our way back after transporting bait from another harbour. The boat was heavily loaded. One man was with me and he was sleeping below deck. I was very tired and sleepy and was beginning to nod at the wheel. Suddenly I woke up and saw her in front of my eyes, just as I saw her while she was still alive and dressed as she used to. I looked at her while I turned the wheel to get away from the shore. I narrowly made it. Her appearance saved me this time and that was not the only time. I saw her in full figure and her bare clear face and the blue cloth she had on her head. (7602)

### Seventy year old fishmonger and former seaman

I was on a fishing boat from Stykkisholm. We were out in the bay in storm and rain and had just laid our nets and should be awakened at six in the following morning. I slept in a narrow cabin with the others and one man was on duty in the deckhouse. About five in the morning I and some others woke up as someone called "Rise." I went up to the cabin door and called to the man in the deckhouse and asked if he had been calling. No, he said, it was not time for that. I went back to my bunk and was not yet asleep when again there was a shout, "Rise, are you not going to get out of bed?" It was as if someone was calling loudly from the cabin door some two meters away. Everyone woke up and jumped out of bed. That surprised me; generally the crew was not that quick. I told the engine-operator to run aft and start the donkey engine to haul in the nets. As the engine-operator went down to the engine room he saw that the generator was on fire. He barely managed to disconnect the electricity so that it came to a halt. I am convinced that if he had been later we would have caught fire and there would have been a fatal explosion in the engine room. I did not recognize the voice. It called in a typical seaman fashion. I had reasons to suspect that it was my deceased grandfather. (7542)

**Seaman in his fifties from the fishing village of Flateyri**

I often saw my deceased father stand behind the wheelhouse of my boat. I got so used to this that I no more paid particular attention to it, nor did it startle me. I had a boat of 15 tons. We were fishing with a Scottish seine and we were drifting in the fjord. A man should have been on watch in the wheelhouse. Then I heard that I was called twice in my bunk below deck. I was sleepy and was not quick to react but when I was called the third time I was thrown out of my bunk and onto the floor. I went up to the deck but thought this was my imaginary nonsense. Then I saw that the boat was almost stranding on the shore. I could not have turned the boat from the shore any later. The man supposed to be on watch and lookout was asleep on the floor of the wheelhouse. I recognised that the voice calling me was my father's voice. I am convinced he saved us. (7011)

**Seaman from Siglufjord**

This happened when I was a teenager. I was alone fishing in a small boat. Suddenly I heard a voice that said I should leave the fishing line and row ashore. I heard this quite clearly. It was said to me in a commanding tone. I did as ordered, I do not know why, but I found it so strange. Just as I was about to arrive at the harbour, there suddenly swept over us a violent storm. I barely managed to dock. I did not recognize the voice but later I connected it with my brother who had recently drowned. (7028)

These accounts are especially interesting because there is a meaning behind the appearance of the being, or deceased person, who intervenes to help living people avoid approaching dangers. In these incidents men are often woken up, but such events have also happened when men are fully awake, sober and at work, just as in both the first and last example above. It appears that the apparitions have a better view of the environment than the person who had the experience. These accounts describe purposeful and intelligent actions.

# 26

## GUIDANCE AND WORDS
## OF WARNING

Words of warning were not only given to fishermen but also to people inland. Just as with fishermen, warning and guidance are given by the departed. Or the perceiver feels they are sent by a person who has died. Here are some examples.

### The call. Reported by a seventy year old lady in Reykjavík

I felt my mother was calling me. I was asleep and I woke up and got out of bed and thanks to that there was not a fire, for the stove was red-hot... (2041)

### An artist tells of an incident which happened when he was in his sixties

I have often experienced things like this. Once I was on my way to town and walked to the bus stop. While I was waiting for the bus I was suddenly touched on the shoulder and a voice behind me said I should hurry home to my mother. I decided not to go to town and run the errand that had been on my mind. I hurried home to my mother and when I arrived the situation was that she had fallen on the stairs between the open steps and was hanging there. She would have fallen down and probably injured herself if she had not got help. There was no one in the house except my sister and she could not help my mother because she was very heavy. (5024)

We asked the artist's sister. She remembered this well: "I was try-ing to pull my mother out but could not. Then my brother unexpect-edly turned up and jointly we managed to pull her out, to our great relief."

### Forty year old craftsman and owner of a business

My father was an alcoholic and caused great difficulties at our home. One early morning my father came in and sat down at the bed of my mother. Everything seemed fine but from previous expe-rience I knew that he had something in mind, namely to get anoth-er bottle of alcohol. He suddenly tried to beat my mother. His arm stopped close to her. I saw a man in a sea officer uniform grasp my father's hand. He tried a second, third and fourth time in vain. Then he stopped and said he did not understand this, it was as if someone stopped him and held his hand when his fist was about to reach my mother. I had no idea who this man was or why he was there, but I realised he was there to protect her. Later I brought this up with my mother. She told me this had been an officer on a freight ship that was shot down during the war and had been her friend. (7636)

### A young manager of a large fishing firm in the countryside

I do not know if this is imagination or reality. I am sometimes aware of a deceased man around me. Perhaps I get anxious about something and then this person comes to my assistance and push-es me on. In this instance I was worried and had little hope about something ahead of us. It concerned financial matters of the com-pany and we needed a great deal of financial support. I went to the bank and was concerned to have to ask for this big sum of money. My superiors had suggested that I ask for a quarter of what I got in the end. On this occasion it was as if someone pushed me to go as far as possible and so I did, successfully. I have often felt at impor-tant moments and decisions that someone stood behind me and helped. It is the clergyman who confirmed me. I often feel his pres-ence. He had unexpectedly died in an accident. (7522)

A ship-owner from Suðurnes drank heavily for a period and believes a friend saved him from dying. This friend had committed suicide at a young age and was found cast up on the shore in Seltjarnarnes a few years before the following incident happened:

### The alchoholic

I was only a little drunk. I wanted to spend the night in a fishing boat that stood in the Daniel slipway for repair. Then there appeared a man in front of me and prevented my entrance up to the boat. His name was Unnsteinn. He seemed pleased when I had to turn away. This night the frost reached 10 degrees Fahrenheit. Had I got onto the boat and slept there, it would probably have been the last sleep of my life. (7007)

### In the warehouse

As a child I was very much attached to mother's foster-father. We enjoyed each others company and spent much time together. After he died he communicated through my sister who sometimes did automatic writing that he kept an eye on me. Once I was fetching goods in the Eimskip warehouse and stood waiting. Then I clearly heard whispered into my ear. "Move away". I did so immediately. Just then one of those lifting vehicles drove by and over a piece of log on the floor that got thrown away at great speed exactly where I had stood. Later I learnt from my sister that there my grandfather had helped me. . . (7546)

### The woman on the road

I was driving near the town of Akranes and just about to enter the town as darkness was creeping in. Then I suddenly saw a woman walking on the road towards the car, saw her clearly by the lights from the lorry I was driving at normal speed. I applied the brakes early enough to stop but had the feeling she disappeared under the lorry. I stopped and got out and looked under the lorry as I thought the woman must be there, but she was not. I walked behind the lorry some distance but no one was there. Ill at ease about this I returned to the lorry and drove on. In just a few moments, still at low speed, a large group of horses come running towards me. Evidently someone had appeared on the road to warn me of the horses ahead. At normal speed I would not have had sufficient time to avoid collision with them. (78A)

### The uncle

I was walking up a hill on my way from the shop. The first or second car that arrived in Borgarnes had recently come, a Buick, almost soundless. As I was walking on the road I suddenly found that a man was close to me, there in the snowfall. I thought how much he looked like my uncle Johann who had died three or four weeks ago. He had on a big otter skin hat, but naturally it could not be Johann. The man kept getting closer and closer and finally he had forced me off the road, into the rubble there. This won't do, I thought, and stopped to let the man pass in front of me, who with skill had made me get off the road, when the car that had just arrived raced passed us with no headlights on and would have driven over the man, and obviously me too if I had still been on the road. I think this was my dead uncle helping me.... (2043)

## Happy call

A young man died who lived in our house. He was not related to us but a delightful man and we were all very sad that he died. After that I felt that he was near. Several months later I had to wake up at 8 o'clock in the morning. We had no alarm clock and the next clock was in the living room, which was the third room from my bed. As I woke up I saw him, as if through the wall, and he called me rather happily; "Inga, it is eight o'clock". I got out of bed and turned on the radio and heard it announced that it was eight o'clock. This seemed so natural. (5008)

## Comfort from beyond

I sat up in bed thinking about a boy who had died recently. Then I suddenly saw my grandmother's sister at my side and felt a touch from her... then she disappeared. I felt that she came to comfort me, to let me know that things were well and I should not be be feeling miserable. (5025)

## The grandmother's warning

I was young and worked in a factory and had to watch a certain machine. One day I was a bit absent-minded and turned away from the machine. Then someone poked at me, although I could not see anyone near. Then I became conscious of a serious problem with the machine. I often feel this, that I was warned and sensed a clear touch. I relate this to my grandmother. (5026)

As in the last example, something strange which happens is traced back to a deceased person without him or her having been perceived in a vivid way. This appears to be quite common.

# 27

# HEALERS AND CURES

IT was quite common for people to feel that a deceased person had appeared to cure somebody. Sometimes it was thought to result from a prayer or a prayer through a medium. People also felt that doctors had come from the other side to help them. In those cases, people have even mentioned syringes leaving marks on the skin from the procedure.

### Granting of a prayer

I was watching over my mother who was sick and I prayed for her. I felt the presence of someone dead that night and this had a good effect on me. I felt as if I was being answered and felt sure my mother's health would improve. Then I saw him as he left the room. (80)

### With my eyes closed

I was in hospital and one evening a tall man wearing a brown suit came to me, right next to the bed. I felt as if he gave me an injection or some other kind of medical care. I saw with my eyes closed or I felt him there. The day after the woman in the next bed told me she had seen the shadow of a man by my bed the night before. (1062)

### The girl with the doctor's bag

My husband was seriously ill of a painful disease and he was being prayed for. One night I saw a girl carrying a doctor's bag enter our bedroom and behind her I saw a man, rather unclearly. (834)

In the next account, a lady senses the strong presence of her father and it sounds like he may have been there to help her son.

### Fish from grandfather

Shortly after my father died my son was taken ill. I attended to him and one time while I was watching over him I suddenly had a strong feeling that my father was present. I thought I saw his face and he indicated with a smile that I need not worry. It made me very happy to feel his presence... and I felt sure that my son would be alright. When the boy woke up the first thing he said was: "Grandfather has given me fish..." (642)

In the next account, a gamekeeper in his forties tells of his visit to a spiritist healer and the events that followed.

### Better back

I had a continuous problem with my back. I went to the late Ragnheidur Gottskalksdottir a well-known healer in Reykjavik. She told me to be still and rest for 10-12 hours. I fall asleep but awake as I feel that some people are with me. I feel that my mother is in the group. I am being lifted and my back is being touched. I did not hear or see anything but I felt touch and was aware of some movement back and forth at my bed. I lay quite still, was not afraid, felt very well and fell into a peaceful sleep. After that my back was better. (2204)

### The old doctor

I had had a pain on my left side and had decided to see a doctor, but my regular doctor had died last fall. This was just before Christmas. That night I dreamt him or rather it was not a dream - I just felt him with me, standing over me and doing something to me. I felt as if I had left my body and followed him to my kitchen, through the hall and he emptied two bowls that he had. Then I entered my room again and saw myself lying in bed and I felt as if I re-entered my body. In the morning when I woke the pain was gone and I have never had it since.

My doctor had told me that he had trouble sleeping or could not sleep at all the night before he came to see me. The spring before he died I had my last child but it died in birth. The night before he had not been able to sleep so his wife did not want to wake him and we could not reach another doctor in time. He was very sorry he had not been woken up... (2049)

## Per request

I had been suffering from back pain for a quite some time but felt I had improved enough to get back to work on the freighter Fjallfoss when it returned from America. This was during the war. Shortly after we started our journey my condition became worse again. We sailed to Scotland where we waited to join a convoy to the States. One night I felt so bad that I could not take my shift. I told the first engineer who said I should take it easy, that another would take my shift. As it turned out, it was not necessary.

I went to bed and must have been sleeping although I felt quite awake and saw all that happened. There entered my cabin white dressed doctors who said they had been requested to examine me. I told them that no such request had been made. I remember this as I wrote it down immediately afterwards when I realised what had happened. They turned me around and examined my back where the pain was. Then they said: 'We are going to operate on you'. I had never heard that this problem was operated upon. They said firmly it did not matter at all. I told them I had the shift at 4 o'clock in the night and it was impossible for me to be bedridden for a longer time. They said I would not be bedridden, could work the next day but should be careful and not lift heavy objects. Then I would be fine for a long time. As they said this I saw them and felt their hands on my back but felt no pain. They said the operation was over and they wished me well as I saw them disappear out of the door. I jumped out of bed and opened the door but saw only darkness outside. I shouted, 'Where are the men'. Then I heard the man on duty call back, 'There have been no men here, you must have been dreaming'. I insisted there were two men dressed in white, doctors...

I had seen them so clearly as fully awake and always believed I had been awake all through this experience, although I was definitely asleep before. As I jumped out of bed, hardly able to move before, I felt no discomfort anywhere, completely healthy and have had no problem since, although I had had this problem for fifteen years and was often bedridden. (7618)

## Operation with a syringe

I had asthma and bad catarrh in the nose. At a séance I was told that I would get assistance, I would be paid a visit and an operation would be done on my nose. That was fine by me. Then one night I woke up and it happened. Some sort of an operation was done on my nose, most likely an injection. My nostril was blocked up so I could not breathe and then I felt something like an injection in my nose. I saw something resembling a white gown moving about the room; it lasted only for a short while. In the morning I woke up at the same time as usual and my nose was sore and there was an injection mark on it. I put this in connection to the operation that had been spoken of and that I thought had taken place in the night. (5078)

**Una in Gardur**

This happened some ten years ago. I rang up Una and asked her for help. I had become sick with asthma. She neither replied yes or no as she was wont to. That was the end of our conversation. I had never seen Una. The next morning I woke up and my husband had gone to work. Then three people entered my room, a short man, somewhat dark-skinned, who reminded me of Indians or someone of the yellow race. He seemed a bit over thirty with a small beard and in a white gown. There was also a nurse or a girl that I cannot describe further. She might be of the same age as the man. A third person entered with them. Then I felt as in a sleepy state but also that they touched and palpated my ribs and chest. The hands were very warm, short, thick and radiated heat. Then I become fully awake again and saw the face of the woman who leaned over me. She seemed to be 150 to 156 cm high, rather short and sturdy and with her hair combed straight. As this warm current goes through me I say suddenly 'You are Una in Gardur'. Then this scene disappeared completely.

Breathing was considerably easier after this, so I rang her up. I asked, 'Are you a short stout woman?' I asked her to describe her hands, and they were like what I had seen. She said she never got cold hands. I never met Una face to face. The people that were with her, I felt, were deceased. (7566)

In our survey from 1975, 41 percent of a representative sample of 902 people had been to a prayer healer or spirit healer, 24 percent of men and 56 percent of women. We interviewed 100 people from this group, who all lived in the Reykjavík area. About half of them had visited a medium to obtain a cure for themselves and a third had gone on behalf of other people. In a few accounts, other people had been to spirit doctors on the behalf of the informant (Haraldsson and Olafsson 1980).

It was most common for people to have sought a cure from "the other side" through a medium who contacted a doctor or doctors (46 percent). The medium was believed to play the part of the intermediary between the patient and the doctor from "the other side".

Prayers were the next most common way to seek a cure (26 percent), either used alone or along with trying to obtain a cure from the other side. In these cases the cure was sought from God or Jesus and the power of the cure was believed to originate there. Other methods were not as common. Some of those who went to mediums and prayer healers did not know what method was being used. The practice of healing in Iceland has spiritual and religious roots, which is obvious from the examples above.

While seeking help from a spiritual healer, two thirds of the patients were also being treated by physicians. The physician was rarely notified of the attempted alternative healing. After 40 percent of the incidents the patient believed he or she had fully recovered; in 32 percent the patient recovered to some degree; and in 28 percent of accounts there was no cure. With regards to the cured individuals, 30 percent of them thought the cure came from a spirit doctor on "the other side" and for 30 percent the cure was due to the prayer. Fewer people (17 percent) believed that the healer, or whoever prayed for them, was responsible for the cure and 10 percent believed it was because they themselves believed in such cures.

What seemed to determine whether the informant felt that they had been cured was whether they had ever had a religious experience and if they read the bible more often than most. Nevertheless, the statistical correlation was relatively low for these factors. The belief in the abilities of mediums did not really have any influence on whether people traced their cure back to mental healers or spirit healers.

### The nearness of a mother

I have had this kind of experience a few times. One of them is especially memorable. My eye had been bothering me for some time. I had something in my eye and I was quite uncomfortable. Then one morning I was awake with my eyes closed when I felt my mother who was deceased, standing at my bed. She bent over me and I thought I could feel her breathing. I was well awake but did not want to open my eyes because I felt sure I would not see her. I am sure she was there and that she was checking how my eye was. I felt her bend down all the way to my face. (2000)

## Backache

I was a sailor but had to give it up because I had a bad back. I went to see a doctor, the spinal column was damaged. I was in some pain. One night I was awakened by what I thought were 3 men in my room. I knew them all quite well; they were my father, my uncle and my brother, all deceased. Firstly they asked if I was better. I said I was. Then they said: "We are glad you are better, we asked for a doctor for you." I saw them as they left. Since then I have not had any trouble with my back. (7526)

## Now I will get better

I had been operated upon a few times at the National Hospital and was once more waiting for an operation. I had been told what would be done. I was with two other patients in a room. My bed was closest to the door. That morning I was awake but not fully when I noticed that the nurse came in and placed something on the table. Then I noticed that there were some people at my bed, two or three close to my bed and bent over me. They had some metal plates in their hands and placed them above me. In the middle was a young man who was in charge. He was a tall man in a pullover made of red and white yarn with a collar around the neck. I saw this clearly, was startled and then the vision disappeared. In a short while, it appeared again and even more forcefully and stayed for a while. Then they went away, and my first thought was; 'Now I will be get better'. (5066)

## In a fog

I have been aware of deceased people but never really anyone I know myself. One night I slept over at the home of an old lady friend who is a patient but has received help from the other side. During the night I perceived that there came to her two men, doctors and rather young men. I did not see their faces but in other ways I could describe them. I saw they bent over her and were trying to help her. I was a little scared this time, probably because they touched my face and seemed to be trying to make me at ease. (2094)

## The healers

I was having an operation in the hospital, when I thought I was awakened by two doctors standing on each side of my bed. Then I was electrified... I felt myself jolt up in bed and I was half-sitting. I became terribly frightened... Later I learned that a healer had been contacted about my illness. (2070)

## The healer doctor

My wife and I were sitting at the bedside of our sick child. Margret from Oxnafell, a famous healer, had been asked to help. One night I woke up and saw the (deceased) doctor that Margret worked with coming to heal our girl. I did not know anything about this doctor, but he came to help and then he suddenly disappeared. (514A)

## Help from a doctor

I was with my sister-in-law. She sometimes took into her home sick people who needed help. We sat in the twilight that night and she spoke to us and there were many healing persons from the other side around us. The following night two doctors came to me whom I knew nothing about other than that they were deceased. They seemed to be examining me. I felt better after their visit. I saw them as I see living people. They seemed natural, wore white gowns like doctors do. (2194)

# 28

# MEDIUMS AND PSYCHICS

IT was fairly common for people to mention mediums, psychics or readings even though we did not include in our collection any phenomenon which had been experienced under such circumstances. Mentioning mediums is not surprising considering the fact that in 1975, our survey showed that about one third of the grown up population, 23 percent of the men and 38 percent of the women, had attended some sort of a mediumistic séance. This number had changed very little when the survey was repeated in 2006. Below are some examples where psychics, mediums or séances are a part of the account.

### Moonlight

I was tired and lay down to rest. I was in such a state that I could not move any limb. I heard and perceived what was around me and saw clearly a doctor who had died. Or I thought I knew it was him. He was Magnus who was one of the persons who regularly appeared at Hafsteinn Bjornson's séances. He was often trying to help me. I saw clearly how he was dressed and I saw his back when he walked briskly away from me. There was some light with him, a special kind of light, like moonlight. Shortly afterwards I attended a séance with Hafsteinn and told Magnus I had seen him. 'I certainly knew about it', he replied. (5035)

Hafsteinn Björnsson (1914-1977) was a popular and prominent medium who became nationally known in Iceland. During his long mediumistic carrier thousands of people attended his séances and some left them deeply impressed. Hafsteinn was a trance medium with a few distinct control personalities. Runolfur was his main control and Magnus was another, a very different character who took on the role of a healer and who often stated he would come and bring healing to people in the night.

Runolfur (nicknamed Runki) first appeared at Holstein's séances as a disturbing entity until a man from Sandgerdi attended one of Hafsteinn's séances. Runolf told this sitter that he could help him by finding his leg in a certain house in Sandgerdi. A leg was found and duly buried. After that Runolfur became an effective and distinct control personality with very clear and vivid personality characteristics. The remarkable story of his life and origin was meticulously investigated by the author and Ian Stevenson of the University of Virginia (Haraldsson and Stevenson 1975). Runki had drowned on the coast near Sandgerdi. His corpse was later found with his femur missing.

A double blind experiment was conducted with Hafsteinn in New York in which he could not know who the sitters were, and the sitters did not know which reading - describing deceased persons - was meant for each of them. A significant number of sitters identified the reading meant for them (Haraldsson and Stevenson 1974).

### The siblings

We were going to a séance with Hafsteinn the medium that evening. I took a nap in the afternoon and when I woke I saw two youngsters standing at the sofa beside me and between them was a great spread of flowers. I looked at this for a little while. Then we went to the séance in the evening and then I asked Runolfur who these people were I had seen. Then he said rather impatiently: "It was your son and hers". We were both at the meeting. It was my wife's daughter who died at the age of nine, the boy died in his mother's womb. He was just about the size he would have been had he lived... (2162)

### Talent

I once visited a woman who had mediumistic abilities. She told me that I might have some experience that evening. I was dissatisfied not to get something more from her than this and felt this was not good enough. In bed that evening I was seized by the neck and drawn down to the floor. I was then again seized by the neck and pushed up into bed and into a sitting position. I was going to scream but could not do it.

### Have you got your pipe?

I was going to take the bus to Vogar in Reykjavik from my home in the same city. As I am walking towards the bus stand this deceased grandfather says to me, 'Do you have your pipe with you?' I searched in my pockets, found no pipe and went back to get it. This is characteristic of how I remember him. Sometimes I did not heed what he told me but it was always right. Now I always heed what he says. I hear him with my inner hearing. Once I was at a séance, he comes forth and I ask him if it is he who is poking me and reminding me. 'Oh yes,' he says 'and I wish you would heed it more'. I have never seen him. He died long before I was born. (2186)

### Strange effect

A well-known psychic healer visited my brother with whom I was living at this time. It was evening and he was playing a musical instrument so I went to the door to receive the guest that knocked on the door. As we enter the living room I ask her if her helper was also with her. She nods with a smile. Then I ask her if she cannot introduce me to him and if we cannot shake hands in the ordinary way. I stretch out my right hand. If I remember correctly I felt his touch. Then he shook my other hand and with greater vigour, and I say, 'He takes both my hands'. The healer laughs and says that is right. This was, of course, not a usual touch. It was more an impression like a current or flow that goes between friends when they greet. It is more than a physical touch. Some heartiness goes between friends which is hard to describe. (2200)

Perhaps the following account belongs to this chapter on mediums and psychics.

### Soul helper

Just last night people from the countryside were sent to me, to give them strength. The funeral had taken place that same day. I sensed a conflict around me and sat down in my usual seat. Then I saw an old woman and she had a young girl with her. First I saw the girl's face and then the rest of her. I saw the old woman completely.

175

My room-mate who was there with me said the girl's father had been there too. The old woman said: "I carried her here so that she may have peace". The girl was putting up a struggle, I could see that, but a good team of helpers came and took my strength, an oriental friend of mine was there to help. I am not completely conscious during these things, but when it is over I am just fine. I knew who the old woman was and I have found out that she is the girl's grandmother. (2080)

The appearance of spiritualism and mediums in Iceland started with the remarkable medium Indridi Indridason (1883-1912) who was discovered by the first group we know of in Iceland who started to sit together in the hope that some phenomena would appear. Accidentally a young man, Indridi Indridason, was invited to take part in a sitting that took place with the family that he was living with. Immediately such violent movements of the table took place that Indridi became scared and wanted to run away. He was persuaded to continue and there gradually followed automatic writing and trans-speech, violent movements of objects, levitation of objects and of Indrida himself, as well as direct speech. These and other phenomena were witnessed by numerous persons who took part in his sittings which were organised by the Experimental Society which was founded by a group academics solely for the purpose of observing and meticulously investigating the phenomena. See long reports on his mediumship by Gissurarson and Haraldsson (1989, 1991), Hannesson (1924), Haraldsson and Gerding (2010) and Haraldsson (2011).

# 29

# Is Someone Watching Over Us?

ACCORDING to the accounts, people often feel as if the dead keep an eye on their lives and their daily activities, watching over them. We asked people whether they thought the deceased were trying to get a point across but not whether they were being watched out for. Here are some examples.

**Watching over**

I had just come home from the hospital with my first child. Suddenly I had this strong intuition that my deceased mother-in-law was standing behind me. I looked around but saw nothing. This was quite comforting and I thought it most likely that she was there to watch over the baby. (61)

**Working**

I was working in a basement in one house. For a whole afternoon I had a strong feeling of the presence of someone. He appeared slowly once in a while and was always behind me, and it was as if he was watching me work..... I found this a bit awkward. (295)

**A landholding matter**

I have once sensed a deceased person. My husband, at that time, was doing some paperwork he had brought home as he sometimes did. He had come home alone and sat down at his desk to work.

We had a cup of coffee and afterwards I lay down on the sofa in the living room because I felt a little tired. All of a sudden I saw a man sitting opposite my husband, a handsome man, I will never forget him because I was so surprised. He was dressed in old fashioned clothes, wearing a maroon coloured suit and a blue striped shirt that looked like it was handwoven. I could tell because I am an old woman. When I was about 10 years old I saw many countrymen dressed in this fashion. Unfortunately I did not know this man but have often hoped to see a picture of him. The man was very sickly, as if he were suffering from a disease. He was pale, had blond hair that was parted on the left side. He sat there right before my very eyes, resting his hands on the desk and he seemed to be worried. He resembled a countryman but there was something about him that suggested he was used to giving orders. He sat there for about 15 minutes and then disappeared suddenly. I think he might have been connected to one of the landholding cases my husband was working on at his desk. I told my husband what I had seen even though he does not believe in such things. (2057)

### On the edge of the bed

I was twenty and pregnant. I wanted to continue my studies but saw no way, and was worried about it. One morning I lay awake in my bed when my landlady told me there was a guest for me, my 'deceased father-in-law'. He then passed her and came into my room and sat on the edge of the bed before I could say I was not ready to see him. I did not feel comfortable seeing someone while I was still in bed. I pulled the bedcover up to my cheek. I saw him with open eyes, I think... He was an elderly man, had a light step, and with him came peace and tranquility, warmth and goodness. I felt he was there to let me know that all would be well. A few months later I recognised his face on a photograph. He was the father of my boyfriend who later became my husband. I gave the child his name although I am skeptical of such things. I never dared ask my landlady if she really had announced his visit or not. (354).

### In the countryside

I have had out-of-body experiences but they are not voluntary. I see myself lying in bed and it usually happens just before I fall asleep. Often I also sensed the presence of a person I did not know and I distinctly heard her voice. I was once out in the fields getting the horses, when I sensed the presence of this person. I clearly heard her voice. She seemed to be telling me that I did not have to worry about the future. This was accompanied by a feeling of peace, then it slowly faded away... (2068)

## The order

Two months after my father died I was in the maternity ward at the hospital. I had not been out of bed for six days and that was rather unusual. Suddenly I felt that my late father was in my room. He seemed to be quite alive right there in front of me, at the foot of my bed. I clearly heard him say: "Maria, is it not about time you got up?" This happened very suddenly and I was quite startled. Yes, he ordered me out of bed and after this I got up. (2060)

## Guitar being played

I have seen this two times. Some time had passed since this person died when it occurred the second time. She was a good friend of my wife and me. I saw her very clearly. She was at the chair of her son-in-law when he was playing the guitar. She seemed very pleased and happy to see this and smiled. She did not say anything, was just letting us know that she was there. My wife also saw her when I saw her the first time. We were then together and it made us happy to see her. (2110)

## On Hjörleifshöfdi

When I was a youngster I spent some years at a farm at a high rocky outcrop on the sands of Myrdal. I had to keep the sheep off the shore. Sometime later when I was living in Reykjavik my foster father, the farmer at Hjörleifshöfdi, died. Sometime after his death I was woken by the feeling that someone was calling me. I did not find this at all strange, got up and went through the house as I thought there was someone there. I looked all over and opened the outside door, then realised that it was my foster father's voice that I had heard. So I went back to my room and fell asleep. A while later I heard that a boat had been cast up onto the shore right below our farm; and this had happened at the same time as I heard my foster father call me. From this I understood that he had been following the event and this was his way of letting me know what had happened. (2168A)

## The wretch

I worked for a few years on board the cargo ship Edda, which was later to become Fjallfoss. Before one trip which was bound for Spain, the first mate was left behind in Reykjavík because of illness. One day – we were in Italy when this happened – my mate and I saw a man standing aft on the ship, where no one should have been at that time, and I said immediately, "You go up that ladder and I will go up the other and we will catch him; it's probably some wretch from on shore looking for something to steal." The man we saw disappeared behind a large ventilator and when I got to that spot I saw the first mate, so I said: "It is just the first mate; I thought it was some wretch or other". We were about three months at sea on that tour, and we heard nothing from home during all that time; but the first mate had died while we were on the way to Spain.

Exactly the same kind of event took place a year later in Canada. I thought that someone had come aboard who had no business being there. I did not recognise the man himself. But it then occurred to me where I had seen this before, the same clothes the same bearing... I had already said to one of my mates: "If he dies before us, he will always be here on board." So I connected the two things ... I took it as a sign that he was watching over us ... (2168)

## Between hope and fear

My daughter took some pills when she was a little girl and had to be rushed to hospital, where her life hung in the balance for a time. The doctors could give us no hope; the quantity she had swallowed had been so great. We been sitting by her for some hours when I had the sensation that someone was in there with us. I felt that my mother was present and that she was trying to indicate to us that our daughter was out of all danger. It was some kind of inner consciousness and absolute knowledge ... and I said to my wife: "Well, will we go home now? I know everything is going to be alright." (2152)

## Sure of winning

I lay in the hospital, and to relieve my suffering I was given painkillers, which did not do much good. I was beginning to be overcome by a sense of hopelessness and to believe that, in this condition, I would never live through the winter. One evening, at visiting hours, I suddenly saw my deceased sister standing by the bed and heard her say, "Have patience." My sister appeared to be very determined, confident and sure of being right and I took this to mean that I would start on the road to recovery. (2138)

### An old friend

I was having a nap in the afternoon when I was awakened by what I thought was my friend standing beside me. She was leaning over me and pressing her hand against me. Her checks were rosy and had a youthful glow. I turned over to the other side with great difficulty but then the girl vanished. At the same moment I heard the door slam shut. Her name was Rikey and she had suddenly became ill of tuberculosis and died. She was 25 years old and had a young child. I often thought of her. I think she was just making me feel good. (368)

The following account is one of the oldest in our collection, the woman who recounted the episode being 96 years old when she was interviewed. She answered all our questions lucidly in spite of her age.

### A father watches over his daughter

I lived with my parents in our home at Brekkuvellir, Bardaströnd. A young girl also lived there who was being tutored for her confirmation. Her father had drowned earlier that spring when his boat Vigga from Patreksfjord went down. One evening, we were arguing about who should sleep on the outside of the bed, for we shared the same bed and I won. During the night, I woke up and saw the girl's father sitting on a chest which stood alongside the bed. It was just as if he had walked in there alive and just as I remembered him in appearance. He was also seen to be dry. I happened to glance away from him and when I looked back he was gone. I think that he had been showing me and letting me know, that I should be friends with his daughter ... (6000)

### Everything was ruined

My younger son was five years old but my elder son six and a half when he died. I wanted very much to see him. This was in the spring. My husband had been a heavy drinker but he had not touched the bottle for eight years. But one spring day he went out and did not come back that day. Then I knew he had started drinking again. In the evening around eight o'clock, I was busy in the kitchen and my son had gone to bed a while ago, I heard some kind of groan coming from the bedroom. I entered the room and I saw to my surprise that my son that was alive went out of focus but the picture of my deceased son appeared instead. He raised himself up and leaned up against me and said: "Mummy, look ,look, just you look, everything has been ruined for me". And I said: "No dear, it has not." "Yes, it's all ruined, you just cannot see it," he said. Then he waved his arm like in a semi-circle and said:"Yes it is, it is all ruined." I knew at once what he meant, it was about his father, and it proved to be true. Then I said to him, "Why do not you lie down dear." He moaned and said: "Yes I will". Then he layed down and I watched his picture fade away and his brother's picture appear instead. I have always wanted to share this experience but never have. It was just like in the movies, when one picture fades away as another one appears. (2035)

Sometimes people feel that a deceased person is keeping an old promise to let people know they are alright or prove themselves by appearing. The following accounts are examples of this.

### A promise kept

I was resting after a hard day's work and had a drink by my hand when the lights in the room suddenly went off and then came on again. Also, the glass which I had just filled was empty and I saw no indication as to where the contents had gone. I suspected that my friend, who had died a few months before at the age of thirty, was there with me, making good his promise of long ago to make himself known after death if at all possible. (807)

### "I will let you know"

There was an old man living at the next farm that came and went as he pleased in our home. We talked of many different things; of this and that and how he, when he had passed away, would let his presence be felt by us. "Oh yes, I will certainly let myself be known", said he. It was over a year after his death when I was out in the sheds with the animals, as I so often was. It had been a custom with him to come upon me unexpectedly and knock three times in his own particular manner. On this occasion, I was alone when I heard these three knocks and I suspected that I knew what they were. I rushed outside. The weather was such that no one was out and about, and there were no footprints to indicate the passage of

anyone or anything. I was quite certain of what it was I had heard
– I knew it so well ... (2202)

## Letting us know

My paternal grandmother had been dead for a year. Once, when
we were approaching our summerhouse, and I had got as far as the
gable in which a large window was set, large enough to see in clearly.
I looked in and distinctly saw my grandmother sitting there, inside
the house. She was dressed in a certain way – in the clothes she used
to wear when out in the country; a long coat and unusual headgear.
She looked straight ahead, pensively and did not appear to be connected to us in any way, as if she was in another world somehow ...
She was 86 when she died, but here she seemed to be around fifty
to sixty. Before she passed away she had been plagued by pessimism
and lack of faith and was afraid of dying ... I think she wanted to let
us know she was there. (5074)

## "I am back home"

My mother was in a hospital and was returning home the next day.
But then she died and we were naturally very sad about her death.
The next day I was at work in the school, sat outside in the break
and was aware of everything around me. Two men walked towards
me in the corridor when I saw her immediately behind them. She
leaned towards the wall and said 'I am back home'. (5044)

## To lighten my grief

I lost my son when he was 25 years old. I have often sensed him.
One morning I was lying in bed. I had been out of bed earlier but
was feeling a little strange, when he came to me and I said to him:
"My dear son, are not you out in the cemetery?" He replied, "Mother
dear I did not think you said things like that. I thought you knew
there are two bodies." Then I said, "Then you do not mind how your
body is treated?" "No mother, I would not say that. I thought you
knew that the body is the means of the soul while we are in this
world. It is the body that we leave behind." He seemed to have some
sort of a dark veil and waved it as if to indicate that he had to be
going. When I saw him he looked grave and sickly but there was
peace and calm over him. I think he was proving himself that he
was not dead out in the cemetery, and that he was trying to relieve
my sorrow... (2088)

# 30

## I'VE GOT A BAD
## FEELING ABOUT THIS

IN two thirds of cases, people felt that they had had a positive experience when they encountered a deceased person. However, in six percent of the cases the experience was negative, 17 percent said it had been neither, and 8 percent did not know whether they had negative or positive feelings about their experience. In the 20 incidents where the informant felt the experience had been negative, they usually felt they had been haunted or were frightened. Some examples:

**On the Lord Fisher**
I was on an English trawler, registered in Hafnarfjörður, one of the Helliers trawlers, as they were called. There were a number of them and on them were both Icelandic and English crew. We had just hauled in the trawl and there was not much catch in it. Then most of the men went down to rest, and what we called a trawl shift was left to keep watch. I was a bit slow in getting into my berth. There were three tiers of bunks, and I was in the top one, around the middle section of the prow cabin. I climbed up into my berth and laid down with my eyes closed. Just then, I heard the side of the bunk creak and looked round. No sooner had I done that, than a man flung himself on top of me. I immediately became paralysed with shock and could think of no other action than to spit in his face – after which he disappeared like dew on a sunny morning. If the incident had been a prank played on me by one of my shipmates,

the perpetrator would not have been able to vanish as he did. I got down from the bunk and told the skipper that I could find no peace there; that a man was bothering me. But he said that he had never been aware of any such goings-on. However, there were others who had seen the man. Especially a man called Sigurd, quite a bit older than I am, from Borgarfjord. Sigurður said he had often seen him in the prow cabin.

It was an old trawler and had been used a great deal, fishing from England. If what I saw was the ghost of a dead person or something like that, then it must have been an Englishman. (7540)

**An unpleasant feeling**

I bought an apartment in which I felt very uneasy for a year and a half. I often sensed that someone was present, and I was scared. It was worst in the kitchen and in the hall; I always had to have the lights on. My three year old child said he often saw a man in the apartment. My mother and two of my friends were aware of this too. One of them once saw a man standing in the doorway when he was on his way out. I did not see or hear anything but had this very unpleasant feeling, and most of the time in the evenings. The apartment had been owned by a man who was murdered about a year before I moved in, but I did not know this until about a week ago... (625)

**Wearing the new clothes**

This happened many years ago. I was a police officer in Siglufjord and my wife and I rented a room from a friend. In the summer his foster-father from Fáskrudsfjord in the eastern part of the country came to visit. He had just had an operation on his eye in Akureyri. In November he came down south for an operation in a hospital in Reykjavík. We went to welcome him and he stayed with us in the apartment we had rented. There were two rooms, one was our bedroom but the other was a small corner of the living-room where I studied. I was studying theology at the University of Iceland. The old man arrived and slept in the living-room on a couch he had brought with him, and he kept his things in a bag under the couch. He stayed with us for two weeks. He often opened his bag and showed me its contents. He went to the hospital, had surgery and died three days later. This was in December. The very same night someone was about in the living-room, someone I had not been aware of before. For a while I could not see anything but I felt something move about in the room. Sometimes it came from behind and bent over my shoulder as I was reading. I thought it must be him coming home to look after his things; the things in his bag were very dear to him. He died in the hospital December 7th and his corpse was kept there because there were not any means of transporting it back to the eastern part of the country until in February. He was always in the living-room. We sensed him especially in the evenings but sometimes also in the day.

Later our family came to stay with us, my parents among others. They slept on the couch but the funny thing was no one felt at peace on it or could sleep on it. In the morning my mother brought her blanket in our bedroom to sleep on the floor. She said she could not fall asleep, someone had been above her, and laid on top of her. My father had the same experience as others who came to visit us did. We put this in connection with the bag and my wife and I were thinking of moving the bag down to the storage-room, but we did not have the nerve, because by doing so we thought we would be throwing the man out of the house. But there was no harm in this and we were not frightened of it.

One morning I was going to school at about 8 o'clock and I was putting my books in my schoolbag. I did not turn on the light in the living-room because some light came from the bedroom. When I looked up I saw him. He was standing on the threshold in the bedroom and he had his back turned to me. I recognized him at once; he had grey hair that was curly. He stood there for a while as I looked at him. Then he turned around and I saw his profile. I looked at him and was thinking of walking over to him and touching him, but I was afraid he would disappear and I did not want him to. This caused me to be late for school. I watched him for a few minutes and it seemed as if I could see right through him, although I could not see anything behind him. One thing I noticed was that his outlines trembled like they were electrified, but he was very clear. Then he entered the bedroom that had another door out to the hall. He walked through the bedroom and out the other door into the hall. He closed the door behind him and my wife who was half-asleep heard him as he shut the door. The door was locked with a key and the key was in the keyhole and the door locked after he was gone.... I did not see him again but he was always moving about. There was something else rather extraordinary. He had two suits, one old and shabby, and the other brand new. He wore his better clothes when he stayed with us, but now he wore the other suit...(7520)

**In the bedroom doorway**

It was in the evening and I had gone to bed, beside me I had a burning candle in a bowl. Then I see a man coming into the doorway. He was tall and had to bend down in the doorway.... I could not move a limb nor make a sound. The man then suddenly disappeared. This had a great impact on me and for quite some time afterwards I was afraid of being alone.... (238)

**At Ulfljotsvatn**

There was a man who, in many ways, was dear to me. He got on well with our children and I was a favourite with him. He was a lot older than I was, about 40 to 50 years. Then, in the middle of summer, he died suddenly of pneumonia. We became aware of him in our home immediately after his death, even in the living room. With the approach of autumn, when the summer workers had gone, he did not think twice about getting into bed with me and I could see him lying above me as it was a bright moonlight night and quite light in the room. I said to him that he should go, he did not belong there, "Yes" he said, mumbling something and sat up: "Oh well, I suppose I must go." He lay beside me in the bed, went past me, onto the landing and disappeared downstairs; it was an upstairs living room. That was the only time that I felt that he answered me. I did not see him again that night but he often came and lay beside me in my bed, first on one side and then on the other.

Many nights I woke up with him in my bed. I saw him clearly and recognised him. When he had stopped coming into my bed, he began to bother others in the same way and the whole thing was becoming a problem in the upstairs living room. So actions were taken to try to stop this, e.g. my father erected a cross on the man's grave and with that he vanished ... (7614)

**Wanted to have a light**

It is some years since my husband's grandfather died at the age of 91 in the hospital. Then he was brought home, where he was laid out and placed in his coffin. We got permission to do this. In the evening when we were going off to bed the lights were put out. When I was in bed I felt him coming to me and he handled me so roughly that there was no peace to be had. I put on the light and this mistreatment stopped. I was not going to give in but he always came back. This went on for a few nights but after his funeral, I was not aware of any further activity. A few years later, my mother-in-law died, and the exact same thing happened again, I got no peace at all after I had turned off the light. It was as if someone had laid dead-weight on top of me. But she was not satisfied even after her funeral, and I had to have the light on all that winter. I thought I recognised them both and the activity always disappeared when I had put the light on. (2134)

## Looked eye to eye

The spirit of a man followed me, seemed always to be where I was. While at sea I woke up in my berth to find him watching me, and when I was wide awake he disappeared, slamming the door of the cabin, or so I believe. I followed him out but of course there was no one to be seen. This also happened at home, usually in the middle of the night – we always had the bedroom door open a crack and a light on in the hallway. He often came to the crack and sometimes I woke to find him standing by the bed, staring at me piercingly. I mostly got up and went to look for him ... It was as if he were asking me for something, but I never knew what it was. This became so persistent that my wife complained about it.

He followed me to where I now live and stayed around for a few years before he vanished for good. Sometimes I saw all of him and sometimes only his head and shoulders. We often looked at each other eye-to-eye. Then I felt that he left; turning away and leaving through the door. He seemed to be a man of around 30 to 40 years, but I never knew who he was ... (7582)

## Old Olof

I am from Keflavík. In that town was a house which was said to be persistently haunted. In this house lived the parents of Petur Sigurdsson who later became a member of parliament. They once took an old woman from the country under their wing who had lost her husband and was said to be a relative of the mistress of the house. She was supposed to spend her old age there, except surprisingly, she was only there a little over two years. It was said, in Keflavik that she had been rather well situated. Her name was Olof and I remember her well. I was always a little bit afraid of her. She was a large woman with a deep voice and when I was fetching water at the pump, she sometimes came walking along with her stick in her hand. My mother said there was no reason to be frightened, she was a good woman and liked children. Then the old woman died, Sigurd left the house and it was rented out. A sister and brother rented the upstairs flat. He was a fisherman and she worked here at the fish factory. It was very cramped for them up there. Once she asked me to stay with her overnight while her brother was at sea. She did not dare sleep alone in the flat. A newlywed couple lived downstairs and we women all knew each other.

Once we were upstairs playing cards, all three of us. Then we were gripped by a bout of silliness and Jónína said to me: "No! You are betraying your colour" and so on. Then Gudrun said to her: "I wish Olof was here to kick your backside." Then Jonina said: "No, no, no! You must not say that." We laughed all the same, and had a lot of fun. Then we went to bed. We slept in the same bed Gunna and I, and I was on the outside. Right after we got into bed I heard that Gunna was fast asleep, but I could not drop off at all. Then I felt as if someone had touched my neck, here, and pinned me down so hard that I seemed totally paralysed: I could not move at all, not even a muscle. I knew someone was standing in front of the bed that seized my throat so hard that it was difficult to breathe. I was conscious and I knew Gunna was asleep. I heard her breathing and I wanted to kick her and wake her up, but I could not move. That is how it was; I cannot estimate how long it lasted. Then all at once I was able to move one of my legs and I kicked Gunna. She turned over and asked "What's wrong with you girl?" "Well. I cannot sleep; let me be on the inside." I did not want to tell her about it. So I clambered over her and turned my face to the corner. I could not sleep and after a bit, I think I heard something odd, I heard such strange breathing. I said to myself, that Gunna could not be going through the same as I had, and I pushed her so vigorously that she woke up and said: "You were SO good to wake me, I felt as if someone was strangling me." "Do not be silly Gunna, you were just having a nightmare", I said. So that had been the exact same thing ... we had both been harassed, one while awake the other in her sleep. We talked about it later, but not until the next day. We concluded that we were probably attacked because of our foolish behaviour the previous evening, talking about Olof and all that ... I thought that maybe she had not liked that ... (5028) (see also 7592)

The same Olof appears in another account (7592), in which the informant described a very powerful experience when he was saved from drowning.

### Strange noises

We have often, my husband and I, heard strange noises and sounds like someone were about in the house that we moved into seven years ago. I have for instance heard someone walking up the stairs from the foyer and down the hall, - but when I have checked to see who it was, no one was there. Others have heard this, as if someone where about in the house. When I went to a séance I found out that my brother who had died as an infant, was causing the racket. It is not as noisy as before and I am not as frightened. (422)

In the following accounts, the informants did not feel they were being haunted but they felt scared.

### Do not mourn

This happened twice as far as I can recall, shortly after the death of my grandfather who was very close to me. I lay in bed in my room and had been thinking a lot about him. It was dark as the light was off. I was about to go out of the room when I think I saw him. I do not know how long this lasted. I was not aware of myself, or so I felt, and I heard nothing around me. I thought he was talking to me, although his mouth was shut. He talked through me in some way. He asked about the family, and said he felt extremely well and asked me to pass that on to my grandmother. He did not want her to grieve for him. I remember that he manifested very clearly and strongly in the corner of the room ... My siblings entered the room at this point and described how I had looked. My body had been rigid and I was staring at something. I was horribly scared after that and did not dare sleep in that room for a very long time. (5046)

### Coffee man

I was in Eskifjord at my brother's. He and his wife were not at home and the oldest daughter had gone to bed. I had been watching television and went into the kitchen to get some coffee. I then became aware that someone was standing beside me. I looked to the side, put my hand on the kitchen table, took a peek under my arm and saw the figure of a grown man up to the waist. I recognised him immediately from his slippers. It was my grandfather who was a great coffee drinker. I made my coffee where I stood, and put the milk back in its place. Then he came back to my side, so I said: "Is that not enough now?" I must admit I was not thinking about anything remotely in connection with my grandfather at the time, and I got quite a nasty shock as I was not expecting it ... (5112)

## Having a look

I was used to having my siblings around me in the bedroom, but this evening I was alone; they were at some summer entertainment. This was in July in the western fjords. I think I had been asleep but I woke up when a woman came into my room, and I seemed to feel her bending over me to examine me. This woman was so like my mother that I thought it was her, but then I saw that she was dressed in completely different clothes. She had on a black crocheted shawl and a dark coloured dress which I realised my mother had never owned. I became very scared and then the woman vanished. (5098)

## In the clouds

The first apparition I ever saw was that of my great grandmother. I spent the summer in the country in my youth. Once I was lying out in the meadow, looking up at the clouds and not thinking about anything in particular, in fact my mind was quite empty. I had been working at the haymaking. Then all of a sudden my great grandmother appeared, and I saw some kind of profile image of her. I got quite a shock and was terribly afraid. I did not tell anybody about this, and when I got back home after my day of haymaking I looked through the photos of my great grandparents that they had at the farm, and saw that it was she who had appeared before me ... (2216)

## My grandfather

I think it must have been about 1974 when my grandfather died. Once around the New Year I was alone at home and was looking after my siblings. The time was about 11pm. I had to go to the toilet and as I was on my way there, I felt as if there was someone behind me. The passage was a long one and when I turned around I saw a man in black clothes with a hat. He was hunkered down in the passage beside me. I recognised him perfectly. I knew it was my grandfather. I felt that there was no other possibility but still I was very much afraid. I did not approach him at all just told him to go. Then I went back into the room and when I reached the door something caught my attention, some kind of rustling noise or something. I felt compelled to look around, and when I did so I saw him walking out of the door, dressed in black and with the same hat ... (7600)

# 31

# They Showed up For Their Own Funeral

IN our collection we have a number of sightings of the deceased incidents which occured at funerals. Here are a few examples of this kind.

**Whole**

I was present when the young man brought up in the same house as I was laid in his coffin. He died at the age of 25 from blood poisoning in an infected tooth. During the ceremony I saw what seemed to be an image of him, from his head down to his shoulders, appear in a window pane opposite me. He ran his hand down from his cheek to his neck, and then he vanished as quickly as he had come. This made me feel glad and I gave a laugh which was considered to be rather inappropriate on such an occasion. But then I explained what had happened to me. I think that he was letting me know that he was well again, and that the stroking movement of his hand symbolised his tooth and the blood poisoning which had had its source there. (451)

**Speaking to the dead with the mind**

I have often made contact with the dead, but this only happened at funerals. I do not see the dead nor am I aware of them in any way. I have spoken to the person being buried, and the conversation takes place in my mind. I get the impression that those who have passed away do not hear what is going on in this world, but that they can see it very clearly. In one case, I was some kind of interpreter, during the eulogy, for the person being interred. The man had died abroad at the age of 73 and had a long history of illness behind him. I have no explanation for this and I have never told anyone about my experiences before. (2021)

## Cured of ills

It has happened quite often at funerals that I have seen the person being interred. I always get a certain feeling beforehand, but it does not always follow that I see the persons or am aware of them in any other way. This characteristic has become less strong as I get older. The most noteworthy occasion which I want to tell you about concerns my sister-in-law, a mentally handicapped girl who was also disabled and could hardly walk. She died when she was twenty. At her funeral, I saw her in the church where she stood by the coffin. I thought she looked as if she had just come out of her bath; her hair was wet and she was dressed in a frock. She was of the height I would have expected her to be in this life had she been in good health. She appeared to be whole and cured of her disabilities. (2023x)

## Talking

My brother died in an accident. His funeral took place from a church in Ísafjord. We arrived ahead of the clergyman and sat there in the peace and quiet. Then I perceived that everything around me disappeared. I then saw a deceased man who had been married to my aunt and his son who went down with a boat from Bolungarvik. They were at each side of my brother. They walked down the aisle of the church all the way to the coffin in front of the altar. They were having a lively chat and were happy. And that was all there was. I can recall other instances. Everything goes blank, like everything is in a haze, but I would not say that I see these things in the usual way. (2074)

## My father's brother

My father's funeral was in the Cathedral in Reykjavík. There, I both saw his brother who was dead and heard him too. But what he said to me I will not reveal as it was of a personal nature. (2142) (see also 6010)

### At Skard on Land

I was attending a funeral at Skard in the county of Land. Many people had gathered and the church was full. Some had to stand outside, so a loudspeaker had been installed on the outside wall of the church. I stood in the church doorway and could hear both the words spoken inside the church and the amplification outside – depending on which source I was listening for. There were also some people in the farmhouse of Skard, where another loudspeaker had been placed. When the last hymn was being sung, those in the house came out, and among them I noticed a man who had previously been a farmer at Land by the name of Sigurd. He came along with that group and took up a position in the churchyard. Then I looked into the church and thought to myself: "No, that cannot be, he is dead." I looked back over the group and he was still there. Then I blinked my eyes and with that he was gone. (398)

### Smiling and happy

I was at a funeral and saw the deceased appear. It was a man who had drowned. I saw him stand by the coffin and he smiled at us where we sat on the pew. He was well turned out, looked happy and pleased ... (5011)

### After the funeral

She was a great friend to us children, especially us siblings. There were eight of us and I was the youngest – she was especially good to me. I wanted very much to attend her funeral. By then I was of course a young man of 22. This was out on Grimsey Island. But it so happened that I was out at sea that day, and could not be present. So one or two days later I was walking on the island and passed the house where she had lived. The next thing I knew, I saw the old woman, walking as she used to do, from the shed and down to the house. I felt she had almost reached me, and I saw her clearly, dressed just as she had been before she died and with a happy expression. But I fell and when I stood up and looked again of course I saw nothing. I took the manifestation to mean that she wanted to let me know that she remembered me, and that she now existed in another world. She was often out and about both in the meadow and somewhere between the buildings. People, at least in days gone by, believed that such phenomena existed, although there is not much of that around nowadays, or people just do not believe in it any more. (6014) (see also 7032)

**I am so happy**

It was in the evening, at the beginning of January. I felt as if I was not asleep when my grandfather appeared to me. He had died on New Year's Day some years ago. I saw him in some strange way, not with my eyes but rather in my mind somehow. I thought I saw only his head. He was a loveable man, at least to me. He smiled lovingly at me and let me know, not with words but rather with some kind of telepathy, "I am so glad because I am allowed to fetch ..." I am not sure whether he said him or her. I found this so peculiar that I fell fast asleep and forgot all about it until my husband arrived home at lunchtime the day after. He told me of the death of my mother's brother-in-law, that is to say the son-in-law of my grandfather; his death had come very suddenly. Then I remembered my grandfather, who had been trying to tell me he was so happy about going to fetch his son-in-law. (5096)

**My husband's brother**

When my husband's funeral was in progress in the Cathedral in Reykjavík, I saw his dead brother standing by the coffin. He appeared to be unhappy, and wanted to break through. He was not pleased with the order of the funeral service; some part of the ceremony did not please him. (6010) (see 2142)

**At the funeral feast**

The first time I had this kind of experience was six years ago at my grandmother's funeral. When we came into the house where refreshments were waiting, I was not thinking about her. This may seem strange because I was just coming from the funeral. I was wandering if the house would accommodate all the guests. When I walked into the house I saw her standing there welcoming us, just as if she was still alive. She trembled a bit like many old people do. She was wearing a dress that was very familiar, it was not a fancy dress, she was not dressed up, just dressed in her normal way. She disappeared suddenly. I did not tell anyone about this until a few hours later. (7510)

And finally an example which is indirectly connected with funerals.

## Problems because of a strike

I come from distant countryside and a good friend of mine died there. She had asked me to come see her there but did not say why. But I knew she had been very ill that spring. I did not make it. Maybe it was because of tardiness on my account that I did not take the time. One always thinks there is time enough, but suddenly I heard of her death. I was very sorry that I did not... What if it had been something important. We were good friends so I decided to write her an obituary. I have often done so.

I sent the obituary to a newspaper, but there was a strike that lasted for a long time. I was sorry that it took so long. It is usually awkward when these things are so late. I was quite worried about this. Well, then I had some kind of intuition that the strike would be over soon but I did not know for sure. Then I had a dream, it was not really a dream, I just saw her, I started up from sleep with the feeling that someone was there with me, and there she was. She was just like she was the last time I had seen her, I felt she was quite content and happy, and she said with a gleaming smile, "Thank you so much for the obituary." I felt her hand touch my bedcover, she stroked it, and I saw her walk about my room quite normally. The obituary was printed in the first release after the strike and it was the day after I had had this experience. She knew about this and was letting me know. That same day my conscience was clear. (2025)

# 32

## Obtaining Information Unknown Before the Encounter

ONE thing which people find interesting is when the perceiver has been given information by the deceased person about something that they had no knowledge of before. Two examples:

**The man with the pigeons**

I was often a guest in the house of my grandparents when I was a teenager. Once when I was running down the stairs on my way out, I saw a young man standing there on the landing below me. I ran past him and then looked back at him and I found it strange to see him with two pigeons, one on each shoulder. I thought I knew this had been my uncle who had died in an accident when I was four years old. When I described him to my family they thought it had been him. I did not know that he had been fond of pigeons and had kept them..... (77)

**Exactly that pink nighty**

I brought my wife to the hospital. She had been sick for several weeks. I visited her that same evening again and she was dressed in a blue nightgown. I had expected to see her again the following day, but she died in the night. The next day my daughter-in-law came to select a gown for her burial. A day later I come home late and take out the psalm book to select the psalms to be sung at her funeral. Then the astounding thing happened. My wife suddenly stands in front of me, bathed in an oval of white light. I saw her very distinctly and vividly as she held both hands around the collar of her nightgown - not the one I saw her in when I saw her the last time, but a pink fancy gown she used only rarely. She held the collar together with both her hands under her cheek. I became startled and then she disappeared. I had not known what gown my daughter-in-law had selected for her but discovered later that it was exactly this dress. (2172)

This man's daughter-in-law also encountered his wife the night she died and described it in these words:

My mother-in-law had been ill for a long while, and my father-in-law and I took her to hospital one afternoon. She had been very good to me and we were great friends. During that night, I woke up with the feeling that she was there in the room with me, looking at my husband and I, and smiling. I thought that was really strange, as I knew she was ill. Then she disappeared ... The morning after, I learned that she had died, had passed away around the time she appeared to me. (5003)

It is important to add that no questions were asked about whether the informants had learnt something from their experiences that they had no knowledge of before the event. There were only a few such accounts and some of them can be found in other chapters.

# 33

# Multiple Witnesses

I N the first round of interviews we did not place much emphasis on trying to verify what the participants reported to us. Therefore, all first 100 cases were not included in the analysis below, although a few examples of these enounters from this group will be described. The numbers quoted below are taken from the 349 accounts where participants had to answer more detailed questions regarding their experience and every avenue was taken that could verify what they reported to us.

In about half of these accounts (174 cases), the perceiver said that another person was present or close by when the incident occurred. Around half of these cases (89 people) were in such a position that they should have been able to make the same observation. Nevertheless, our informants said that in 41 out of these 89 incidents, the other person also had the same experience; that is, they experienced the same perception as the informant. Seven of these witnesses had passed away and two could not be contacted. That leaves us with 32 accounts. For three incidents, the witnesses could not remember the incident or would not give their opinion on the matter. In 29 accounts, the witness said they had experienced the same perception as the informant.

That is, in several accounts, there was more than one witness to the incident. There were also cases where the perceiver told people close by about the experience before the news of the death was received. As such these people indirectly shared the experience with the informant.

We will discuss those cases in more detail in the next chapter. Let us first take a look at the accounts where there is more than one witness to the incident. First we have an example from a lawyer who was widely known in Iceland.

### Nationally renowned lawyer

It was just after graduation in 1939. I was coming home from a dance. I had not tasted a drop of alcohol. It was about four o'clock in the morning and full light as we were in the middle of summer. I was walking over a bare hill on my way home from town. Then there comes a woman towards me, kind of stooping, with a shawl over her head. I do not pay any attention to her but as she passes me I say "Good morning" or something like that. She did not say anything. Then I notice that she has changed her course and follows me a bit behind. I got slightly uneasy about this and found it odd. When I stopped, she stopped also. I started saying my prayers in my mind to calm myself. When I came close to home she disappeared. I lived in a house on the compound of a psychiatric hospital where my father worked. I go up to my room. My brother Agnar wakes up and says half asleep, "What is this old woman doing here? Why is this old woman with you?" And I tell him not to speak such nonsense but to continue sleeping, although I knew what he meant. I did not see the woman at that time but my brother appeared to see her when he woke up. I go out to get me some coffee. When I return to my room, Agnar gets up again and says, "Why has this woman come back?" And I tell him not to act like that, that there is no woman in here, that he is confused and should go to sleep.

At lunch the following day I say to my brother, "What nonsense was that last night? You thought you saw a woman in our bedroom." "Yes," he said, "I felt as though an old woman came with you into the room." Then our father became attentive and said to me "Did you see something last night?" I told him that I had seen this woman. "That is strange," he said, "around three o'clock this morning old Vigga died." What I had seen fitted her description perfectly. (2196)

The brother of the informant, said he remembered the incident. Asked whether he had seen the woman he replied, "I saw the outlines of some woman... but not clearly... when I woke up I saw a woman come in with him. She was a patient and always locked inside I think, if that was her". Here two witnesses perceive the same person at a similar moment in time though not at the exact same time.

A close scrutiny of our cases reveals that often collective observations do not take place at exactly the same time. This is exemplified by the case above, reported by a well-known attorney in Iceland. It still seems reasonable to consider such a case collective.

### Sixty year old doctor from Akureyri tells of his experience.

Shortly after our father died I came to his house with my brother. We knew that there was nobody in the house and then we heard the old man at his desk. He was walking around, opened the door and closed it again. Both of us stopped and listened when we entered and then I remarked, "I guess there is no doubt who is up there." "No, there is no doubt about it", my brother replied. Both of us went upstairs, no one was there. We had heard this so clearly. He was 85 years when he died, walked slowly you know, had the typical old man's way of walking. (2198)

The informant's brother, told us in an interview that he remembered the incident well and fully confirmed the account.

### A lady teacher in Akureyri in her forties

I was around twenty. My father and I sat in the kitchen around noon. Then I saw clearly a woman coming toward us. I was not going to mention it but notice that my father also saw this. I asked him what he was looking at and he replied, "Surely the same as you." Then he said he knew this woman. She had died a while back. Three or four hours later there was a phone call for my father who was a clergyman. The husband of the deceased woman we saw had died. We had seen the woman around the time her husband had died. (5102)

The informant's father was asked about the incident and he confirmed his daughter's description of the event and gave a detailed description himself.

### The mother

My mother died in February 1946. I think it was in 1947 that I once saw her very clearly. She entered the bedroom where my husband and I slept and I saw her and so did my husband. She put her finger to her lips as if she wanted us to be quiet. In our room there was a dresser my mother had had since she was a young girl. (2002)

The lady's husband gave this description of the event:

> This incident happened around 1950 in Hrutafjord. I was there with my wife visiting some of her relatives; her mother's sisters among others. One of these ladies had given up her bedroom for us and we slept in there. The set-up in the room was that there were two beds, each standing at its own gable wall. There was a chest of drawers between them, facing a wall with a window. We locked the door before we went to sleep, but left the key in the lock. During the night, I woke up suddenly and saw a woman in Icelandic costume fiddling with something at the chest of drawers, which stood in the room. She put a finger to her lips as if to silence me and let me know she was not going to bother us. I took her to be my wife's aunt, and therefore normal, thought no more about it and went back to sleep. It was the morning after, when we started talking together, that we discovered that we had both seen the same thing. The room was still locked, so it could not have been the aunt we had seen. It had been my mother-in-law, who I had never seen while she was alive ... (6018 A) (see 2002)

## The passenger, reported by an engineer under forty years of age.

My wife comes from the Westfjords and when we were engaged we drove there in my car. I left in the evening in the hope that I would find a place to sleep on the way if I got very tired. On the way I parked the car and was going to sleep as it was already late and getting dark. In the morning I was going to go to the post-office to give notice of my whereabouts. During the night I let the motor run so I would not be cold. Then I woke up because it was uncomfortably hot. I glanced to the back of the car and saw a man there who seemed to be in his forties. He had on a hat with a brim that masked his face so I could not see him clearly. Even if I had met him again the next day, I would not have recognized him in the street. He wore dark trousers and a blue sweater, the kind sailors wear. He sat there and did not say a word. I was in such a state of mind that I thought this was quite normal. I was glad the poor man had managed to get in the car and have some rest and keep warm, and I went back to sleep.

When I woke up the morning the sun was up and the weather was fine, but the man was gone. I found it hard to believe that I did not wake up when he left. I had to pinch myself to see if I was awake. I thought it was so unbelievable. When I arrived back home my foster mother laid the table for two. She said I was lying when I told her I was alone. Later I took the back seat out of the car and put it in a storage room. I passed the kitchen-window and my foster mother saw me and the man behind me. Her description of his clothes matched what I had seen and she said his height was similar to mine. I knew nothing about this man. The only person who had owned the car before me was a taxi-driver from whom I had bought the car. (7532A)

The informants foster mother confirmed the account. She said she had seen the man just as the informant said but she also saw him in the house. She said that he had followed the informant.

### The woman in the sofa

It so happened that three couples, including us, were invited to visit a house in Isafjord. When we went in, I saw a woman sitting in a chair in the living room. I must have looked away from her for when I turned to greet her she was gone. It turned out that four of us had seen the woman, and we mentioned this to the couple who lived in the house. They replied that there had been no one in the house except the two of them. When we compared our experiences and found that our accounts of what the woman looked like tallied, we realised who she was. She was the grandmother of the woman who lived there, and the sister of one of the two men who had also seen her. (7554)

The informant added that one of those present, a man from Reykjavík, had mentioned that he thought it was strange that when he entered, a lady was sitting in the sofa but she was gone when he turned around to greet her. We managed to contact this man. He said that four of them had seen the woman sitting in the lounge but when they went to say hello she was gone. He said, "I believe that I did not realise when I saw the woman sitting there that it was my sister who had passed away twenty years earlier, but when I think about it, the clothes were just as when she dressed up nicely". It may be added that one of the couples was Swedish and we were given their addresses but they were never contacted.

**Woman around sixty and shopkeeper in Reykjavík**

We were in rather a strange mood, maybe a little vulnerable, but I was concentrating on some work I was engaged in, and was not thinking about this kind of thing at all. I looked into the sitting room and saw a man. I saw his head and hands unclearly and he was dressed in very fine, well-tailored clothes. He was a well-dressed man of the old school, a gentleman or a diplomat. I did not think at the time that this had anything to do with us, but later began to wonder what it meant; whether someone was fated to die or if something was wrong. I went in to my sister's room – she had gone to bed long before – and told her about the incident. She was shocked and said that she had seen exactly the same thing earlier that evening. (6003) (see 5005,2)

The informant's sister gave us her account of the incident:

It was maybe two or three years ago. We sat in our sitting room. First of all, I saw a man standing here, who, to tell the truth I did not recognise; nor could I bring to mind who he could be. I did not tell my sister anything about his appearance; just said, as I went off to bed, "There is a man in the sitting room". I said no more after that. Later that evening, she was doing something in here and saw some man and started to describe him. And truthfully it was rather a shock. Her description fitted the man perfectly. We were, perhaps in a somewhat unusual mood. A man we both knew well had just passed away, our brother who died suddenly ... We did not, and have no way of knowing, who the man we saw was, we did not recognise him. She described him exactly as she saw him, as did I. (5002,2)

**Seaman from Isafjord, less than thirty years of age**

We were on our way home. There was no one home, the heating system was turned off, and the house was quiet. We passed along the corridor, at the end of which was a room. When we got to the door we heard the sound of heavy breathing coming from inside loud and distinct, as if from a man who was in a deep sleep. I walked into the room and the sound stopped. I connected it with my father who died in an accident when he was only 45. He had a lot of hair in his nostrils and his breathing was very noticeable because of this. I knew that breathing very well ... (7624)

We contacted the man's wife who confirmed the seaman's account.

Below is the case of a young man who was seen by more than two people at a time when he was living in a far away part of the country. However, the apparition was never seen by two people at exactly the same time and place.

### On ice

I was skating on ice in the open when I felt I saw my friend Erik. I thought this was some misperception and skated on. A little later I saw him again close to me, and thought again this cannot be, I must be hallucinating and tried to shake it off. I felt a strange feeling going through my body and I looked behind and saw his face. Then I felt sure he must have died. I went home and told them. They said of course that I was talking nonsense. The next morning there came a telegram announcing his death. We did not have a telephone. (7616)

Erik had been living at a tuberculosis sanatorium where he died at the age of sixteen. When we asked the percipient's half-sister, she remembered that her brother had looked shocked when he had came home and told them that Eirik had come, he had seen him and he had been so pale and poorly and all dressed in rags. She thus certified that the primary witness had told her about his experience before Erik's death was known.

She told us also that some other people had seen Erik more than once after the incident, although it was never more than one person at the same time. One incident that she experienced herself is particularly interesting:

There were more of us who were aware of his presence. He just appeared and then wandered away. I saw him more than once; usually here on the farm. There was a silage pit towards which he often walked backwards, stepped aside and disappeared into a mist ... I well remember one time, it was during winter. The sheep were grazing along the whole length of the valley. I went to gather the animals and had herded them home; was about to let them inside. But they refused to go into one of the pens, no matter how I tried to get them to do so. They just shied away, so I went to find out what was wrong. And there he stood in the doorway of the sheep shed. I told him sharply to go to God and stop wandering about here on earth.

Then he left and the sheep entered the pen. He pointed to the west, in the direction of the farm where his mother lived. She was to die of tuberculosis later that winter. (6026).

The sister believed that by pointing to the farm where his mother was living, Erik was expressing concern about his mother's health or indicating that she might soon die, which she did, although not immediately.

And finally a mother describes an incident that she experienced with her husband. He had passed away at the time of the interview and therefore it was not possible to confirm the account.

### Saw husband and two children

I lost two infants and then my husband and I have sensed them all. Before my husband died he also sensed the children and at the same time as I did.

I was at home ironing. I sensed something behind me and I was always looking back and I saw two little children, there was no doubt about it. I knew they were my children. They seemed to be about the same age they would have been had they lived. Then my husband came home from work just after five o'clock and I noticed he was always looking over his shoulder, so I said to him: "Tell me, do you see anything in here?" "It is evident" he said, "there are two little children here." (2027A)

There are other accounts with two witnesses spread throughout the book: See account numbers 424, 759, 2001, 2004, 2056, 2058, 2110, 2130, 2142, 2154, 2190, 2200, 5017, 5034, 5043, 5054, 6004, 6010, 6012, 7542, 7560 and 7612.

# 34

## INDIRECT VERIFICATION

I n some cases the informant told someone present about their experience before they received verification of the death of the encountered person.

### A graduate from the Maritime College, in his fifties

I lost my boy at sea in mid winter. He came to me in the night and I saw him, the expression on his face and everything; I saw him beside me in my bed. It was as if someone was trying to go through me. My heartbeat was terrifying. I woke my wife and we went into the sitting room, and when I stood in front of the photo of him there I collapsed. It was as if someone had pulled a rug from under my feet. I said to my wife that some terrible thing must be about to happen, and I rushed into the children's bedroom; they were fast asleep. When I had pulled myself together a little I went back to bed but felt that the same sensation was about to engulf me again and I began to pray ... (7512)

The man's wife confirmed his story. She said she remembered it well. They had discussed what happened to him over a cup of coffee after the incident occurred. Their son drowned that same night at sea. The incident occurred around two years before we interviewed the couple separately.

### Thirty year old engineer living in Njardvik.

I was at home, and was about to go to bed. A man appeared to me dressed like an officer in the US marines. He stood in front of me and was trying to talk to me. It was very strange. I did not much like this and said to him "Listen here mate, I cannot hear a word you are saying, there is no point standing there in front of me moving your mouth." Then he made a motion with his hands, a kind of sign like people make when they are going to pop out to use the phone or something, and he was gone. Then he came back with four others. These others I saw only dimly, they looked like brown columns, or like when you see people in the darkness of the night, although the room was brightly lit. When they were with him they kept very close to him and he managed to get the words across to me, speaking in Icelandic. He was against my plan concerning where I was going to study, wanted me to abandon my idea of going to Europe and go to the US instead.

He babbled on about this for some time, and I must say I did not like it one bit, the way the man was acting, although I had had some experience of this kind of thing before. I reached out my hand and said: "Listen to me now, if you have some money to pay for a trip to America, then I will go to America, but if you do not, then there is no point talking about it." Then he disappeared. It was as simple as that.

When I was telling some people about this event, a friend of mine asked what he had looked like. I gave him a detailed description, that he had been about 1.76 metres tall, aged about forty, grey haired, clean-cut, with a wide jaw, broad features, you know, a sort of roughly-hewn man ... Then this friend of mine recognised him as a man he had pulled out of the sea. There had been an accident here, to the west of Reykjanes near the Keflavik airport where they were constructing some military buildings. He was a frogman and was diving somewhere around there. A boat they were on capsized and one took a chance on swimming ashore while the others waited behind for the helicopter to collect them. He probably misjudged the rough waves among the rocks in Icelandic weather conditions and was knocked out. Two men on the shore, C.M. and S.O. ran to the scene and pulled him out, but he was dead. I understand that that must have been the man, the description fitted. The man who told me had had some dealings with him for they had been working on the same job for a long time. (7596)

We were able to interview one of the two men mentioned in the story. He confirmed that he remembered when the American had died and that he had been there when his mates were saved. He could not remember our informant telling him of his encounter with the deceased person or his description of the American. He could not remember recognising the description either. However, he pointed out that a long time had passed and at that time they worked together a great deal and therefore it may be difficult to remember single conversations that they had.

### Sixty-year old lady in Hafnarfjord.

I had sensed my husband many times before. Shortly after he died one of my daughters was staying with me. We had a glass to drink before we went to bed. We had laid down and were just about to fall asleep when we heard someone enter the house and go straight into the kitchen. The glass I had been drinking from was lifted and placed on something that made quite a loud noise. I did not say anything because I thought my daughter was asleep, but then she said, "Mother did you hear that?" I asked her to come with me to check what was going on, otherwise I would not be able to sleep. We both went into the kitchen and saw that my glass had been moved from the table and into the sink. (2058)

This woman's daughter tells of her experience here. It does not look like the accounts are of the same event:

It was more like hearing than seeing ... My father died at the age of 55. I heard noises and it sounded like the kind of noise he used to make, more purposefully than when someone fumbles to open the door and closes it again. There is a pane of glass in that door, and you hear it more than you do any of the other doors. And then there was the mirror in the hall. One night my mother and I were just sitting there when we heard someone come in and stop by the mirror ... I got a real shock; I recognised these footsteps so well. (6004A) (see also 2058 and 6002)

The daughter tells of another incident with her father.

I saw my father just a few days after he was buried. I slept in the same room as my mother. There was a chair which always stood by my father's bed, and he used to sit on it while undressing. When I had got into bed I saw him there, sitting on the chair. He was leaning forward as if he was dressing, or taking off his shoes. I did not care much for this, and every night I moved the chair to the foot of the bed, but my mother always moved it back. This went on until one night my mother asked me why I always moved the chair. So I told her what was going on, and she said that she had suspected that, although she had not seen anything herself ... I saw the whole of him – just as you would see any man sitting on a chair. I did not see him clearly. It was as if he was enveloped in some kind of white mist. (6002)

### "Hello there"

I did not know the place, had newly taken up my post as housekeeper for a man who owned a fishery in Holmavik. I was coming out of a shop at about 12 noon. I saw a woman come out of an alley, from a house where, I learned later, she had once lived. She was extremely thin, some of her molars were missing and there were deep hollows in her neck. She was very tall, high-waisted and terribly long from the waist down. She had light red hair and she doddered. She was dressed as she used to be dressed, as I was told later. I did not, at that point in time, realise that she was dead, just thought that she was mad or crazy. I looked around me, as I was beginning to get concerned. Then I saw a woman leaning over a fence looking towards us. This strengthened me in my conviction that the woman was not normal. She held out her hand, grasped my fingers hard and said: "Hello there." I looked away and after we parted I saw her walk up some steps into a house where her foster son lived. She and her husband had no children.

When I reached home I sank down and was gripped by a terrible coldness. I said: "There are only two possibilities, either ghosts or crazy people are walking about in these streets." Everyone laughed at me except the man I worked for because he himself had been clairvoyant as a child. There were siblings living in the village who had been schoolmates of mine. I went to see them, described the woman in every detail and asked, "Who is that woman?" They were amazed and said that I had given them an exact description of a woman from the village who had died a little while back. "I do not believe it" I said, for, as I had seen spirits before, I had never seen the like of this and never touched one, not one which seemed to be of flesh and blood.

The woman in question had been an active spiritualist and had said that she was going to manifest when she had passed over.

I said to the aunt of one of my schoolmates, "Will you do me a favour, and get the photo album where there is a picture of the woman, but do not tell me anything?" This was quickly done and she did as I asked. I flipped through the album until I found her and said: "That is the woman but she is plumper there." Her mother was alive and also psychic, and they took me along to see her. She said, "Yes I knew that, I had a message from her today." (5082A)

One of the siblings visited by the informant said in an interview: "The informant was a stranger in the village and was only there during the summer. I can confirm that she was telling the truth. I especially remember that I could not have described the lady as well as she did even though I had known her very well.

### The skipper from Flateyri

I was at home with my brother. He and his wife had raised a girl who had lost her mother. I looked into the hall and saw a woman walk into the room where I knew the little girl was. I sat in a chair and the doorway was quite wide. I saw her from the second she appeared from behind one door until she disappeared behind the other. A little later, I said to my sister-in-law: "Who was that woman who just walked in there?" She asked me to describe the woman and I did so. She said that it was the girl's mother; she had been dead for 10 years. (7038)

The informant's sister-in-law confirmed that the skipper had told her of the incident. She herself had been aware of the presence of the deceased lady. His description matched the knowledge she had of the woman but she had never seen her alive. She had only heard descriptions of the woman and seen a picture of her.

### In the cow shed at Vogar

I was fourteen year old and tended the cows at a farm in Vogar. I had just brought in the cows and was tying them in their booths. I was in the innermost booth and saw a woman standing in the booth of the cow that was furthest away from me. She had a dignified look and was dressed in the national costume. She walked across to the cows on the other side of the aisle, and disappeared into the wall.

In an excited mood I ran into the house and told about this. They seemed to recognise the woman.

A man we contacted who was partly raised at Vogar told us that he had often been aware of the same thing and he had often felt that he was not alone in the shed or in the house.

### A thirty year old lady from Flateyri told this story:

I was not the only person to become aware of this. It was very obviously a deceased man. I saw how he looked, but not like one sees a living person in day-to-day life, but rather as if one somehow feels and accepts that someone is there, without actually seeing them. There were two families in the house and the children were also aware of this. They often talked about the man who was there beside them. We saw him practically every day and we could almost make a joke out of it. It was as if he had become one of the family. He almost always appeared in the same place in the room; just stood there. We made it a custom to avoid that area ... I knew that his hair was dark and wavy, and that he was a handsome man with broad shoulders, but I cannot describe how I saw him. I thought he could have been about 35, in the prime of life ... We lived there from September until the following May and we saw him almost every day, always in a similar way. (7020) (see also 6012)

The informant especially mentioned one woman who had witnessed this. She lived in Bolungarvík at the time. This is her account:

### The grandfather's sister

I was along with others baking and doing things around the kitchen at Hotel Reynihlid by Lake Myvatn. We were preparing coffee for the gathering after a funeral, which was to take place that day. Both I and some others there felt that there was a presence among us, that of a deceased woman, our grandfather's sister who had been a great baker and housewife and had known her way around the house in which we were working and had worked there on special occasions. My sister was also with us and she felt the presence of this great aunt of ours even more strongly. (424) (see also 6024)

The sister of the above account said that on that occasion the women had been preparing the coffee and other refreshments for a funeral. This case is typical for sensing a presence:

I felt on and off that someone was standing behind me, sometimes as if in my way. I thought first that my brother's daughter was teasing me. But it was not so. Then I felt that this was a certain woman who had died six years ago. Then the presence suddenly disappeared. The man who was being buried on this occasion had been the brother of this woman and they had always been particularly close. (6024)

### The man with the hat

My grandmother lived in a wooden house on the second floor. On the first floor there was a timber storage or a shop There was a rather dim stairway leading up to the second floor. On one occasion when I was going to see my grandmother, a man walked up the stairs ahead of me, the staircase made a creaking, hollow sound. Naturally I bade him good day but was puzzled by his rudeness, for he did not answer. My grandmother was in the kitchen which was at the end of the hallway. I rushed in and told her how rude this man had been, not returning my greeting. "Oh my God, it is the man with the hat" she said and hurried up to the loft apartment. I had no idea what was going on. "There is not anyone there, I know they went on vacation. No one went up to the loft, it is just the man that I have also seen," said my grandmother when she came back downstairs.

She had often seen this man and spoken of him. Then I come there and saw him clearly. He did not answer me, and avoided looking me in the eye. That man was very real to me. I had no idea who he was.

I often see phenomena of this kind and am very psychic. I have also seen apparitions of living people just before I meet them. I can often predict the death of people. (2029)

The grandmother had passed away so it was not possible to check the account with her.

### Thorbjorg's husband

I was down in the cellar finishing the laundry and was washing out the boiler. I heard someone coming down the cellar steps but did not pay any attention to this. Then, I heard someone coming along the corridor to the door. I looked round but saw no one and carried on with my work. I glanced away towards the washing machine, which was to my right and saw a man standing there.

I saw his feet first. He was wearing boots, high leather ones up to his calves and black trousers. I do not think the style is in fashion now, rather something from a long time ago. The cut of the trousers and the back pocket which had a flap you could button from the outside, like in the old days. I very slowly ran my eyes upwards and saw he was dressed in a blue sweater, English style, like many seamen wore here, and maybe still do ... I continued to look, and when I got to his shoulders he vanished right in front of my eyes. I did not get to see his head. I began to wonder what he was trying to convey to me and thought that his appearance most likely meant that a death was imminent; that must be what it meant. I tried to think who owned such a sweater and remembered two people, but he was neither of them.

The morning after I went down into the cellar again and I did not sense anyone, but heard someone saying from behind my right shoulder: "I am Thorbjorg's husband, I came here yesterday." That was it – nothing else. After a while my daughter's son came down to me and said: "My great grandmother died yesterday". His great grandmother was Thorbjorg and her husband had died in the prime of life in England. I did not know him; had never seen him or spoken to him. (7550)

The son of this woman from Reykjavík confirmed in an interview that his mother had told him when she first saw the stranger, but not when she saw him in the morning. Her daughter's son could not be contacted.

We have tried to present each account only once, although some of the accounts easily could have been placed in different chapters. In this chapter we actually include some accounts which have already been presented before. The following account can be found in the chapter on suicide and manslaughter and is therefore presented here for the second time as it is particularly relevant for this chapter.

### All bloody in the face

I worked in a sanatorium. There was a patient there who was suffering from a mild depression. I tried to liven up his stay by light-hearted chatting. I said that he could visit us, me and my husband, for they were both from the same district and they could indulge in some nostalgic memories from the place of their youth. He agreed happily with all this and I said to him: "You promise to come tomorrow then?" and he replied "Yes, yes I promise." The night after, I woke up feeling as if all the strength had been sucked out of me, I could not move. I suddenly became aware of the bedroom door opening and on the threshold I saw the man from the sanatorium. His face was all covered in blood. I stared at this for a little while and could say nothing – nor could I move. Then he disappeared and I had the feeling that he closed the door after him. I came to my senses and called out to my husband saying:"I could swear something has happened at the sanatorium." In the morning I rang down to work and asked the nurse whether everything was all right with that man. I said I had seen him with blood on his face. "Yes and that is not all," answered the nurse "he committed suicide during the night." (5076)

We contacted the woman's husband shortly after the interview. He said he remembered the incident well. His wife had woken him up in the night and described her experience just as she told us about it. That was before they knew anything about the tragic incident that had occurred. The post-mortem report described two severe head injuries and a broken skull.

# 35

## REPRESENTATIVE SURVEYS
## ON APPROACHES TO
## THE AFTERLIFE

W E have been describing and discussing people's reports of encounters with the deceased. Let us now turn our attention to some facts regarding the belief in life after death, in Iceland and in other countries. The results of the 1975 survey revealed that 68% of our representative national sample believed in life after death whereas disbelievers were a clear minority, with only 7% considering life after death unlikely or impossible. A few years later the European Values Survey revealed that belief in the afterlife is more common in Iceland than in the culturally related and neighbouring Scandinavian countries where about half of the population believes in life after death. The belief in afterlife in Iceland (71%) resembles more what nationwide surveys reveal for the USA (81%) than for Scandinavia.

The European Human Values Survey is a remarkable survey as it allows international comparisons between numerous countries. It was organised by scholars in various fields and assesses the values and views of Europeans. The original purpose was to find out how much the European nations are alike, and how much they differ. It was first conducted around 1980 in Western Europe and around 1990, 1999 and 2008-2010 in Eastern as well as Western Europe. The author took part in the preparation of the survey in Iceland.

The 2008-2010 results reveal that about half of the populations of the European countries believe in life after death. However, there are great national differences; The Irish, Poles, Italians and Icelanders showing the highest degree of belief in life after death, 71-74%. The Germans (only after unification of East and West Germany) and the Danes being lowest (31-36%) among the West-European countries. A representative selection of survey results is given in table 14.

In the published results of the Human Values Survey, those who answered with "I do not know" were not included in the calculations (Inglehart etc. 1998, 2004). It was assumed that 'don't know' answers show uncertainty whether to choose yes or no. This kind of analysis gives higher values for yes and no than when the 'don't knows' are included.

From the beginning of time humans must have speculated about whether anything continues on after death. The simplest idea is that consciousness, mind, spirit, soul, or whatever name we choose to call the life we feel within us, is dissolved and extinguished forever at the moment of death. The opposite belief is that our consciousness lives on in some from after we die. From ancient times we also have the idea that we will be born again and have lived before we were born into our present bodily existence. Let us look at table 14 to see how these approaches are present in our time.

**Table 14. Percentage of people who believe in life after death and reincarnation in a selection of European countries, according to the Human Values Survey 2008-2009.**

| | Life after death | Reincarnation | Believers in life after death also believing in reincarnation |
|---|---|---|---|
| **Western Europe** | | | |
| Ireland | 74 | 31 | 42 |
| Italy | 71 | 19 | 27 |
| Austria | 61 | 29 | 47 |
| Greece | 60 | 17 | 28 |
| Great Britain | 55 | 28 | 51 |
| Switzerland | 53 | 28 | 55 |
| Holland | 51 | 19 | 34 |
| Portugal | 51 | 31 | 60 |
| Spain | 50 | 23 | 46 |
| France | 43 | 23 | 48 |
| Germany | 31 | 18 | 58 |

**Northern Europe**

| | | | |
|---|---|---|---|
| Iceland | 71 | 36 | 52 |
| Finland | 50 | 25 | 51 |
| Norway | 46 | 18 | 33 |
| Sweden | 46 | 23 | 54 |
| Denmark | 36 | 18 | 44 |

**Eastern Europe**

| | | | |
|---|---|---|---|
| Rumania | 74 | 22 | 30 |
| Poland | 73 | 17 | 23 |
| Lithuania | 69 | 37 | 54 |
| Slovakia | 66 | 13 | 20 |
| Croatia | 59 | 16 | 25 |
| Ukraine | 51 | 37 | 73 |
| Latvia | 50 | 42 | 84 |
| Russia | 46 | 33 | 72 |
| Belarus | 44 | 31 | 70 |
| Slovenia | 36 | 19 | 53 |
| Hungary | 35 | 23 | 66 |
| Serbia | 34 | 23 | 68 |
| Estonia | 33 | 31 | 94 |
| Czech Republic | 31 | 18 | 58 |

The mean for the whole of Europe is 52% believing in the after-life. If we split Europe between the Western and Eastern part (former communist countries), we find the West-Europeans slightly higher with 56% and the East-Europeans lower with 50%. The difference is probably due to attempts in the communist era to suppress religion in Eastern Europe. Of individual countries Ireland, Rumania, Poland, Italy and Iceland are high above the average, whereas the British and the Swiss are amongst many who hover around the mean. Way down are the Danes, Germans (after unification) and the Czechs, again to mention just a few.

It is intesting to look at the relatively – perhaps unexpectedly - high figures on belief in reincarnation, especially if we keep in mind that reincarnation is definitely not one of the dogmas of the Christian Church and is considered a non-Christian belief. Like belief in an afterlife, belief in reincarnation also varies greatly among the European countries, from 13% to 36%. We notice, probably with some astonishment, the high percentage of those who belief in life after death who also believe in rebirth. It is way above half in some countries. Among the moderates, like the British, full half of those who belief in afterlife also believe in reincarnation. That is certainly not in line with the tenets of the Christian Churches, Anglican, Catholic or Protestant, nor is it in line with the dominant thinking of the scientific establishment (Haraldsson, 2006).

In table 15 we present figures from North and South America and three Asian countries. The figures are from the World Survey which grew out the European Values Survey, the European Values survey being older. In the Americas we find much higher figures than in Europe. Particularly prominent is the high belief in reincarnation among Brazilians where 80 percent of those who believe in life after death also believe in reincarnation.

**Table 15. Percentage of people who believe in life after death and reincarnation, for a selection of countries in the Americas and Asia, according to the the Human Values and World Values Surveys 1999-2002.**

|  | Life after death | Reincarnation | Believers in life after death also believing in reincarnation |
|---|---|---|---|
| **America** | | | |
| Chile | 82 | 49 | 60 |
| United States | 81 | 25 | 31 |
| Mexico | 76 | 43 | 57 |
| Canada | 73 | 32 | 43 |
| Brazil | 71 | 57 | 80 |
| Argentina | 63 | 39 | 62 |
| | | | |
| **Asia** | | | |
| Turkey | 90 | 54 | 60 |
| India | 66 | 92 | ? |
| Japan | 51 | 50 | 98 |

Two Canadian scholars made an interesting multi-dimensional study of people's approaches and beliefs about the hereafter, and developed a special Afterdeath Belief Scale to measure it. They write that "core variations in post-mortem beliefs can be described in terms of the fate of consciousness (awareness), identity (memory and personality) and physicality (the body) beyond the death event" (Burris and Bailey, 2009). Consciousness is the determining factor; if it continues, there is life after death, if not, there is annihilation or extinction.

If consciousness survives it opens up the important question of the fate of memory and personality after the great transition. Does memory and personality fully survive, or only certain parts or traces of it? Our cases indicate that much of it survives. It is also conceivable that identity is lost and consciousness flows into a sea of conscious life (global consciousness?) and loses its individuality, but continues to exist as a purely spiritual essence. The European Values Survey did not ask their participants about their views on what survives after death so we will leave these questions here.

A study conducted by two theology professors at the University of Iceland (Björnsson and Petursson, 1990) enquired after people´s views about a life after this life. Most people chose the option that "something takes over after death, but nobody knows what that will be".

There are two Christian theories on what happens to us after we die. In one people go after death, "straight to heaven or to hell, depending on how prepared they are for death, and can never return from either place", to quote an Icelandic clergyman (Jonasson, 1961, p.419). This theory is harks back to the words spoken by Christ to one of the robbers who was crucified beside him; "Today shalt thou be with me in paradise" (St. Luke, 23, 43).

In the other version we live on after death in a dreamless sleep until the end of time, when we rise again and are judged and given life in a new body to live with God. This is the resurrection of the dead, and is described in the apostle Paul´s writings to the Corinthians (ch.15, 35ff). In this view there emerges a new physicality, as a resurrected body in a heavenly abode. Or alternatively, in non-Christian religions, a new physicality is formed through rebirth, by being born into physical and bodily existence again. This, our surveys show, is commonly believed today, as it has been throughout history in various parts of the world.

There is not a general consensus amongst Christian Churches and scholars which theory on life after death is the right one. In Islam we find similar beliefs but also exeptions among some groups who believe in rebirth such as the Alevis (at least 15 millions in Turkey and Syria) and the Druze (half a million in Lebanon and Syria).

Belief in rebirth or reincarnation is predominant among Buddists and Hindus. According to this belief we live on in the world of the dead for some time after death. After that we are reborn and begin a new life in the material world just as we lived on earth before we were born.

Before the time of Christianity this belief was widespread among Greeks, Celts, and Germanic and Nordic peoples. It is described in the writings of Plato and Julius Caesar (on the Gallic Wars); in pre-Christian Irish poems, in the works by Appianus from Alexandria about the Germanic people, and in poems of the Nordic Edda.

If we jointly analyse the questions on life after death and reincarnation in the European Values Survey, we get a more comprehensive view of contemporary approaches to the afterlife. How many reject any form of personal survival and believe that we are extinguished forever when we die? Burris and Bailey call them Extinctionists. How many are the doubting Thomases - the Agnostics - who think we can never know what happens when we die? How widespread is the Christian kind of belief that we come into existence when we are born and after death we continue to live forever after? These are the Immortalists. Finally, how widespread is the ancient belief that we have lived before we were born, we will continue to live after we die and will be born again into physical bodily existance? Burris and Bailey call them Reincarnationists.

**Table 16. The percentage of people in selected countries who believe that death is the end of our existence (extinctionists), do not know what to believe (agnostics), believe in a Christian kind of eternal life (immortalists), or that we have lived before and will be born again (reincarnationists).**

| | Extinctionists | Agnostics | Immortalists | Reincarnationists |
|---|---|---|---|---|
| **Western Europe:** | | | | |
| Ireland | 18 | 16 | 41 | 25 |
| Italy | 20 | 18 | 45 | 17 |
| Iceland | 24 | 10 | 34 | 33 |
| Austria | 29 | 15 | 31 | 25 |
| Greece | 29 | 18 | 37 | 15 |
| Great Britain | 34 | 15 | 30 | 21 |
| Switzerland | 34 | 17 | 25 | 24 |
| Spain | 37 | 16 | 27 | 20 |
| Portugal | 37 | 16 | 20 | 27 |
| Sweden | 37 | 26 | 20 | 17 |

| | | | | |
|---|---|---|---|---|
| Netherlands | 41 | 11 | 31 | 18 |
| France | 51 | 6 | 14 | 22 |
| Denmark | 53 | 10 | 20 | 17 |
| Germany | 56 | 15 | 14 | 16 |
| **Eastern Europe** | | | | |
| Poland | 21 | 10 | 53 | 15 |
| Ukraine | 28 | 24 | 19 | 29 |
| Latvia | 31 | 17 | 17 | 35 |
| Russia | 33 | 23 | 18 | 26 |
| Belarus | 41 | 23 | 11 | 24 |
| Bulgaria | 41 | 23 | 11 | 24 |
| Estonia | 49 | 16 | 8 | 27 |
| Hungary | 54 | 7 | 17 | 22 |
| Czech Republic | 54 | 18 | 13 | 16 |
| **Mean of 44 European countries (N = 62.223)** | 36 | 15 | 28 | 21 |

In table 16 we show the results for several European countries. Europe as a whole is about equally divided between believers in survival (49%) and those who are not sure about it (51%). Over a third (36%) reject the survial idea completely and 15% are agnostics. We find that 28% are immortalists and thus comply with the dominant Christian view, but a surprising 21% are reincarnationists. The last number is interesting and not in line with the dogmas of the Christian Churches. This means that 43% of those who believe that we continue to live after the dissolution of our physical body, also believe in reincarnation. In our Western culture the concept of reincarnation is a major concept of continued life. Of survival believers, only 57% hold to the official Christian view.

We do not have surveys on these issues going far back in time. It is not unreasonable to assume that with the emergence of the physical and biological sciences, particularly in the 19th century, the believers took a considerable, if not heavy, toll. Then reincarnation was either more resistent, and probably also received some support from the eastern religions as they became more widely know in Europe, and people became more aware of their pre-Christian past.

Among the European nations there is obviously considerable variability. The Catholic countries tend to be greater believers than the

Protestant countries, and Anglican Britain is somewhere in between. There is only a slight difference between Western and Eastern Europe when we combine the results for all participating countries and not just those listed in table 16. The percentage of extinctionists is the same (36%), there are slightly more agnostics in Eastern Europe, 17% versus 14% in the Western part. Immortalists are more numerous in Western Europe (30%) than in the East (25%), and the reincarnationists are slightly more in the East (22% versus 20%). Because of the huge samples these differences are significant but such significances are not very meaningful when the difference in percentages is so small.

# 36

## BELIEF IN LIFE AFTER DEATH AMONG PARTICIPANTS

OBVIOUSLY the attitudes towards an afterlife were very positive, or became very positive, among the 449 participants who shared with us their experiences: 91% said they believed in the afterlife and only 7% were not certain about it. Oddly enough we obtained accounts from three men and one woman who said they did not believe in life after death but nevertheless reported the following experiences:

### Nightmare

I took a nap in the afternoon and had a terrible nightmare. I was half asleep / half awake and was calling for help in the dream. Then someone grabbed me by the shoulder and told me to wake up. I was wide awake in a flash and saw an old woman, my grandmother, who was deceased, dissappear. (6005)

### In the old living quarters

Behind the farmhouse where I lived at Hofteig in Jökuldal, which was made from wood, was an old living room. It was long and quite wide but had not been used for a long time as a main room but it was used to boil ‚slátur' (a form of Icelandic black pudding or sausage) and to make and keep all sorts of things. I was probably about seven or eight years old when they decided to put a new door on the old living room. They put the door in a wall that was about 2 metres thick. The wall had probably got thicker through the years but the house must have been ancient.

I did not know until later that many of my siblings had heard singing in the wall after they made the door. One day, when I was twelve years old, they were washing wool in the stream, which was some distance from the farm. There was nobody at home. I remember, it was about five o'clock, the sun was shining bright and the weather as good as it could possibly get. I was sent home in a hurry to get more soap. I was going to take a short cut through the old living room since there was nothing to fear there but as soon as I got to the door I heard singing to the left of me. I stopped suddenly and realised that it was not an unusual sound although it is not quite as it should be. I stopped and listened and I could hear three female voices singing. I stood there for quite a long time and listened, I had never heard such singing, I have heard similar voices since but never exactly the same... I stood there and listened and the voices started moving away from me. Then I thought to myself that I was not supposed to hang about, I was sent for soap and had been told to hurry. I set off but the voices followed me and that gave me such a terrible fright, I realised that it was something that was not supposed to be there and I ran back up to the stream without soap. I have never heard it since. (7024)

**My father's father**

When my grandfather died I was living in the east of the country. I went into a house, an old house where my grandfather and grandmother used to live. That's when I saw the old man, right in front of me, in a hallway of the old house, for a few seconds. It was as if we had looked at each other, I saw the face very clearly. I did not perceive anything other than just what I saw. I cannot remember having experienced any other sensations. But afterwards, when I thought about it, I was most surprised that I had not been scared. I thought you would get so scared when you saw something like that... (7608)

**Wearing dark clothes**

I have seen a man here in my house and so have both my son and my husband. All three of us have seen the same man. We see everything but the head and we can see that he is wearing dark clothes. When we are upstairs in the evening we can hear somebody switching the lights on and off in the rooms and in the hall. When we are sitting in the kitchen we can see his shadow move across the floor in the hallway. He is about average in height... (7612)

Not everybody agreed that having an encounter with the deceased had increased their belief in life after death. Perhaps this was usually because their belief was already strong before the experience. Nevertheless, 38% reported that their experience had increased their belief in life after death, whereas for almost half (45%) it changed nothing.

# 37

# CRUCIAL FEATURES OF
# AFTERLIFE ENCOUNTERS

W E have in the previous chapters discussed important characteristics of encounters with the deceased. They suggest that some of the experiences may be something more than a mere imagination or hallucination. Let us briefly look at how these characteristics appear in our collection. Most of what follows is difficult to explain through normal means.

1. In our collection, 28% of the appearing deceased had suffered a violent death. However, only 8% of the Icelandic population suffer a violent death. In Stevenson's (1982) analysis of such incidents in *Phantasms of the Living*, 28% of the cases turned out to involve persons who had suffered violent deaths. In our collection we find the same result. The findings stem from two different countries and the cases are collected over a century apart. Are we not dealing here with universal human experiences? There is now substantial evidence for this from different countries. In many instance in Iceland as well as in Great Britain the experiencing persons did not even know about the death of the person that was encountered. This may be most easily explained as due to a high motivation to communicate by the prematurely deceased person. It seems that the departed thrust his or her image on the mind and senses of the perceiver.

2. Statistically an extraordinary high number of incidents occur within 24 hours of the death of the perceived person. Why are so many more perceived or encountered on the day they die, than at other times? In our study, such cases made up 14% of the whole case collection. By chance, this number should be much, much lower, since the incidents that happen within a year from the time of death should be spread equally over the 365 days of the year, and be below 1%. In many of these cases the experiencing persons was not aware of that the person had died or was likely to die. Again, comparable results were found in British studies conducted more than a century earlier. In this fact we see the motivation of the deceased at work, apparently eager to communicate with the living close to the time of death. To do that the communicator must exist and hence exist somewhere. This is an argument for continued life after death and for the existence of the alternative reality that William James wonders about.

3. In foreign data collections, sometimes more than one person witnessed the same experience at the same time and in the same place. We also find examples of this in our collection. Collective experiences make the theory of hallucination less likely to be true, and they support the theory that there is something real in these experiences.

4. The informants sometimes perceived a person they had never seen. From their description of this person's appearance the deceased person was identified. Many such examples are found in our data collection, and are scattered throughout the book.

5. Sometimes the informant discovered something during the experience that he or she had no knowledge of before experiencing the incident. Later, or following some enquiries, this observation was found to be true. This is also found in our data.

6. In some incidents, the appearances of the deceased are obviously purposeful. This can be found in our collection, for example, in the accounts in the chapter "Warnings and rescue at sea". One of these examples is account number 7592, which came from a nationally known leader of seamen. The lady who appeared saved him from drowning. This looks like a supernatural intervention. Since there

are many such cases it seems farfetched to explain them away as illusions, imaginations, or intentional exaggerations. Such cases have also been investigated in other countries in the past few decades (Osis, 1986; Haraldsson, 1987).

The reality of apparitions of the dead, encounters with the deceased, phantoms or ghosts, has remained a puzzle. People who experience them instinctively feel that they represent something that is not of this world although the responses can be quite variable. Those who have not experienced it will often reject it as imaginary, joke about it, fear it, or have an inner conviction that the essence of it is not real.

When all the accounts we have collected are considered, it seems impossible to reject all of them as deceptions and mistaken perceptions. Something real is there, at least in some of the accounts. The main characteristics of these occurrences, summarised above, indicate that they do indeed have some basis in reality. Furthermore, these major characteristics have also been found in China (Emmons, 1982; McClenon, 1988), in the United States (Guggenheim, 1995; Archangel 2005), in Great Britain (Gurney, Myers, & Podmore 1886; Green and McCreery 1975), Germany (Schmied-Knittle 2003) and in other European countries (Bozzano 1919; Flammarion 1922-23). These characteristics are independent of whether the cases occurred a century ago, or in our time. The author hopes that the great number of cases presented here make it easier for the reader to reach an informed opinion of these experiences that have accompanied humanity down through the ages.

# 38

# ARGUMENTS FOR AND
# AGAINST AN AFTERLIFE

A RGUMENTS against the afterlife go back to Greek philosophers, as are the arguments for it. The generally pro-survival Plato wonders if the soul could be like a tune that is played on a musical instrument. If the strings get broken the tune comes to an end.

The Roman Epicurean philosopher Lucretius Carus (99-55 BC) succinctly formulated, two thousand years ago, the main naturalistic arguments against survival:

- Mind matures and ages with growth and decay of the body.
- Wine and disease of the body can effect the mind
- The body is stunned by a blow.
- If the soul is immortal why does it not have memories of its previous existence?

These arguments are worthy of serious consideration. The opposing view is that mind and body are separate but interacting entities. The mind or soul can under normal circumstances only be manifested to the extent that is made possible by the condition of the body. This has to involve some kind of dualism.

Up into the 19th century there were only philosophical or religious arguments for survival. This changed with the arrival of spiritualism and psychical research around or shortly after the middle of the 19th century. Thereafter we see empirical arguments emerging with the study of mediumistic communications and extraordinary physical phenomena occurring in mediumship. This was followed by studies of apparitions of the dead and death-bed visions.

After the middle of the 20th century two further areas of research opened up, near-death experiences and investigations of cases in which children claim memories of episodes from a past life. These investigations have substantially strengthened the arguments for a life beyond the bodily existence. Studies of numinous or mystical experiences, such as those discussed by William James, should also be mentioned. They usually bring a deep conviction of an all-pervasive, superior, non-physical reality and life beyond the bodily one.

With the researches of the 19th and 20th centuries there emerged considerable empirical findings that are relevant for the question of life after death. Even Lucretius would have had a partial answer to his question about memories of previous existences. Scientifically these findings are obviously indicators rather than proofs, but they still represent an important step forward.

In this area of research there are still many unresolved methodological issues and open questions. Among them is the ongoing debate about the merits of the survival hypothesis versus the so-called super-psi hypothesis, which assumes that all evidence for life after death is explainable as due to the psychic abilities of the perceiving individual. This would mean that the experiences of our participants could all be explained by a psychic gift they are assumed to have, rather than to stem from deceased persons that appear to them. The author will not get into this beyond expressing his view that he finds that the super-psi hypothesis fails to adequately explain the motivational (such as expressed purpose) and behavioural features that are an essential part of many apparitional cases. For an in-depth analysis presenting further arguments against the super-psi hypothesis the reader is referred to Rousseau (2012).

The fact is that now – in the author's view - there are from different areas of empirical research, rational reasons for taking the possibility of life beyond bodily existence seriously. The time has passed when we only had philosophical or religious arguments.

Further research – far too little unfortunately, and rather sporadic - is being conducted in some of these areas, particularly on near-death experiences, deathbed-visions and claimed past-life memories. The author has been deeply involved in investigating deathbed-visions and past-life memories. It is beyond the purpose of this book to deal with them extensively, but let us mention a few relevant characteristics.

**Deathbed visions.** Their essential features can be thus summarized: While fully aware of their surroundings some people see, shortly before they die, deceased friends and relatives. The deceased persons often say they have come to take the dying person away into the realm of afterlife. These patients become willing to die and become "ready to go". Such experiences often occur to patients when no normal medical explanation can be found that might cause them to hallucinate (Osis and Haraldsson, 1977; Fenwick & Fenwick, 2008).

**Near-death experiences.** These are their essential features: They occur mostly in life-threatening situations. The persons may feel they are dead, and are separated from or out of their bodies. They may see the physical body that they are separated from. These experiences are often accompanied by feelings of peace and calm and may have transcendental features. A brilliant light is sometimes seen at the end of a tunnel. While in this state, the person may encounter deceased friends, relatives and/or "beings of light". This feature resembles what takes place in deathbed-visions. For reviews see Greyson, 2012; Kelly, Greyson, and Kelly, 2007.

**Memories of a past life:** Prof. Ian Stevenson at the University of Virginia started up a new field of inquiry half a century ago. He began to investigate claims that some children appear to remember episodes from a past life. In the course of half a century he investigated in great detail some two thousand cases in many countries and wrote numerous articles and books about his findings. The author has also investigated over ninety cases of this kind and found the same basic features as Stevenson did. These features can be summarised thus: The child claims to have memories of a past life. Most children talk about remembering how they died, mostly how they suffered a violent death. Many have phobias and fears related to their memories of death in the previous life. Many are gifted, do well in school and have a larger vocabulary than their peers. Some have birthmarks/deformities or physiological features that they relate to their past-life experiences. They often say that their parents are not their real parents and want to find their previous home. In rare cases there is evidence of skills or knowledge of how to do something that a child would not normally have. For reviews see Stevenson, 2001; Tucker, 2005 and Haraldsson, 2012.

We should also mention **terminal lucidity**. These are cases of un-expected return of mental clarity and memory shortly before death in patients suffering from severe psychiatric and neurological disorders. They might not have been able to communicate with people around them for a long period of time. This is an important but so far largely a neglected area of research (Nahm et al., 2011; Nahm, 2012).

All these areas are open for further research and hold promise of new findings that might shed more light on the question of life after death.

# 39

## PERSONAL EXPERIENCES

FTER lectures on apparitions and encounters with the deceased I am frequently asked: Have you had any experience of those who have died? The thoughtful reader is also likely to ask if the author has had any experiences of the kind that we have been discussing. What are his personal views of the possibility of an afterlife? Such experiences - or lack of them - might cause him to have biases for or against. These are therefore reasonable questions to ask.

Let us first discuss personal experiences. Two are memorable from my student days. They will be related in the first person as the participants did:

In the mid 1950s I spent some months in Copenhagen as a student. I rented a room in the apartment of an elderly lady who lived alone in a large apartment house. After I had gone to bed in the evening and turned off the light, I suddenly felt, like perceiving it with my inner eye, that an elderly man opened the door just enough to look into the room to see who was there. I saw his face clearly and he was dressed in dark clothes or overcoat. After a while this inner vision faded away as the man seemed to vanish. This happened a few times on different nights. I was not entirely at ease about this but kept my peace of mind and soon fell asleep afterwards. This was a very vivid experience as if it was thrust upon my mind. In those days I was certainly not thinking about experiences of this kind nor did I have any particular interest in them. I was not very communicative in those years and never asked the old lady if she was a widow – which seemed likely - or who had lived in the room before me. If this had happened a few years later I would have asked her and wanted to see a photo of her late husband or get a description of the person who had lived in the room before me. After that I would have told her of my experience. Perhaps this was someone concerned about her well-being. This was not a remarkable case in any way and might not even have fulfilled our criteria for a case. No attempt was made to verify it, but it was interesting for me. Could it have been hypnagogic, that is, associated with sleep onset? It did not appear that way to me. I felt fully alert and awake. It was also a bit odd that it occurred exactly the same way on more than one occasion.

The following year I was again in Copenhagen for a few months. I rented a room in Öster Farimagsgade in the older part of the city. It was on the first floor, a few steps up from the street level. Two ladies had a sewing repair shop in the two rooms facing the street. In the middle of the flat was a short corridor with a door to a kitchen and my room both of which were facing the backyard. The ladies went home around six and I never saw them later in the evening or at weekends.

One night I heard some people going around in the corridor and the kitchen. I assumed this were the ladies. After a while I thought I should say hello to them for they were always very nice to me. I opened my door but to my surprise there was no light in the corridor and dead silence, nor did I hear anyone walking through the outer corridor towards the entrance. I found this quite strange but did not then think further about it and went back to my studies. Later in the evening, I heard again that there were some people in the corridor and the kitchen. This time I listened carefully to convince myself of what I was hearing correctly. There was no doubt that the noise came from across my wall and from the other side of the door. Strangely, I was not able to distinguish any words. After I had listened for a while I decided to open the door again. I did so with a quick jerk. Again there was no light in the corridor or kitchen, and quite suddenly there was complete silence. I was quite struck by this.

What was this? Was it a misperception? It definitely did not appear that way to me. Was it some kind of an echo of sounds from a distant past? Were former inhabitants of this old house making me aware of them?

An hour or so later I went to bed. I slept on a sofa that served me also as a bed. I turned off the light and soon fell asleep. When I had slept a very short while I was suddenly thrown out of my sleep by a strong blinding light that shone directly into my eyes. It took me a few seconds to orient myself and turn my head away from the blinding light. Then I realized what had happened. I had been lying on my right side facing a chair and on it stood a light that I used on my bicycle. It had been switched on and was directed straight into my eyes. This light was never switched on at any other time during my stay in Copenhagen unless I did it myself.

I am not easily upset, but this time I was a bit shaken, especially when I thought about the two strange events that happened earlier in the evening. I could not help connecting the three phenomena that occurred to me and which only occurred that one night. Somehow I intuitively felt this was not of this world.

Not of this world? That is the question that begs for an answer in many cases throughout this book. Is there another sphere of existence that we only sense briefly and vaguely on rare occasions? Is it like what William James, the father of American psychology, asked and wondered about? If it is, then "what we call visible nature, or this world, must be but a veil and surface-show whose full meaning resides in a supplementary unseen or other world" (James, 1895).

In my early youth I had had some vivid numinous or mystical experiences of the kind that William James described in his classic book "The Varieties of Religious Experiences". They deeply influenced my sense of reality and made me more open to the possible existence of an otherworldly and transcendental living realm or reality. It might be "just around the corner" and a part of us. Deathbed visions and near-death experiences occur at the threshold between life and death, and in them we often find awareness of the same kind of 'deeper' reality. More research in these areas holds the promise of important further insights into the nature of persons and reality.

In the previous chapter we briefly reviewed the major findings of some survival research, and the author's substantial and prolonged involvement in some areas. There certainly are considerable limitations and pitfalls in some of this research and many buts and ifs one could raise. Nevertheless, on the whole the author finds in this substantial body of research increasingly suggestive - if not convincing - evidence for life beyond the physical body.

# Appendix A

## Comparison of the Two Surveys

P ARTICIPANTS who shared their experiences with us originally took part in either of two surveys. Firstly, 128 participants were obtained via a random representative survey that was conducted in 1975 on psychic experiences and beliefs (Haraldsson, 1978). Secondly, 321 participants represent a self-selected sample that was obtained by placing a brief questionnaire in five popular magazines. All these 449 persons reported a personal experience of a deceased person when they were in a waking state.

### The 1975 representative sample.

We interviewed all persons that could be reached in the Reykjavik area and in Akureyri who had given an affirmative answer to the question on an encounter with the deceased. A questionnaire was constucted for this purpose. Face-to-face audio-recorded interviews followed. First, participants were asked to describe what had happened. Then we went through the questions on the questionnaire. Two senior students conducted the interviews under the supervision of the author. A few years later we interviewed participants from the rest of the country, then using a revised and more detailed questionnaire with 79 questions, instead of the 40 questions which were used in the original interviews. This questionnaire is reprinted in Appendix B.

A total of 128 participants from the representative sample gave us accounts of their experiences. Some persons could not be reached or

declined an interview, and a few reported experiences that did not ful-
fill our criteria, such as experiences in dreams or with mediums. These
were excluded as we only collected cases of direct personal experience
in a waking state.

Participants who had more than one experience to report, were asked
to recount the most vivid and memorable incident. In a few instances
we recorded more than one account from the same person, but the ad-
ditional accounts have not been included in our analyses.

### A larger self-selected sample

Five popular magazines with widely differing readership allowed
us in 1980 to include a brief questionnaire containing the following
question: "Have you ever in a waking state perceived the presence of
a dead person?" Those who did were encouraged to fill in their name
and phone number so that we could contact them. A reply envelope
was included that could be posted free of charge.

These magazines were the seamen's magazine *Aegir; Víkingur*, for the
fishing industry; *Morgunn*, published by the Icelandic Society for Psychical Research; *Gangleri*, published by the Theosophical Society; and
*Heima er best*, which has a wide distribution in rural Iceland. Readers
of the these magazines included very different groups of people.

Around 9000 people subscribed to these magazines. We received
some 700 positive responses. Three senior psychology students conducted the interviews, this time by phone, as the costly face-to-face
interviews were beyond our means. As in the earlier interviews the
respondants were first asked to describe their experience and then we
went with them through our long questionnaire. They were always
asked if another person was with them when they had their experience
and if he or she had shared their observation. We made every effort to
trace and interview such witnesses. Some participants were contacted
a second time to obtain further information.

After interviewing over 350 respondents we concluded our survey.
The interviews were conducted in the years 1980-1986. It took several
months for three interviewers to conduct the interviews. 100 participants responded to the shorter questionnaire and gave cases that fulfilled our criteria, and 349 were interviewed with the longer version.

A total of 449 cases were collected, 128 from the random representative sample and 321 from the self-selected sample of magazine readers. Some 400 accounts are briefly described in this book. At the end
of each account is number in brackets. Account numbers 2-1053 stem

from the representative sample of 1975; 2000-2216 were from readers of *Morgunn*; 5000-5794 from readers of *Gangleri*; 7000-7048 from *Aegir*; 7500-7636 from *Vikingur*, and 6000-6026 from readers of *Heima er best* .

## Gender, age and education

When the second wave of interviews were conducted, we aimed for an equal number of men and women. In the representative sample a greater number of women than men reported encounters with the dead. A good response from the predominently male readers of the magazines for fishermen and sailors enabled us to obtain overall an equal number of accounts from men and women.

The participants were born in the years 1884 to 1961, and 65% of them between 1920 and 1939. The great majority of our informants (72%) lived in the Reykjavík area, and the rest in rural areas or towns across the country. It may be added that in the 1975 survey, 35% of those from the Reykjavik area said they had encountered a deceased person compared to 25% of those from the countryside.

Of the total sample, 29% had only a primary school education, 56% had attended a secondary school, and 13% had obtained some university education. These figures are fairly representative for the educational level of this generation.

**Table 17. Comparison of some characteristics of after death encounters in the random (128) and self-selected sample (321).**

| | Random sample | Self-selected sample |
|---|---|---|
| **Senses** | % | % |
| Visual | 48 | 49 |
| Auditory | 13 | 12 |
| Olfactory | 4 | 4 |
| Tactile | 4 | 4 |
| More than one sense | 17 | 22 |
| Sensing a presence | 15 | 9 |
| **Cause of death** | | |
| Illness | 71 | 72 |
| Violent death | 29 | 28 |
| **Relationship with the deceased** | | |
| Family | 57 | 49 |
| Friendship | 14 | 8 |
| Co-worker/ Colleague | 2 | 3 |
| Acquaintance | 15 | 11 |
| Stranger | 13 | 30 |
| **Gender** | | |
| Male | 80 | 66 |
| Female | 20 | 34 |

## Comparison of characteristics in the random and self-selected sample

Could there be a radical difference between the two samples? Let us have a look at some of the characteristics of the incidents that have been discussed in the first chapters of this book. Generally speaking there is only a minor difference between the two samples. For example, visions make up 48% of the experiences in the random sample and 49% of the self-selected sample. We rejected more accounts in the self-selected sample in which people only sensed a presence. It is also interesting that the percentages of those who suffered violent deaths and those who died of an illness are about the same in both samples, as can be seen in Table 17.

A notable difference is found in the relationship between the informant and the encountered deceased people. The random sample encountered significantly more family members (57%) than the self-selected sample (49%) and the self-selected sample had significantly more encounters with strangers (30%) than the random sample (13%). If we divide the encountered dead into two groups: those who were close to the informants and those who were not, we find a statistical difference between the two samples. The people in the random sample perceived more relatives whereas the self-selected sample perceived more strangers. Furthermore, the random sample encountered more men (80%) than the self-selected sample (66%).

What about attitudes such as the belief in the afterlife? There was little difference between the groups as 85% of the random sample and 92% of the self-selected sample believed in an afterlife. On the whole, there was little difference between the two samples. This suggests that the total sample should give a fairly accurate view of the experience that Icelanders have of the deceased.

# References

Archangel, D. (2005). *Afterlife encounters*. Charlottesville: Hampton Roads.

Björnsson, B. and Pétursson, P. (1990). *Trúarlíf Íslendinga*. Reykjavik: Háskóli Íslands.

Burris, C. T. and Bailey, K. (2009). What lies beyond: Theory and measurements of afterlife beliefs. *International Journal of the Psychology of Religion, 19,* 173-186.

Bozzano, Ernesto (1919). *Dei fenomeni d'infestazione*. Roma: Casa Editrice Luce e Ombra.

Crookes, Sir William (1874). *Researches in the phenomena of spiritualism. Crookes and the spirit world*. Edited 1972 by R. G. Medhurst, K. M. Goldney and M. R. Barrington. London: Souvenir Press.

Dunraven, Earl of (1924). *Experiences in spiritualism with D. D. Home*. Proceedings of the Society for Psychical Research, 35, 1-284.

Emmons, C. F. (1982). *Chinese ghosts and ESP*. Metuchen, NJ: Scarecrow Press.

Flammarion, Camille (1922-1923). *Death and its mystery*. New York: Century.

Gissurarson, L. R. and Haraldsson, E. (1989). The Icelandic Physical Medium Indridi Indridason. *Proceedings of the Society for Psychical Research, 57,* 53-148.

Gissurarson, L. R. and Haraldsson, E. (1995). Indridi Indridason. In Alexander Imich (ed.) *Incredible Tales of the Paranormal,* 95-140. New York: Bramble.

Greyson, B. (2012). Near-death experiences. In Cardeña, E., Lynn, S., Krippner, S. (eds.). *The varieties of anomalous experience: Examining the scientific evidence* (2nd ed.). Washington, DC: American Psychological Association.

Greeley, A. M. (1987). Hallucinations among the widowed. *Sociology and Social Research* 71(4), 258-265.

Greeley, A. M. (1975). *The Sociology of the paranormal: A reconnaissance.* Beverly Hills, CA: Sage Publications.

Green, C. and McCreery, C. (1975). *Apparitions.* London: Hamish Hamilton.

Guggenheim, B. and Guggenheim, J. (1995). *Hello from Heaven!* Longwood, Florida: The ADC Project.

Gurney, E. & Myers, Fredric W.H. (1887-88). On apparitions occuring soon after death. *Proceedings of the Society for Psychical Research,* 5, 403-485.

Gurney, E. & Myers, F. W.H. & Podmore, F. (1886). *Phantasms of the Living.* London: Trübner.

Hannesson, G. (1924). Remarkable phenomena in Iceland. *Journal of the American Society for Psychical Research,* 18, 239-272.

Haraldsson, E. (1985). Representative national surveys of psychic phenomena: Iceland, Great Britain, Sweden, USA and Gallup's multinational survey. *Journal of the Society for Psychical Research,* 53, 145-158.

Haraldsson, E. (1978). *Þessa heims og annars. Könnun á dulrænni reynslu Íslendinga, trúarviðhorfum og þjóðtrú.* Reykjavik: Bókaforlagið Saga.

Haraldsson, E. (1987). The Iyengar-Kirti case. An apparition case of the bystander type. *Journal of the Society for Psychical Research,* 54, 64-67.

Haraldsson, E. (1988-89). Survey of claimed encounters with the dead. *Omega, the Journal for Death and Dying.* 19, 103-113.

Haraldsson, E. (2006). Popular psychology, belief in life after death and reincarnation in the Nordic countries, Western and Eastern Europe. *Nordic Psychology.* 58, 171-180.

Haraldsson, E. (2009). Alleged encounters with the dead. The importance of violent death in 337 new cases. *Journal of Parapsychology.* 73, 91-118.

Haraldsson, E. (2011). A Perfect Case? Emil Jensen in the mediumship of Indridi Indridason. The fire in Copenhagen on November 24th 1905 and the discovery of Jensen's identity. *Proceedings of the Society for Psychical Research,* 59 (223), 195-223.

Haraldsson, E. (2012). Cases of the reincarnation type and the mind-brain relationship. In A. MoreiraAlmeida and F. S. Santon (eds.): *Exploring the Frontiers of the Mind-Brain Relationship.* (pp. 215-231). New York: Springer.

Haraldsson, E. and Gerding, J. L. F. (2010). Fire in Copenhagen and Stockholm. Indridason's and Swedenborg's 'remote viewing' experiences. *Journal of Scientific Exploration*, 24, 425-436.

Haraldsson, E and Houtkooper, J. M. (1991). Psychic experiences in the multinational Human Values Study. *Journal of the American Society for Psychical Research*. 85(2), 145-165.

Haraldsson E. and Olafsson, Ö. (1980). A survey of psychic healing in Iceland. *The Christian Parapsychologist*, 3, 276-79.

Haraldsson, E. and Stevenson, I. (1974). An experiment with the Icelandic medium Hafsteinn Björnsson. *Journal of the American Society for Psychical Research*, 68, 192-202.

Haraldsson, E. and Stevenson, I. (1975). A communicator of the "drop in" type in Iceland: The case of Runolfur Runolfsson. *Journal of the American Society for Psychical Research*, 69, 33-59.

Inglehart, R., Basanez, M. and Morendo, A. (1998). *Human values and beliefs. A cross-cultural sourcebook*. Ann Harbor: The University of Michigan Press.

Inglehart, R., Basanez, M., Diez-Medrano, J., Halman, L. and Luijkx, R. (2004). *Human values and beliefs. A cross-cultural sourcebook based on the 1999-2002 values surveys*. Mexico: Siglo XXI Editores.

James, W. (1897). *The Will to Believe and Other Essays in Popular Philosophy*. New York: Longmans, Green & Co. Republished by Cosimo Inc, New York in 2006.

James, W. (1902). *The Varieties of Religious Experience: A Study in Human Nature*. London & Bombay: Longmans, Green, and Co. Numerous reprints.

Jonasson, Jónas frá Hrafnagili (1961). *Íslenskir þjóðhættir*. 3rd ed. Reykjavik: Ísafoldarprentsmiðja.

Jung, C. G. (1995). *Memories, dreams, reflections*. London: Fontana Press.

Kelly, E. W., Greyson, B., Kelly, E. F. (2007). *Unusual experiences near death and related phenomena*. In Kelly, E. F., Kelly, E. W., Crabtree, A., Gauld, A., Grosso, M., Greyson, B., *Irreducible mind: Toward a psychology for the 21st century* (pp. 367-421). Lanham, MD: Rowman and Littlefield.

Kuld, J. J. E. (1979). *Í lífsins ólgusjó*. Reykjavik: Ægisútgáfan.

Magnus, G. M. (1967). *Eiríkur skipherra*. Hafnarfjord: Skuggsjá.

Nahm, M. (2012). *Wenn die Dunkelheit ein Ende findet*. Amerang: Crotona Verlag.

Nahm, M., Greyson, B., Kelly, E.W. und Haraldsson, E. (2011). Terminal lucidity: A review and a case collection. *Archives of Gerontology and Geriatrics*, in press, electronic pre-publication: doi:10.1016/j.archger. 2011.06.031.

Níelsson, Haraldur (1924). Remarkable phenomena in Iceland. *Journal of the American Society for Psychical Research*, 18, 233-272.

McClenon, J. (1988). A survey of Chinese anomalous experiences and comparison with Western representative national samples. *Journal for the Scientific Study of Religion*, 27, 421-426.

Olson P. R., Suddeth J. A., Peterson P. J., Egelhoff C. (1985). Hallucinations of widowhood. *Journal of the American Geriatric Society.* 33(8), 543-7.

Osis, K. (1986). Characteristics of purposeful action in an apparition case. *Journal of the American Society for Psychical Research*, 80, 175-193.

Osis, Karlis and Haraldsson, E. (1977). *At the hour of death.* New York: Avon Books.

Puhle, A. (2006). *Mit Goethe durch die Welt der Geister.* St Goar: Reichl Verlag.

Rees, W. D. (1971). The hallucinations of widowhood. *British Medical Journal*, 4, 37-41.

Rousseau, D. (2012). The Implications of Near-Death Experiences for Research into the Survival of Consciousness. *Journal of Scientific Exploration*, 26(1), 85–123.

Schmied-Knittel, I. (2003). Todeswissen umd Todesbegegnungen, Ahnungen, Erscheinungen und Spukerlebnisse. In Eberhard Bauer, Michael Schetsche (ed.). *Alltägliche Wunder. Erfahrungen mit dem Übersinnlichen – wissenschaftliche Befunde*, pp. 93-120.

Stevenson, I. (1982). The contribution of apparitions to the evidence for survival. *Journal of the American Society for Psychical Research*, 76, 341-358.

Stevenson, I. (2001). *Children who remember previous lives. A question of reincarnation.* Revised edition. Jefferson, NC: McFarland.

Tucker, J. (2005). *Life before life.* New York: St. Martin's Press.

# Acknowledgments

THANKS go, first of all, to those who shared their experiences with us.

Interviews were conducted by Magnus Jonsson, Kristin Valdemarsdottir, Haukur Hjaltason, Jon Ingi Björnsson and Julius Björnsson. The interviews were transcribed from audio recordings by my uncle Olafur Elimundarson. Several persons translated the accounts and the text into English; Liv Anna Gunnel, Rafn and Frances Kjartansson, Ingunn Hansdottir, Haraldur Thorsteinsson and the author. Fern Galloway made useful comments for the improvement of the text. The author is deeply indebted to all these persons. The author rewrote in English some chapters for this edition.

# Appendix B

## The Questionnaire

Questionnaire on experiences of appartitions and contact with the dead
Sample number...

Case number

Name of interviewer

Date

Sex 1=male 2=female

Name of interviewee, experiencer

Address

Phone

Year of birth

Please give a short description of what happened:

## INFORMATION ABOUT EXPERIENCE.

**1. In what way was the deceased (D) perceived?**
1. seen                                    2. heard
3. a smell characteristic of D, what?
4. by touch, of what kind and where?
5. felt only presence                   6. seen and heard
7. seen - heard - touched              8. seen - touched
9. other

**2. Did D bear any signs of cause of death or symptoms of sickness?**
1. yes                                      3. don't know
2. no                                       4. not applicable

**3. Was D seen completely or just a part of him/her?**

1. completely
2. only partly, which part(s)?
3. don't know
4. not applicable

**4. Did D appear to be at a different age than when he/she died?**

1 no
2. younger
3. older
5. don't know
4. not applicable

**5. If D was heard, the sound was:**

1. talk
2. other vocal sounds
3. other sounds, which?

**6. In what mood was he/she?**

1. calm
2. excited
3. happy
4. sad
5. threatening
6. Helpful
7. kind
8. frightened
9. peaceful
10. some other mood

**7. Did D indicate anything?**

1. yes, what?
2. no
3. not certain

**8. How did D indicate this?**

1. in words
2. facial expression
3. in other ways, how?

**9. Do you think that D was trying to convey something only by being there?**

1. yes
2. no
3. not sure

**10. Was there something special about the appearance or behavior of D?**

**11. How often was interviewee (I) aware of D?**

1. once
2. 2 - 3 times
3. 4 times or more
4. don't know/recall

**12. If once**

1. only a few moments, a few seconds
2. minutes
3. longer, how long?
4. don't know/recall

**13. If more than once, how long intervals between the occurences?**
1. only a moment, a few seconds    2. minutes
3. less than 24 hours                       4. longer, how long?
5. don't know/recall

**14. If more than once, how long did the clearest occurrence last?**
1. only a few moments, a few seconds    2. minutes
3. less than 24 hours                              4. longer, how long?
5. don't know/recall

**15. What was the shortest distance between D and I?**
1. within reach from each other    2. further apart indoor
3. further apart outdoor              4. something else/don't know

**16. Was D still or moving?**
1. still                    2. moving
3. don't know        4. something else

**17. Did D appear to be:**
1. in front of I          2. beside the I
3. somewhere else    4. behind the I
5. not applicable

**18. If D was seen, was he/she seen with:**
1. eyes open                      2. eyes closed
3. as with the mind's eye    4. somehow else
5. not certain

**19. At what time of day did the occurrence take place?**
1. in the morning      2. during day
3. in the evening        4. during the night
5. at various times     6. not certain

**20. In what kind of illumination did the occurrence take place?**
1. in dusk indoor          2. in dusk outdoor
3. electric illumination   4. in darkness
5. in full daylight           6. something else/various illumin.

**21. How did D appear?**
1. suddenly                             2. slowly
3. was present when noticed    4. don't know/recall

**22. Did D seem brighter than the surroundings (illuminated from within)?**

1. yes
2. no
3. not certain
4. not applicable

**23. How did D disappear?**

1. suddenly
2. slowly
3. not certain

**24. Did D disappear normally?**

1. yes, how?
2. unnormally, how?

**25. How real was the occurrence (if visual)?**

1. D was physically there, until he/she disappeared
2. D was partially physical (e.g. was transparent (seen through), only seen part of etc.)
3. D was never physically real, why?
Short description of answer:

**26. Did any physical occurences take place at the same time?**

1. moving objects
2. sounds
3. reactions from animals present
4. something else
5. no

**27. How long is it since the occurrence?**

1. less than a year
2. 1 - 2 years
3. 3 - 4 years
4. 5 - 7 years
5. 8 - 10 years
6. 11 - 15 years
7. 16 - 25 years
8. 26 years or more
9. do not recall D

**28. During what season did the occurrence take place?**

1. summer
2. winter
3. spring
4. autumn
5. various seasons
6. don't know

**28a. Where did the occurrence take place?**

**29. Was the place in any way connected with D?**

1. D died there
2. place connected with D
3. place not connected with D
4. place familiar to D
5. don't know

**30. Have others witnessed anything similar in that place?**
1. yes            2. no
3. don't know

## INFORMATION ABOUT THE DECEASED.

31. Have you any idea who D was?
1. yes            2. no
3. not sure

**32. How was the relationship between D and you?**
1. very intimate        2. close
3. minor            4. None

**33. Connection between I and D:**
1. family ties, which?      2. friendship
3. co-workers           4. acquainted
5. strangers            6. Other

**34. Age of D at death:**
1. 0 - 9 years          2. 10 - 19 years
3. 20 - 29 years       4. 30 - 39 years
5. 40 - 49 years       6. 50 - 59 years
7. 60 - 69 years       8. 70 or older
9. not known

**35. How long after D's death did the occurrence take place?**
1. within an hour (before or after)
2. within 24 hours
3. less than a week      4. less than a year
5. 1 - 5 years          6. 6 - 10 years
7. longer, how long?     8. don't know

**36. Cause of death?**
1. illness            2. homocide
3. suicide

**37. If illness:**
1. died suddenly       2. after short illness
3. after long illness      4. don't know

**38. Place of death?**
1. hospital                    2. home
3. at sea

**39. Did D's death come very unexpected to you?**
1. yes -                       2. no
3. not sure/don't know         4. not applicable

**40. Do you think D believed in life after death?**
1. yes                         2. no
3. not certain                 4. not known

**41. Do you think D was:**
1. very religious              2. moderately religious
3. little religious            4. not religious at all
5. not known

**42. How much do you think you know about the religious beliefs of D?**
1. very much                   2. a little
3. very little                 4. nothing

**43. Had you ever thought about D after he/she died?**
1. often                       2. sometimes/seldom
3. very seldom                 4. don't know
5. not applicable

**44. When did you last think of D before the occurrence?**
1. a short time before         2. thought of D once in a while
3. not for a long time/not at all   4. don't know
5. not applicable

**45. Why did you think of D?**

**46, Had D have any young children when he/she died?**
1. yes                         2. No
3. if yes, how many?           4. don't know

**47. Did D have special problems before he/she died?**
1. mental problems             2. heavy drinking
3. difficulties ahead          4. did not want to live
5. Other                       6. don't know/not applicable

**48. Did D have much unfinished business when he/she died?**

1. yes
2. no

if yes, what?

3. don't know

**49. The name of D was**

**50. Sex and perceived age of D:**

1. male
a) 0 - 40 years
c) over 65 years

b) 41 - 65 years

2. female
a) 0 - 40 years
c) over 65 years

b) 41 - 65 years 1

**51. Date of birth of D:**

1. 1850 - 1880
3. 1901 - 1920
5. 1931 – 1940
7. 1951 – 1960
8. 1961 or later

2. 1881 - 1900
4. 1921 - 1930
6. 1941 – 1950

9. not known

**52. Educational status of D:**

1. primary school
3. college
5. University degree

2. secondary school
4. Not known

# INFORMATION ABOUT THE INTERVIEWEE

**53. What were you doing when the occurrence took place?**

1. working/active, what kind?
2. at rest, where?
4. just after awakening
6. unclear if asleep or awake

3. just before falling asleep
5. sleeping
7. various

**54. Your physical state at the time of the occurrence?**

1. healthy
2. sick in bed
4. on medication/drugs, which?
5. something else
6. in hospital

3. had fever, how high?

**55. Your mental state at the time of the occurrence?**
1. normal
2. sad
3. depressed
4. not fully concious
5. something else/don't know

**56. Did you grieve for D at his/her death?**
1. yes, very much
2. a little
3. not
4. somewhat
5. don't know
6. not applicable

**57. Were you grieving or did you miss D just before the occurrence?**
1. yes, very much
2. a little
3. not
4. somewhat
5. don't know
6. not applicable

**58. Prior to the occurrence, did you think you could experience something of this sort?**
1. yes
2. perhaps
3. No
4. don't remember

**59. Did this experience change anything of your ideas of experiences of the dead?**
1. yes
2. no
3. don't know

**60. What effect did the occurrence have on you?**
1. strong
2. moderate
3. no effect
4. not sure

**61. Did you find the experience:**
1. positive
2. negative
3. neither negative nor positive
4. don't know

**62. Were other persons present when you perceived D?**
1. yes
2. no
3. don't know

**63. Did others present observe the phenomenon?**
If yes, were they;
1. asleep
2. awake
3. turned towards D
4. Turned away from D
5. Something else

**64. Did they have a similar experience as you did?**
1. yes                                      2. no
3. don't know if yes, who?

**65. Did those who were with you experience the phenomenon:**
1. before you did                    2. at the same time
3. after you did                       4. don't know

**66. Were others told about the experience?**
1. yes, who and when?           2. no,
3. why?

**67. Did you learn about D's death:**
1. before the experience        2. after the experience
3. not known                           4. not applicable

**68. Have others experienced D at other times?**
1. yes, who?                            2. no
3. don't know                          4. while awake
5. in a dream                          6. at a mediumistic seance
7. not applicable

**69. What possible explanation can you give of the phenomenon?**

**70. Have others in your family had experiences of deceased persons?**
1. yes, who
a) closest relatives                b) other relatives
c) not known
2. no

**71. Have you experienced other paranormal phenomena?**
1. yes                                       2. no
3. not sure, if yes, what?

**72. Do you believe in life after death?**
1. yes                                       2. no
3. not sure

**73. Did the experience enhance your belief in life after death?**
1. yes                                       2. no
3. not sure

**74. Do you read books about psychic phenomena?**
1. often
2. seldom
3. never

**75. Do you believe the existence of telepathy or clearvoyance is:**
1. unlikely
2. likely
3. no opinion
4. not sure

**76. Do you believe that the ability to know the future or to have dreams about it is:**
1. unlikely
2. likely
3. no opinion
4. not sure

**77. Date of birth of I:**
1. 1910 or before
2. 1911 - 1929
3. 1921 - 1930
4. 1931 - 1940
5. 1941 - 1950
6. 1951 - 1960
7. 1961 or younger

**78. Education of I:**
1. primary school
2. secondary school
3. college

**79. Interviewer's impression of the case:**
1. no comment
2. doubtful

# Paperbacks also available from
# White Crow Books

Elsa Barker—*Letters from a Living Dead Man*
ISBN 978-1-907355-83-7

Elsa Barker—*War Letters from the Living Dead Man*
ISBN 978-1-907355-85-1

Elsa Barker—*Last Letters from the Living Dead Man*
ISBN 978-1-907355-87-5

Richard Maurice Bucke—*Cosmic Consciousness*
ISBN 978-1-907355-10-3

Arthur Conan Doyle—*The Edge of the Unknown*
ISBN 978-1-907355-14-1

Arthur Conan Doyle—*The New Revelation*
ISBN 978-1-907355-12-7

Arthur Conan Doyle—*The Vital Message*
ISBN 978-1-907355-13-4

Arthur Conan Doyle with Simon Parke—*Conversations with Arthur Conan Doyle*
ISBN 978-1-907355-80-6

Meister Eckhart with Simon Parke—*Conversations with Meister Eckhart*
ISBN 978-1-907355-18-9

D. D. Home—*Incidents in my Life Part 1*
ISBN 978-1-907355-15-8

Mme. Dunglas Home; edited, with an Introduction, by Sir Arthur Conan Doyle—*D. D. Home: His Life and Mission*
ISBN 978-1-907355-16-5

Edward C. Randall—*Frontiers of the Afterlife*
ISBN 978-1-907355-30-1

Rebecca Ruter Springer—*Intra Muros: My Dream of Heaven*
ISBN 978-1-907355-11-0

Leo Tolstoy, edited by Simon Parke—*Forbidden Words*
ISBN 978-1-907355-00-4

Leo Tolstoy—*A Confession*
ISBN 978-1-907355-24-0

Leo Tolstoy—*The Gospel in Brief*
ISBN 978-1-907355-22-6

Leo Tolstoy—*The Kingdom of God is Within You*
ISBN 978-1-907355-27-1

Leo Tolstoy—*My Religion: What I Believe*
ISBN 978-1-907355-23-3

Leo Tolstoy—*On Life*
ISBN 978-1-907355-91-2

Leo Tolstoy—*Twenty-three Tales*
ISBN 978-1-907355-29-5

Leo Tolstoy—*What is Religion and other writings*
ISBN 978-1-907355-28-8

Leo Tolstoy—*Work While Ye Have the Light*
ISBN 978-1-907355-26-4

Leo Tolstoy—*The Death of Ivan Ilyich*
ISBN 978-1-907661-10-5

Leo Tolstoy—*Resurrection*
ISBN 978-1-907661-09-9

Leo Tolstoy with Simon Parke—*Conversations with Tolstoy*
ISBN 978-1-907355-25-7

Howard Williams with an Introduction by Leo Tolstoy—*The Ethics of Diet: An Anthology of Vegetarian Thought*
ISBN 978-1-907355-21-9

Vincent Van Gogh with Simon Parke—*Conversations with Van Gogh*
ISBN 978-1-907355-95-0

Wolfgang Amadeus Mozart with Simon Parke—*Conversations with Mozart*
ISBN 978-1-907661-38-9

Jesus of Nazareth with Simon Parke—
*Conversations with Jesus of Nazareth*
ISBN 978-1-907661-41-9

Thomas à Kempis with Simon
Parke—*The Imitation of Christ*
ISBN 978-1-907661-58-7

Julian of Norwich with Simon
Parke—*Revelations of Divine Love*
ISBN 978-1-907661-88-4

Allan Kardec—*The Spirits Book*
ISBN 978-1-907355-98-1

Allan Kardec—*The Book on Mediums*
ISBN 978-1-907661-75-4

Emanuel Swedenborg—*Heaven and Hell*
ISBN 978-1-907661-55-6

P.D. Ouspensky—*Tertium Organum:
The Third Canon of Thought*
ISBN 978-1-907661-47-1

Dwight Goddard—*A Buddhist Bible*
ISBN 978-1-907661-44-0

Michael Tymn—*The Afterlife Revealed*
ISBN 978-1-970661-90-7

Michael Tymn—*Transcending the
Titanic: Beyond Death's Door*
ISBN 978-1-908733-02-3

Guy L. Playfair—*If This Be Magic*
ISBN 978-1-907661-84-6

Guy L. Playfair—*The Flying Cow*
ISBN 978-1-907661-94-5

Guy L. Playfair —*This House is Haunted*
ISBN 978-1-907661-78-5

Carl Wickland, M.D.—
*Thirty Years Among the Dead*
ISBN 978-1-907661-72-3

John E. Mack—*Passport to the Cosmos*
ISBN 978-1-907661-81-5

Peter & Elizabeth Fenwick—
*The Truth in the Light*
ISBN 978-1-908733-08-5

Erlendur Haraldsson—
*Modern Miracles*
ISBN 978-1-908733-25-2

Erlendur Haraldsson—
*At the Hour of Death*
ISBN 978-1-908733-27-6

Erlendur Haraldsson—
*The Departed Among the Living*
ISBN 978-1-908733-29-0

Brian Inglis—*Science and Parascience*
ISBN 978-1-908733-18-4

Brian Inglis—*Natural and Supernatural:
A History of the Paranormal*
ISBN 978-1-908733-20-7

Ernest Holmes—*The Science of Mind*
ISBN 978-1-908733-10-8

Victor Zammit—*Afterlife: A
Lawyer Presents the Evidence.*
ISBN 978-1-908733-22-1

Casper S. Yost—*Patience
Worth: A Psychic Mystery*
ISBN 978-1-908733-06-1

William Usborne Moore—
*Glimpses of the Next State*
ISBN 978-1-907661-01-3

William Usborne Moore—
*The Voices*
ISBN 978-1-908733-04-7

John W. White—
*The Highest State of Consciousness*
ISBN 978-1-908733-31-3

Stafford Betty—
*The Imprisoned Splendor*
ISBN 978-1-907661-98-3

Paul Pearsall, Ph.D. —
*Super Joy*
ISBN 978-1-908733-16-0

**All titles available as eBooks, and selected titles available in Hardback and Audiobook formats from www.whitecrowbooks.com**

CPSIA information can be obtained at www.ICGtesting.com
Printed in the USA
BVOW08s0247070816

458167BV00003B/183/P